DATE DUE

			PRINTED IN U.S.A.

SCHOOLING
HIP-HOP

SCHOOLING
HIP-HOP

Expanding Hip-Hop Based Education Across the Curriculum

EDITED BY

Marc Lamont Hill
Emery Petchauer

Foreword by Jeff Chang

Teachers College, Columbia University
New York and London

Published by Teachers College Press, 1234 Amsterdam Avenue, New York, NY 10027

Previous versions of Chapters 2 and 5 appeared in *Urban Education* and are reprinted here with permission.

Library of Congress Cataloging-in-Publication Data

Schooling Hip-Hop : expanding Hip-Hop based education across the curriculum / edited by Marc Lamont Hill, Emery Petchauer ; foreword by Jeff Chang.
    pages cm
Includes index.
ISBN 978-0-8077-5431-3 (pbk. : alk. paper) —
ISBN 978-0-8077-5432-0 (hardcover : alk. paper)
    1. Education, Urban—United States—Sociological aspects. 2. Hip-hop—United States—Influence. I. Hill, Marc Lamont.
LC5131.S375 2013
370.9173'2—dc23   2013003856

ISBN 978-0-8077-5431-3 (paper)
ISBN 978-0-8077-5432-0 (hardcover)

Printed on acid-free paper
Manufactured in the United States of America

20   19   18   17   16   15   14   13   8   7   6   5   4   3   2   1

Contents

Foreword

Hip-hop saves. At least that's what we tell ourselves sometimes. So it is one morning at a high school assembly in a rust-belt city, where I find myself being presented to the assembled students as "the voice of hip-hop."

The vice principal, the corporate community liaison, and the local university administrator who are hosting me have been stingy in describing what they want me to talk about before this group of perhaps two hundred Black students. They all laugh, "That's on you."

We stand in a beautiful theatre of perhaps 700 seats, built in the 1950s, well kept, the stage-curtain still a rich red. The hallways we had just walked through were spacious, and outside the grounds sprawled. There were fenced-off gardens, dormant in the winter chill.

After all the students have filed into the theatre, they fill only the top section at the back of the theatre.

My three hosts have been much more generous in talking about the problems the school is facing. The problem, they say, is that this central neighborhood in this aging city has suffered dramatic and absolute White flight in the past decade.

When each of them had attended the school, it had been the pride of the county—athletes had gone on to the professional leagues, scholars had gone on to elite universities. Back then it was about half White and half Black, and the school ran as well as any big school would, as if it would grow forever, a beacon of success, a wonderland of integration.

But then the White flight started—belatedly, three decades late. Now the school sustains a population a third of its size during the 1980s. The city itches to sell the property, most likely to the highest-bidding private school. These students I now stand before will probably not return. They are being educationally Hope-Sixed out of their own neighborhood. To civic leaders, they are already ghosts.

"You're the hip-hop guy," the vice principal, a former star athlete at the school, says with a gallows humor smile. "Talk about it."

So I begin with the familiar story—abandoned children in an abandoned borough, no other ambition than to have fun, taking their forms of play with focus and seriousness, building a futuristic culture of the Afrodiasporic forms to which they are heirs.

They do it under the radar of parents, elders, the state. They take it into the public and begin to transform their surroundings. They enlist thousands of others and make a movement. It succeeds beyond their wildest imaginings. They are the reason that I—a Chinese Hawaiian guy who lives in Berkeley—can even come speak to you here today. It is truly a beautiful and wondrous thing.

Those who haven't already covered their heads in fake-sleep simply stare at me blankly.

I press on. The movement they created is a movement of transformation, I say, raising the pitch. Hip-hop celebrates and enacts desegregation where politics still fails to. It connects the world. It changes the world. It's a movement of hope.

I ask them, have any of you heard what may be happening to you and your school?

Silence.

I wait. The teens slump in their chairs. They stare at the ceiling. They giggle over private jokes.

I ask, Are you concerned about the designs that local politicians have on your school? I ask, Where will you go? They slump even deeper.

So I hasten to the conclusion. If these abandoned kids from these abandoned boroughs could change the world, I say, so can you. So can you. Ok, done. I have skipped the part about asking them if they believe me. I ask, Any questions?

A teen in the back row raises his hand: "You say you from Berkeley?" I nod. "What do you think of Lil' B?"

Some laugh. Now I have a reason to smile too.

"Oh you up on Lil' B, huh? He's crazy. He's from my neighborhood in Berkeley and even there he come off crazy."

The room explodes in laughter. The teachers and administrators look at each other, puzzled. But now we're talking.

We're talking Lil' B. We're talking Doughboyz Cashout and Chief Keef and rust-belt rappers that they are into. We're talking ratchet this and ratchet that. Suddenly the room is alive. We're laughing, we're interrupting each other, we're talking about the strange dances teens do in the strange places teens do them.

The conversation has slipped the bounds of piety and propriety, platitudes and attitudes. When the bell rings I am feeling that it has all ended too soon.

"That was great," says the university official. "But what just happened here?"

After most of the students have filed out, two students come down, eager to talk. The first explains that actually Doughboyz Cashout really can't rap and they live kinda foul, and he can't understand why anyone would actually listen to them. He has a list of other artists I should be checking for: Dizzy Wright, Ab-Soul, Hopsin.

The second waits until the other is gone, and then he quietly asks, "How can I be an artist?" The adults and I stare at him. I ask him what kinds of art he enjoys.

He explains that he lives with his grandmother and he loves to dance and he enjoys acting. The university administrator asks him if he has been able to see any of the plays they have been presenting downtown. He shakes his head. He's never seen a play outside of those he has been in in this school.

The university administrator and the corporate community liaison begin to make plans with him. Now they can talk.

I do believe in hip-hop. But now I have to ask myself also, what just happened here?

Hip-hop saves. That's what we believe. It saved many of us. We believe it might save many more, even some of the students we see every day.

But hip-hop is not the conclusive solution. It is not free of contradictions. It is not a substitute for good teachers, adequate resources, supportive communities, and wise leaders. But it's more than fizzing images on a screen, more than an amalgamation of passing fads, more than the rhythms and rhymes inducing a kind of mass social hearing impairment.

Hip-hop is a body of knowledge and a worldview more vast and encompassing than even many of its practitioners—one that students often comprehend much better than their teachers.

The field of education is no less susceptible to faddism, groupthink, and hustling than any other mass project of human endeavor, perhaps it is more. Hip-hop education offers the real possibility of exchange. And in exchange is the possibility of transformation. That is where the authors in this volume begin.

—Jeff Chang
Stanford, CA
2013

Acknowledgments

here are numerous community-level hip-hop organizations and crews that contributed to this volume in many indirect ways. Most importantly, these contributions include hosting and maintaining hip-hop cultural spaces where young and not-so-young people can participate in and create hip-hop. Without these kinds of spaces, many of the ideas and practices that authors take up in this volume and connect to pedagogical practice would not have developed. These community and hip-hop organizations include 5e Gallery in Detroit, Freestyle Session in San Diego and worldwide, Flow Mo Crew in Finland, Hip-Hop Congress, Mighty 4 Arts Foundation, Relative Theory Records, Rock Steady Crew, Session 31, The Gathering in Philadelphia, The Rotunda in Philadelphia, Tools of War Grassroots Hip-Hop, Urban Artistry in D.C., the Universal Zulu Nation, and every other individual and group who creates such spaces.

On a more technical level, we are grateful for the work of Katie Avesian, Bianca Baldridge, and Ieisha Patterson for helping assemble this volume.

Finally, we are grateful to the contributing authors of this volume as well as the larger cypher of scholars and practitioners who continue to push this work forward.

Introduction

O ver the past 40 years, hip-hop culture has become a central feature of both youth culture and American popular culture. During this time, the educational community has attempted to make use of hip-hop within a range of formal and informal learning contexts. Drawing theoretical and methodological insights from a range of intellectual traditions, scholars and practitioners in the field of education have demonstrated how hip-hop cultural texts can be used to produce more favorable educational processes, outcomes, and environments (Petchauer, 2009). As a result of this work, the field of hip-hop based education (HHBE) (Hill, 2009) has become a rich and vibrant site of inquiry.

As the field of HHBE has taken form, its scholarship has undertaken several key shifts. In the nascent stages of the field, HHBE scholarship (as with the field of hip-hop studies more generally) consisted largely of historical analyses of hip-hop culture and descriptive accounts of the educational potential of rap lyrics (e.g., Powell, 1991; Smitherman, 1997). Such work was necessary because many educators were unfamiliar with hip-hop culture or unaware of its educational possibilities. This early work also provided a necessary counternarrative to the dominant public conversation about hip-hop, which focused primarily on the socially corrosive effects of so-called "gangster rap," particularly during the apex of the subgenre in the 1990s.

After these initial historical and descriptive accounts, subsequent scholarship provided concrete curricular and pedagogical strategies for linking hip-hop to effective educational praxis. Often drawing from the principles of critical pedagogy (e.g., Freire, 1970) and culturally responsive teaching (e.g., Gay, 2000; Ladson-Billings, 1994), such work demonstrated how rap songs could be used to teach academic skills and content (Alexander-Smith, 2004; Hallman, 2009; Morrell & Duncan-Andrade, 2002; Wakefield, 2006), as well as different dimensions of critical literacy (Akom, 2009; Alim, 2007; Duncan-Andrade & Morrell, 2005; Ginwright, 2004; Hill, 2006; Morrell, 2004; Parmar, 2005; Stovall, 2006). From this thread of HHBE scholarship came systematic and standards-based hip-hop curricula to support these kinds of educational efforts (e.g., Irby, 2006; Runell & Diaz, 2007) as well as initiatives and annual events at higher education institutions nationwide.

More recently, scholars have drawn from a wider range of academic disciplines in order to move beyond narrow and technocratic questions and launch broader, more critical investigations about HHBE in relation to questions of

1

culture, power, identity, and policy. This iteration of scholarship has uncovered how knowledge of rap music and videos can function as a form of cultural capital (Clay, 2003; Dimitriadis, 2001) and a resource for racial and generational identity formation among African American students (Alridge, Stewart, & Franklin, 2010; Dimitriadis, 2001; Hill, 2009). As hip-hop has expanded into a global phenomenon, research has also explored the implications of hip-hop outside of the United States with particular attention to how it shapes racial identity formation among youth (Condry, 2006; Forman, 2001; Ibrahim, 1999, 2004; Porfilio & Viola, 2012). Appropriately, scholars have also expanded these inquiries into broader samples of the hip-hop generation, including women (Brown & Kwakye, 2012; Henry, West, & Jackson, 2010; Love, 2012; Richardson, 2006) and college students (Iwamoto, Creswell, & Caldwell, 2007; Petchauer, 2010; Wessel & Wallaert, 2011). As a whole, these more recent scholarly avenues have illustrated that when valued on its own terms or used as a curricular/instructional resource, there is a variety of unintended and unpredictable effects surrounding hip-hop.

EXPANDING HIP-HOP BASED EDUCATION

Despite its remarkable growth, both in terms of intellectual rigor and the number of scholars actively engaging hip-hop based research, the field of HHBE is at an intellectual crossroads. While the current literature has produced a clear and compelling argument for HHBE projects, the overwhelming majority of HHBE scholarship has failed to broaden the bounds of possibility for theorizing, researching, or implementing hip-hop based educational practices. To fully realize the potential of HHBE, we must raise new theoretical questions, deploy new methodological approaches, and identify new units of analysis. These kinds of changes necessitate three distinct areas of expansion.

First, HHBE scholarship must locate and engage a wider range of hip-hop cultural production. Although hip-hop culture is comprised of multiple expressive elements, HHBE scholarship has focused almost exclusively on rap music texts. As a result of this narrow focus, we often lose sight of the ways that youth and young adults create and consume other dimensions of hip-hop culture, such as DJing or turntablism, b-boying/b-girling, graffiti writing and visual art, fashion, language, or spoken-word poetry. These other expressive elements are not relics of the 1980s but thrive both through and outside of commercial culture around the world today. Additionally, an exclusive focus on rap music overlooks the role of knowledge (what is described as the fifth element of hip-hop) and obscures the ways that youth continue to expand the boundaries of hip-hop by crafting new products, texts, and practices that fit within the cultural logic and aesthetics of hip-hop. To respond to this, we must not only expand our methodological purview to account for a broader range of cultural spaces but also engage in careful and deep analyses of a wide range of cultural products, texts, and practices.

An additional component of expanding the notion of hip-hop cultural production requires conceptualizing hip-hop engagement beyond the level of textual interaction. Instead of merely framing hip-hop as a text with content to be encoded or decoded (e.g., investigating how youth make sense of rap lyrics), HHBE scholars must also understand the ways in which hip-hop culture functions at more complex aesthetic and epistemological levels. For example, HHBE scholars must consider the ways that practices like sampling, battling, and freestyling reflect unique sensibilities and worldviews that are not only endemic to hip-hop but are also applied by adolescents and young adults in everyday life (Hill, 2009; Petchauer, 2012). Such insights are critical for reimagining educational spaces in ways that take seriously the cultural orientations and lived realities of students.

Second, HHBE must embrace a wider range of disciplinary locations. Early HHBE practices have taken place most often in language arts and English education classrooms because of rap music's clear and intuitive connections to the written, spoken, and poetic word. However, researchers and practitioners must forge meaningful connections to other disciplines, including those (like math and science) that are alleged to be culturally neutral, and to the entire organization of schools (e.g., Seidel, 2011). In calling for such expansions, we are not alluding to the recent phenomenon of "rappin' teachers" and educational entrepreneurs who use live and recorded rhymes to promote the rote memorization of facts or adherence to dress code policies. Instead, we argue for a deeper understanding of the aforementioned aesthetic and epistemological forms of hip-hop and their connections to students' lives, specific disciplinary practices, and related bodies of knowledge (e.g., Emdin, 2010; Irby & Petchauer, 2012).

Third, HHBE scholars must move beyond teacher-researcher accounts in urban schools. Despite the importance of current HHBE research, the bulk of the literature focuses nearly exclusively on individual teacher-researcher accounts of local curricular interventions (Petchauer, 2009). Although such studies are indispensable, an exclusive focus on them produces the risk of merely compiling more case studies without raising new theoretical questions, developing new methodological approaches, locating new units of analysis, or addressing broader policy concerns. This gap is particularly problematic given the increased demographic and contextual divide between HHBE researchers and the practitioners who express interest in implementing HHBE within their classrooms (Irby & Hall, this volume). In particular, while much of HHBE research has been conducted by classroom teachers and community educators who often possess deep personal, social, and cultural connections to hip-hop culture, we know little about the lives of the preservice and in-service teachers for whom HHBE scholarship is intended. By failing to attend to this gap, HHBE scholars squander valuable opportunities to connect hip-hop based educational projects to the needs and interests of teachers and teacher educators.

Absent of these three areas of expansion, the field of HHBE runs the risk of merely compiling additional empirical cases of student engagement without forging new sites of possibility for HHBE research, theory, policy, and practice. It is at this crossroad that we offer this volume, *Schooling Hip-Hop: Expanding Hip-Hop Based Education Across the Curriculum.*

NEW APPROACHES TO HIP-HOP BASED EDUCATION

Drawing from new and veteran scholars in both the United States and international settings, this volume directly responds to the need for expansion outlined above in order to push the field of HHBE into a wide range of new intellectual directions. These directions include disciplinary ones such as science education, social studies education, teacher development, and college composition, but they also include areas such as classrooms at minority-serving institutions and learning spaces outside of the United States. Table I.1 illustrates the collective breadth of these chapters and some of the different fields, themes, and topics they address. Through this volume, the contributors stop short of offering lesson plans or scripted procedures, for such rigidity is antithetical to the intellectual spirit and aesthetics of HHBE. However, they nonetheless offer clear and explicit strategies for tethering these new directions in HHBE to classroom practice in both secondary and higher education levels.

We have organized these chapters into two main sections that highlight the essential areas of expansion for HHBE. Although there are some common elements—such as curriculum—among all the chapters, these two main sections of

Table I.1. Areas and Fields Addressed by Chapters

Areas and Fields	Chapter							
	1	2	3	4	5	6	7	8
College students		X	X	X				
Critical literacy/ pedagogy				X		X		X
Culturally responsive pedagogy	X				X			X
In-school learning	X	X	X	X	X			X
Out-of-school learning						X	X	
Science education	X							
Social justice		X		X				X
Social studies education								X
Teacher development		X			X			
Writing/composition			X	X		X		

the book highlight the collective influence that these chapters have upon the field of HHBE. Part I of this volume, under the heading "Aesthetics, Worldviews, and Pedagogies of Hip-Hop," organizes chapters in which authors locate their analyses at the intersections of hip-hop aesthetics and educational practice in a variety of disciplines and settings. In this way, authors look to the sensibilities and worldviews endemic to hip-hop's creative expressions and unpack how these can operate for educational purposes. This fundamental shift in focus from hip-hop products to hip-hop aesthetics is a much-needed move toward hip-hop theory. We unpack this move and these distinctions more fully in our introduction to this section later in the volume. Overall, in this first section, authors challenge us to expand our collective understanding of hip-hop culture beyond printed rap texts and other products. By doing so, we are able to broaden our units of analysis when engaged in HHBE research, as well as draw from a wider range of cultural resources when implementing HHBE in classrooms.

Part II of this volume, under the heading "Curricula, Courses, and Pedagogies with Hip-Hop," organizes chapters in which authors describe the workings of cutting-edge HHBE programs and explore the contours and complexities that arise in these programs. Like the work in Part I, these chapters go beyond classroom-based practices to explore and present more expansive applications of hip-hop in which various aspects of hip-hop culture are the primary organizing agents. These aspects include the intertwined expressions of hip-hop, historical and counternarrative interpretive frameworks, and the intended and unintended consequences of these. In these two sections, readers will notice some different spellings of hip-hop terms (such as *DJing* and *deejaying*) as well as the term *hip-hop* itself. These differences represent regional lexicons, personal preference, or nuanced authenticity claims. We include these differences rather than impose a standardized form to underscore the variability that hip-hop has when taken up by different people in different places.

Overall with this volume, we aim to chart new directions for HHBE, build on existing areas of research and practice, and enable new possibilities for linking hip-hop culture to the educational lives of our children, youth, and young adults. While we hope to provide critical insights and address pressing problems of theory, research, and practice, our goal is not to offer the final answer on HHBE. Rather, in the spirit of hip-hop culture, we hope to challenge, critique, explore, inform, and inspire a global community of engaged teachers, cultural workers, students and, of course, hip-hop heads.

P.E.A.C.E.

—Marc Lamont Hill
Emery Petchauer

REFERENCES

Akom, A. A. (2009). Critical hip-hop pedagogy as a form of liberatory praxis. *Equity & Excellence in Education, 42*(1), 52–66.

Alexander-Smith, A. C. (2004). Feeling the rhythm of the critically conscious mind. *English Journal, 93*(3), 58–63.

Alim, H. S. (2007). Critical hip-hop language pedagogies: Combat, consciousness, and the cultural politics of communication. *Journal of Language, Identity, and Education, 6*(2), 161–176.

Alridge, D. P., Stewart, J. B., & Franklin, V. P. (Eds.). (2010). *Message in the music: Hip-Hop history and pedagogy.* Washington, DC: Association for the Study of African American Life and History.

Brown, R. N., & Kwakye, C. J. (Eds.). (2012). *Wish to live: The hip-hop feminism pedagogy reader.* New York: Peter Lang.

Clay, A. (2003). Keepin' it real: Black youth, hip-hop culture, and Black identity. *American Behavioral Scientist, 46*(10), 1346–1358.

Condry, I. (2006). *Hip-hop Japan: Rap and the paths of cultural globalization.* Durham, NC: Duke University Press.

Dimitriadis, G. (2001). *Performing identity/performing text: Hip hop as text, pedagogy, and lived practice.* New York: Peter Lang.

Duncan-Andrade, J. M. R., & Morrell, E. (2005). Turn up that radio, teacher: Popular culture pedagogy in new century urban schools. *Journal of School Leadership, 15*(3), 284–304.

Emdin, C. (2010). *Urban science education for the hip-hop generation: Essential tools for the urban science teacher and researcher.* Boston: Sense.

Forman, M. (2001). "Straight outta Mogadishu": Prescribed identities and performative practices among Somali youth in North American high schools. *Topia, 5,* 33–60.

Freire, P. (1970). *Pedagogy of the oppressed.* New York: Continuum.

Gay, G. (2000). *Culturally responsive teaching: Theory, research, and practice.* New York: Teachers College Press.

Ginwright, S. (2004). *Black in school: Afrocentric reform, urban youth, and the promise of hip-hop culture.* New York: Teachers College Press.

Hallman, H. L. (2009). Dear Tupac, you speak to me": Recruiting hip-hop as curriculum at a school for pregnant and parenting teens. *Equity & Excellence in Education, 42*(1), 36–51.

Henry, W. J., West, N. M., & Jackson, A. (2010). Hip-hop's influence on the identity development of Black female college students: A literature review. *Journal of College Student Development, 51*(3), 237–251.

Hill, M. L. (2006). Using Jay-Z to reflect on post-9/11 race relations. *English Journal, 96*(2), 23–27.

Hill, M. L. (2009). *Beats, rhymes, and classroom life: Hip-hop, pedagogy, and the politics of identity.* New York: Teachers College Press.

Ibrahim, A. (1999). Becoming Black: Rap and hip-hop, race, gender, identity, and the politics of ESL learning. *TESOL Quarterly, 33*(3), 349–369.

Ibrahim, A. (2004). Operation under erasure: Hip-hop and the pedagogy of affective. *Journal of Curriculum Theorizing, 20*(1), 113–133.

Irby, D. J. (2006). *Do the knowledge: A standards based hip-hop learning and activity guide.* Retrieved from http://artsanctuary.org/wp-content/uploads/2011/12/Do-The-Knowledge-A-Standards-Based-Hip-Hop-Learning-Guide-Updated-11-06.pdf

Irby, D. J., & Petchauer, E. (2012). Hustlin' consciousness: Critical education using hip-hop modes of knowledge distribution. In B. Porfilio & M. Viola (Eds.), *Hip-hop(e): The cultural practice and critical pedagogy of international hip-hop* (pp. 302–321). New York: Peter Lang.

Iwamoto, D. K., Creswell, J. W., & Caldwell, L. (2007). Feeling the beat: The meaning of rap music for ethnically diverse Midwestern college students—A phenomenological study. *Adolescents, 43*(166), 337–351.

Ladson-Billings, G. (1994). *The dreamkeepers: Successful teachers of African American children*. San Francisco: Jossey-Bass.

Love, B. (2012). *Hip hop's li'l sistas speak: Negotiating identities and politics in the New South*. New York: Peter Lang.

Morrell, E. (2004). *Linking literacy and popular culture: Finding connections for lifelong learning*. Norwood, MA: Christopher-Gordon.

Morrell, E., & Duncan-Andrade, J. M. R. (2002). Promoting academic literacy with urban youth through engaging hip-hop culture. *English Journal, 91*(6), 88–92.

Parmar, P. (2005). Critical studies and rap: The poetry of an urban lyricist. *Taboo, 9*(1), 5–15.

Petchauer, E. (2009). Framing and reviewing hip-hop educational research. *Review of Educational Research, 79*(2), 946–978.

Petchauer, E. (2010). Sampling practices and social spaces: Exploring a hip-hop approach to higher education. *Journal of College Student Development, 51*(4), 359-372.

Petchauer, E. (2012). *Hip-hop culture in college students' lives: Elements, embodiment, and higher edutainment*. New York: Routledge.

Porfilio, B., & Viola, M. (Eds.) (2012). *Hip-hop(e): The cultural practice and critical pedagogy of international hip-hop*. New York: Peter Lang.

Powell, C. (1991). Rap music: An education with a beat from the street. *Journal of Negro Education, 60*(3), 245–59.

Richardson, E. (2006). *Hiphop literacies*. New York: Routledge.

Runell, M., & Diaz, M. (2007). *The hip-hop education guidebook: Volume 1*. New York: Hip Hop Association.

Seidel, S. (2011). *Hip-hop genius: Remixing high school education*. Lanham, MD: Rowman & Littlefield.

Smitherman, G. (1997). "The chain remains the same": Communicative practices in the hip-hop nation. *Journal of Black Studies, 28*(1), 3–25.

Stovall, D. (2006). We can relate: Hip-hop culture, critical pedagogy, and the secondary classroom. *Urban Education, 41*(6), 585–602.

Wakefield, S. R. (2006). Using music sampling to teach research skills. *Teaching English in the Two-Year College, 33*(4), 357–360.

Wessel, R. D., & Wallaert, K. A. (2011). Student perceptions of the hip hop culture's influence on the undergraduate experience. *Journal of College Student Development, 52*(2), 167–179.

PART I

AESTHETICS, WORLDVIEWS, AND PEDAGOGIES OF HIP-HOP

One important context for understanding the growth and key shifts in HHBE is the larger area of hip-hop studies. A significant strand of growth within hip-hop studies over the past 10 years has been a focus on the emic sensibilities, norms, and mindsets that are endemic to hip-hop. In this way, scholars have looked beyond the specific linguistic, kinesthetic, auditory, and visual elements of hip-hop expressions to understand the deeper aesthetics and worldviews at work within and among these expressions. These sensibilities include appropriative sampling, competitive battling, affective engagement, freestyle improvisation, and more. This area of growth has been enabled primarily through scholars looking beyond the products of hip-hop (i.e., rap songs, videos) and going to the specific spaces, places, and communities where people create hip-hop. The quintessential space in which people create hip-hop—called a *cypher*—is thus a fundamental unit of analysis in hip-hop scholarship. Examining hip-hop in this way and attempting to understand it on "its own terms" has enabled this fundamental shift and allowed scholars and practitioners to move toward hip-hop theory.

This shift in hip-hop studies more generally has had clear implications for HHBE specifically. Instead of using hip-hop products (once again, most often rap songs) to teach different academic content and skills, educators and scholars have seen that it is fruitful to use the aesthetics, sensibilities, and worldviews of hip-hop as pedagogies. If these aesthetics have made hip-hop the compelling, evocative, and global phenomenon that it is today, then they have incredible pedagogical potential.

Each chapter in this section operates in varying degrees on this shift. They use the aesthetics of hip-hop as the basis for teaching and learning in a variety of educational settings. Although the chapters indeed touch on courses and curricula (the focus of Part II of this volume), the organizing principles of work in this section are hip-hop aesthetics. In Chapter 1, Christopher Emdin connects communication and argumentation in the urban science classroom to one of the most unifying threads of hip-hop: the battle. Emdin provides the framework of "Reality Pedagogy" in order to facilitate more effective and culturally responsive science education. In Chapter 2, Emery Petchauer takes up the aesthetics of kinetic consumption and autonomy/distance in context with justice-oriented teaching and urban teacher development. Petchauer unpacks the nature and design of learning experiences based upon these two aesthetics as well as their usefulness and challenges when employed among preservice teachers. In Chapter 3, James Braxton Peterson draws a parallel to the traditional four elements of hip-hop culture by framing four educational elements of hip-hop based education. He then draws from the aesthetic practices of sampling, freestyling, and remixing to establish a pedagogical and theoretical foundation for hip-hop based composition courses at the university level. With this foundation, Peterson describes how composition instructors can amplify disciplinary practices and course design through the aesthetics of hip-hop. Finally, in Chapter 4, Joycelyn A. Wilson unites three frequently overlooked areas of HHBE: southern hip-hop, higher education, and historically Black institutions. She draws from the aesthetics infused within the HipHop2020 Curriculum Project to illustrate leadership development pedagogy among young adults in college.

As with all of the work in this volume, these chapters stop short of making prescriptive outlines for educators. However, readers will be able to take specific lessons from the accounts in each chapter and use them to envision these kinds of pedagogies of hip-hop in other educational settings. Ultimately, these chapters should inspire additional, innovative uses of hip-hop aesthetics to improve both the immediate educational experiences and long-term educational outcomes of students.

CHAPTER 1

The Rap Cypher, the Battle, and Reality Pedagogy

Developing Communication and Argumentation in Urban Science Education

Christopher Emdin

H ip-hop based education is a field of study that is long overdue for validation as an approach to teaching and learning. This is because of the seemingly perpetual achievement gaps between urban youth of color who are deeply embedded in hip-hop and their counterparts from other settings. In efforts to explore effective approaches to improving instruction, contemporary researchers have called forth the traditions laid by progressive educators such as Dewey (1902) that discuss the significance of teaching from the perspectives of the learner. In response, since the mid-1990s, approaches to education such as culturally relevant pedagogy have reemerged as a viable option for addressing the issues that plague urban schools. Leading the charge in implementing these approaches is hip-hop based pedagogy that specifically targets hip-hop youth and their culture.

An age-old ethos that guides the Deweyan tradition of "culture-focused pedagogy" is that "the subordination of the life and experience of the child to the curriculum" is the "source of whatever is dead, mechanical and formal in schools" (Dewey, 1902, p.14). When this philosophy is brought into and used to analyze issues in contemporary schools, researchers who work with urban youth of color begin to make sense of the reasons why urban youth see schools as boring, unimaginative, and unrelated to their everyday experiences. In a sense, contemporary schooling has inflicted some level of subordination of hip-hop culture, and students have reacted to this process by expressing disinterest in conventional schooling. Unfortunately, even among educators who are rooted in the Deweyan tradition and those who support the immersion of student culture into curriculum, the approaches to instruction they implement (that are intended to reflect youth culture), are ineffective in reaching urban youth of color. This is because there is a flaw in creating culturally relevant approaches to instruction if teachers misidentify the culture of students who are disconnected from school. In essence, culturally relevant approaches to the academic needs of urban youth will inevitably result in ineffective teaching when they do not consider that these youth are deeply immersed in hip-hop culture. Furthermore, the misperception of hip-hop as "just a musical genre," and not a culture, limits research and practice in urban schools from moving beyond the "dead, mechanical, and formal" approach to instruction that is prevalent in urban schools.

In response to the omission of hip-hop culture from education, educators like those who have contributed to this book have begun to focus on utilizing hip-hop as a tool for teaching and learning. Although this work is progressive in relation to the existent work in culturally relevant pedagogy, the superficiality of the general approaches to implementing hip-hop pedagogy has proven to be just as ineffective as approaches that do not consider hip-hop at all. Only a small piece of hip-hop culture has been explored in the field of education, and the oversaturation of this small piece necessarily disengages youth who are deeply involved in a much more complex understanding of the culture. Hip-hop based education, despite its good intentions, will be perceived as disingenuous and a feeble attempt to connect to youth rather than as a genuine attempt to transform teaching and learning if it rests only on segments of youth culture that have already been saturated by popular media and commercial interests.

For the most part, academic work that considers hip-hop as a tool for improving instruction has considered rapping about a topic, or using rap lyrics as text to be studied, as the primary mode of hip-hop based education. This process usually involves the creation of raps that contain academic content and/or the use of text from rap songs as the anchors of classroom lessons. Although these efforts to bring rap into the classroom reflect a step in the right direction in regard to utilizing hip-hop as a tool for instruction, the use of rap lyrics as the sole element of hip-hop based education has become such a widespread practice that it truncates the potential of hip-hop based education to truly reflect the complexities of hip-hop culture. Much of what is described as hip-hop based education is merely rap-based instruction that is misnamed as hip-hop based. Rap is an artifact of hip-hop that holds much symbolic value in hip-hop culture because it has been the chief means of providing a voice for the hip-hop community. However, it represents neither the full spectrum of hip-hopness (i.e., being hip-hop) nor the various modes of communication within hip-hop culture.

While the analysis of rap text reflects a certain level of complexity in instruction, the more prevalent approach to instruction that is referred to as hip-hop based education merely uses rap as a way to help youth memorize information. This use of rap as a memorization tool calls forth archaic modes of instruction like rote learning and bastardizes the potential of a cultural art form whose legitimacy as a learning tool is yet to be fully explored. I argue that the use of rap as the primary way to support hip-hop based instruction, particularly in a culture such as hip-hop that is largely based on oral traditions with deeper meanings than words, misrepresents hip-hop culture and reflects a superficial rendering of hip-hopness.

In an effort to expand the potential of hip-hop based education in this chapter, I challenge established approaches within the field of study by calling forth aspects of hip-hop that have yet to be fully explored in the field of education. Rather than focus on the use of rap text in subject areas like English or social studies, my work focuses on dimensions of hip-hop such as the cypher and the battle, and the academic field of science education. I utilize the battle and cypher both as new areas to explore in teaching and learning, and as the next step in using rap in a more constructive and complex fashion in classrooms. I pursue the connection between hip-hop and science education because science has traditionally been ignored by hip-hop based education, despite the fact that it is the field of study that is least represented by students of color. My work intends to break the stereotypes that science is an older White male discipline that is separated from real people, or that it is a field of study that is too academically rigorous to align with the culturally rich dimensions of hip-hop. Furthermore, I argue that the complexity of hip-hop not only lends itself to scientific ways of thinking but also has the potential to support youth who are a part of hip-hop to become more successful in science than their counterparts who are not exposed to the multimodal ways of knowing and being that are inherent in hip-hop.

In this chapter, I explore pieces of hip-hop culture that go beyond rap text. I reveal the potential of elements of hip-hop such as the rap cypher and the battle, I explore an approach to pedagogy that is rooted in the communicative aspects of hip-hop, and I utilize an approach to writing that is rooted in hip-hopness by merging storytelling, autobiography, and traditional writing in discussing hip-hop and urban science education.

STORYTELLING IN HIP-HOP: BEGINNING WITH THE BATTLE

In the fall of 2000, the entire hip-hop community was in the midst of an intense battle. Shots had been fired across the landscape of New York City hip-hop, and when the smoke cleared, everyone was forced to take sides. Anyone with even the most remote interest in hip-hop culture and/or rap music was forced to pledge allegiance to one faction or another. Tempers rose everywhere the battle was discussed, and the air was thick with either support or opposition for the warriors involved. After each strike by one of the combatants, anticipation for a response attack would build until it reached a fever pitch. Then, unexpectedly, a response would come that ushered in a new barrage of exchanges. These exchanges were always accompanied by deep analysis by each rapper in the form of deconstructions of the claims being made by each of the warring factions and arguments about who was winning or losing the battle.

The battle described above was a war of words between Jay-Z and Nas, two of the most prolific and highly respected artists in hip-hop. The engaging nature of their battle propelled anyone within earshot not just into hip-hop history but also into becoming a witness to and participant in argumentation at its finest. Not only did the battle between these artists allow audiences to witness argumentation, but it also encouraged the audience to engage in the process. As songs by each artist were played all over radio stations and broadcast from playgrounds to barbershops, heated debates about who was winning the battle were heard everywhere. Words from and references to the battle were woven into everyday conversations and rap lyrics by everyone from amateur rappers on street corners to renowned rappers in multimillion-dollar recording studios. People took sides, debated, and worked diligently to convince others about the merits of each of the rappers engaged in the battle, consistently working to create logical arguments for why they supported one rapper over the other.

FROM JAY-Z AND NAS TO THE POSITIVISTS AND RELATIVISTS

About a decade before this epic battle between Jay-Z and Nas, the world of science was entrenched in a war of its own. The "Science Wars," which in a vernacular way can be described as a battle between realists and relativists (Gould, 1981), was a conflict between scientists who believed in an objectivist, noncultural science (realists) and those who believed that what we consider to be scientific facts are culturally embedded and constructed (relativists). Within this battle, scientists who support indigenous knowledge and a nonpositivistic approach to science argued for the consideration of "local ways of knowing and being" in science. To support their views, these scientists often cited Einstein and the fact that his work added much to science despite the fact that it did not rest exclusively within established paradigms and empirical evidence. In response, relativists argued that the focus on new approaches to science that realists called for were often a result of an inability to grasp the complex mathematics and science in which realists are well versed.

The constant exchange between these two groups of scientists provided a wonderful example of argumentation and drove home the following point:

> The theories around which consensus forms do themselves come and go [and] . . . science offers us the remarkable spectacle of a discipline in which older views on many central issues are rapidly and frequently displaced by newer ones. (Laudan, 1986, p.4)

This replacing of older views by newer ones when a convincing and agreed-upon argument is made is part of science and also part of hip-hop.

The battle between Jay-Z and Nas, and the shifting of opinions on who was the better rapper based upon their arguments in the midst of the battle and the general public is evidence of the constant displacement of previous views by newer and more properly supported ones. However, despite these facts about the connection of science to hip-hop, the instruction of science in urban schools that serve hip-hop youth of color often extracts this kind of dialogue and argumentation from classroom instruction. This is often because students are not perceived as being able to understand the complexities of argumentation or to handle the heated debate that comes with it. I have argued elsewhere that this is the case because deficit-laden perspectives of (and general teacher misconceptions about) urban students' propensities for poor behavior mask the fact that students who are interested in science may also express attributes traditionally associated with hip-hop that are viewed negatively by teachers (Emdin, 2010).

The work presented in this chapter looks at aspects of, and pedagogical approaches inspired by, hip-hop. It then follows the tradition of transformative pedagogical approaches such as critical and culturally relevant pedagogy by questioning the general perspectives that people hold of hip-hop youth. The pedagogical approaches I draw from, and the work of considering the validity of a hip-hop based approach to urban science education, considers the social, symbolic, and cultural capital that students bring into the classroom as the point from which pedagogy is birthed (Freire, 1970; Ladson Billings, 1994). The work in this chapter emphasizes communication and argumentation in hip-hop and is therefore rooted in hip-hop based education. These roots are evident through my focus on using artifacts from students' lifeworlds, connecting them to school curriculum (Morrell & Duncan-Andrade, 2002), and framing students' investment as a form of cultural capital (Clay, 2003) to be expressed in urban classrooms.

ARGUMENTATION: COMMUNICATION AND SCIENCE EDUCATION

In contemporary science education research, science talk and argumentation are two approaches to improving student understanding of science that consistently emerge as viable methods for connecting students to science. Brown (2006) has discussed the importance of using students' ways of communication as a tool to use in the expansion of their scientific vocabulary. In addition, Rivard and Straw (2000) have discussed the importance of both writing and talking science and their significance to scientific understanding. These studies as well as many others that address scientific communication in the classroom ultimately support the notion that deep communication in and about science can evolve into such comfort that science talk can develop into worthwhile argumentation. Ideally, exchanges in the classroom foster argumentation, active debate, complex thinking, deep questioning, demonstration of mastery, and the ability to defend one's position with appropriate words and content knowledge (Driver, Newton, & Osbourne, 2000). However, for various reasons, urban educators usually find it challenging to accomplish these goals.

In hip-hop, exchanges among rappers that support argumentation, active debate, complex thinking, and deep questioning are the norm. Rap battles like the one described earlier in this chapter, freestyle sessions where rappers create impromptu raps that have to be both coherent and insightful, and various songs that pose profound questions about life address argumentation and debate, complex thinking, and deep questioning, respectively. Consequently, I argue that science teaching and learning that incorporates hip-hop provides students with opportunities to express skills and talents that are ideal for learning science and would not be expressed in classrooms otherwise. In particular, when science communication and, more specifically, argumentation are supported in the classroom through tenets of hip-hop discourse, not only are hip-hop youth provided with opportunities to learn, but they also receive support to demonstrate mastery of scientific concepts.

PEDAGOGY FOR HIP-HOP YOUTH

Hip-hop youth, which is a term I use as a variant throughout this chapter, refers to youth who listen to and engage in hip-hop music and practices on a regular basis. These are youth who can be identified by the hip-hop practices in which they engage and their embodiment of hip-hop characteristics in their everyday interactions. Urban youth who are engaged in hip-hop are usually immersed in distinctly hip-hop affiliated practices related to the four main components of hip-hop (rapping, b-boying/b-girling, deejaying, and writing graffiti). However, youth who are not classified as hip-hop youth may also benefit from the approaches to pedagogy designed for or inspired by hip-hop youth. The inclusive nature of hip-hop culture and the fact that the approaches to instruction developed from hip-hop simply expand limited approaches to instruction.

This ability of hip-hop based pedagogy to connect youth from varying backgrounds must be considered in light of recent federal initiatives, newly designed curricula, and transformative research targeted toward improving interest and participation in science for *all* students (National Research Council, 1996; Obama, 2009; Roth, 2009). It also fits into the recent focus on exposing access to science and science journals to the general public through nonconventional and even commercial sources so as to widen the readership in, and public consumption of, science (Evans & Reimer, 2009). In each of these efforts, interest and participation in the sciences are framed as larger goals that require activities or processes that foster full engagement and conversation about and within the discipline (Tobin & Gallagher, 1987). In other words, there is a general understanding that in order to meet these generally agreed-upon goals for improving interest and participation in science and science education, an increase in the general populace's involvement in science must occur. I argue that increasing involvement in science requires a concerted effort to attract those who are most marginalized from success in the discipline. This is particularly the case because certain marginalized groups enact practices that support science success, but they only do so when they are outside of the classroom. Intense debate and argumentation about who is the better rapper can very easily become an argument about whether Einstein or Newton was a better contributor to science (a debate among scientists that still occurs today) or whether or not a physics problem can be solved with a certain formula or another. However, if hip-hop argumentation (a science-supported attribute in which youth are well versed) is not welcome in the classroom, it will never be used to support student learning, despite its immense potential to do so.

THE RESULTS OF A NON-HIP-HOP BASED
APPROACH TO URBAN SCIENCE EDUCATION

Populations who are marginalized from science success despite possessing the attributes to be successful in the discipline are predominantly socioeconomically deprived urban youth of color who also happen to be deeply immersed in hip-hop and concentrated in urban settings. Historically, urban youth of color have only been successful in science in small numbers and earn college degrees in science at lower rates than their counterparts (Council for Graduate Schools, 2008; NCES, 2006). However, this population is highly engaged in hip-hop in ways that go beyond just consuming or purchasing hip-hop music (Ginwright, 2004). They spend a tremendous amount of time memorizing, creating, and indulging in hip-hop and, consequently, have found success in creating hip-hop at a higher rate than people from other racial, ethnic, and socioeconomic backgrounds (Samuels, 1992). I argue that both the statistics that point to the low achievement of youth of color in science and those that address their level of involvement in hip-hop are significant for various reasons. The former reminds science educators of the seemingly perpetual achievement gaps that exist between urban African American youth and their peers from other contexts and racial backgrounds and the fact that they must be addressed (Norman, Ault, Bentz, & Meskimen, 2001). The latter points to the significance of hip-hop for urban youth of color and the reciprocal relationship between interest and success. Considering these two factors, the extraction of hip-hop from science teaching and learning only serves to continue the pattern of low achievement for hip-hop youth and causes them to have feelings of success only in realms that are outside of school and science. This is particularly troubling because of the strong connections and similarities between hip-hop and science alluded to earlier. In a sense, there is a forced separation between hip-hop and science that causes the expression of any type of hip-hopness (e.g., debating, asking more profound questions, critiquing the thoughts and ideas of others through possible counterexamples, or even talking, dressing, or interacting using gestures) to become seen as antischool. Over time, the expression of hip-hopness becomes a justification for low expectations of urban youth and the seedbed for a general belief among educators that urban youth are innately unable to develop the tools to be successful in science.

TEACHING AND LEARNING HIP-HOP YOUTH WITH REALITY PEDAGOGY

In order to counter the misperceptions of urban youth and understand the potential of hip-hop based education in urban science education, I call for an approach to instruction called Reality Pedagogy. This approach considers students' realities to be the primary point from which teaching and learning must begin. It is rooted in the belief that everything that exists within the life experiences of a person or group of people is their reality. It also considers that in many cases, those who are from similar racial, ethnic, and socioeconomic demographics are locked into spaces where they all have experiences that are either similar to or understood by those who exist within similar spaces. A hip-hop reality is the sum of all the experiences of those embedded in hip-hop. Therefore, Reality Pedagogy for hip-hop youth is teaching and learning based on the strands of hip-hop that dictate the ways that those embedded in the culture make sense of the world. Although hip-hop realities may vary because of the complex nature of human experience, even for those who inhabit the same spaces, for urban youth who are embedded in hip-hop, there are certain strands of their collective experiences that serve as constants (in the sense that they are a piece of the lifeworlds of hip-hop youth across the globe). By this, I mean that while difference exists among participants in hip-hop from across the globe, there are many similarities with the age range of participants, types of music listened to, and the collective oppression they endure at the hands of a dominant other group. Reality Pedagogy makes it the responsibility of the educator to discover what the similarities are across participants in hip-hop and develop approaches to instruction that derive from these realities.

As mentioned earlier, prior work in science education that considers hip-hop as a tool for instruction has focused on creating science raps or studying rap lyrics. In science education, the perception that these lyrics do not necessarily discuss science in detail causes more of a focus on the creation of rap lyrics, or what I call "rapping science." This approach has gained traction with many progressive urban science educators and involves students or teachers taking science content and placing them into rhymes. The practice usually begins with instruction in science content that is followed by an opportunity for students to create these kinds of raps. Less frequently, rapping science requires the teachers' creation of a rap prior to the lesson that is then performed for students. Most recently, rapping science has evolved to include songs where rappers who have a background in the sciences create songs that incorporate science concepts or are about science. This work blurs the lines between hip-hop and science and serves as entertainment for the layperson, a way to demonstrate the artists' knowledge about science, a way to showcase rap skills, and most important, a teaching tool for science teachers. In my most recent work, I have worked with science teachers in New York City public schools by teaching them how to create science raps that are both scientifically accurate and true to hip-hop. This focus on rap in science helps expand their perspectives of hip-hop youth beyond deficits perspectives and indicates a necessary progression in instructional strategies for urban youth.

This is why I returned to the ancestry of hip-hop based education and began developing Reality Pedagogy, which is an approach to instruction that feeds from the structures of hip-hop while using hip-hop as a pedagogical tool. This approach forces the educator to look into more nuanced ways of incorporating students' culture into the classroom because its beginning point is based on the fact that hip-hop youth reality is complex and cannot be addressed with only one artifact of hip-hop. If focusing on the needs of the hip-hop generation in science classrooms only focuses on rapping science, it is apparent that the needs of the students are only being partly met. Although rap music is the voice of hip-hop, it is merely one component of the culture. Therefore, approaches to instruction for hip-hop youth must consider the nuances of their culture that go beyond just rap. Reality Pedagogy considers rap, uses the battle and the cypher in urban science education, and realizes that other approaches to improving science education exist and can only be understood by delving deeper into urban youth realities.

The tools for delving into these realities come from adopting culturally relevant pedagogy's focus on developing teachers' cultural competence by working with them and their students to challenge the social order (Ladson Billings, 1995). Additionally, these tools are formed by embracing critical pedagogy's focus on highlighting inequalities of power and bringing to light the role of educators in a social order that relegates already marginalized youth to subaltern positions (Burbules & Berk, 1999). These two approaches then become the point from which educators are set in motion on the quest to experience students' realities and teach from them. This process involves abstract suggestions for educators, such as living in students' neighborhoods, listening to the same music they listen to, visiting and volunteering in the same community organizations and afterschool programs they attend, and engaging in the same social activities that they do. However, it does not provide teachers with specific tools for delving into student realities and connecting the information they derive to support their academic success.

THE 5 C'S OF REALITY PEDAGOGY

In response to this disconnect, Reality Pedagogy focuses on five main concepts/ steps (The 5 C's) in which teachers can engage. They are: cogenerative dialogues/ cyphers, coteaching, cosmopolitanism, context focusing/incorporation into instruction, and content development.

The first C, cogenerative dialogues, involves structured dialogues in which a teacher and four to six students discuss the science classroom (Emdin, 2007; Tobin, Zurbano, Ford, & Carambo, 2003). In these conversations, issues related to science content are interrogated and students are asked about their suggestions for improving instruction. In my work, I structure these dialogues like rap cyphers: Participants are positioned in a circle, have equal turns at talk, and support each other in their specific roles that move the dialogues forward. The goal is that ultimately, pieces of the students' culture become a part of the dialogue, and the teacher gains insight into students' suggestions for improving the classroom. Because these dialogues are structured like rap cyphers, they call forth the traditions of hip-hop and support communication in ways that go beyond the rigid structures of classrooms or other similar meeting spaces where students have to raise their hands to be acknowledged, or wait for a leader or teacher to acknowledge them. Like cyphers, these dialogues may occur in an impromptu fashion and always have a goal of allowing students to showcase their perspectives on a given situation that has occurred in the classroom.

The second step, coteaching, involves allowing students to take on traditional teacher roles by planning and then teaching lessons. This process includes the teacher's provision of the time and space for students to familiarize themselves with the science content to be taught and then the teacher observing how students plan for and then deliver the content (Emdin, 2010). This step takes the structure of a hip-hop performance where artists prepare a track and then perform it for an audience. Students are introduced to the subject matter in cogens (i.e., groups) and are introduced to the science content as if they are preparing for a performance for an audience. These students then teach the subject matter to their class while the teacher studies the ways that the students interact with each other as they deliver the content. In this process, the teacher observes the ways that students teach and uses these observations as opportunities to learn how to teach more effectively.

The third C, cosmopolitanism, is based on the philosophical tenet that everyone is responsible for each other (Appiah, 2006). In regard to education, it is refocused to include individuals' responsibility for each other's learning. In my work, I suggest that cosmopolitanism "is evident in the classroom when a co-responsibility for one another and a valuing for each other's realities is part of everyday experiences in the classroom" (Emdin, 2012, p. 62). I argue that a cosmopolitan way of thought is part of a hip-hop existence, and if teachers are able to see how hip-hop youth exhibit cosmopolitanism in their lifeworlds, it is possible for them to bring this way of being into the classroom. Therefore, a part of understanding how to foster a cosmopolitan classroom is to study hip-hop youth's exhibition of cosmopolitanism outside of the classroom and then use out-of-school structures that support this communality within the classroom. For example, if hip-hop youth engage in similar activities outside of school, such as rapping together, riding the train together, or living in the same building, these students should be encouraged to work together in the classroom. Furthermore, part of their classroom activities must incorporate their joint everyday experiences into their classroom presentations.

The fourth C, context incorporation, involves using physical and symbolic artifacts from the students' communities in classroom instruction. For example, a teacher would bring in a picture of the trains in a subway station in New York City in order to teach a lesson about Newton's laws of motion to students from this area. A different teacher could bring in a rock from a local park to teach an earth science lesson about weathering. This process could then be expanded if hip-hop artifacts are used as an integral piece of science instruction. For example, spray cans and graffiti can be used to teach about solutes and solvents in chemistry, and microphones and speakers can be used to teach about sound waves in physics. By bringing those items into the classroom and connecting their use in hip-hop culture to science, the instruction becomes relevant, and youth are more keyed in to the content. This fourth C also involves using analogy and simile in the same ways that rap artists use them in lyrics. In science, this involves providing understandings of science concepts by first connecting them to concepts related to student culture.

The final C, content development, involves the teacher's consistent quest for expertise on science content and his or her willingness to show this process to students. This process requires the teacher to share with students that he or she does not have all the information but is always looking to gain more knowledge on the content discussed in class. This last C also involves the teacher's willingness to admit when he/she does not have a command of the subject matter and a willingness to model for students what the process of gathering new knowledge looks like.

In previous research within urban schools (e.g., Emdin, 2009; Emdin & Lehner, 2008), implementing the steps of Reality Pedagogy has resulted in the emergence of hip-hop themes in each of the above steps, and then a more robust understanding of how to implement hip-hop based pedagogy that goes beyond rapping science or just using rap text. For example, cogenerative dialogues/cyphers evolve into outright rap cyphers where students rap to each other or provide suggestions for how the classroom could be more like out-of-school fields where students interact with each other more meaningfully. Coteaching takes on a spitfire, back-and-forth, question-and-answer process that mirrors out-of-school communication. Cosmopolitan connections from out of the school, such as "having one's back" when adversity arises outside of the classroom, becomes a way of instruction where students "have each other's backs" when they solve a question at the blackboard. The focus on context in instruction enhances the students' thoughts about science as they gather artifacts from their neighborhoods that they can bring to the classroom and use to explain science concepts. Content knowledge gets implanted in students and they expend more time and energy than ever before studying the science content because they learn that the process of gathering information is just as complex as the process of creating a rap.

SCIENCE TALK AND THE CYPHER

Through the descriptions of the rap and science battles earlier in this chapter, I have alluded to some of the similarities between hip-hop and science and discussed the possibilities for looking at the battle as a way to connect hip-hop youth to science. Here, I present another key component of hip-hop, and the chief piece of Reality Pedagogy, and explore its relationship to science and its potential for improving urban science education. This part of hip-hop is the rap cypher: where people stand in a circle and those who rap take turns doing so until everyone who is present gets an opportunity to participate. In cyphers, some people rap, others provide background rhythms to be rapped to, and others support the rappers by providing feedback when they rhyme. During cyphers, the multifaceted nature of the cultural and verbal exchanges among participants leads to the building of communality among members of the cypher that is indicative of the positive attributes of hip-hop. As rappers take turns rapping and other participants enact their roles, members enact certain rules of engagement that are not formally stated but are clearly understood by all participants. In the cypher, these unwritten rules and established norms include subtle words and gestures that alert the person who is rapping that it is time to pass the verbal baton to another rapper, supportive noises made by listeners at certain parts of a rapper's rhyme, and the filling in of words or phrases when a rapper is out of breath.

In certain cyphers, the exchange between rappers (who may not personally know one another prior to the cypher) is so seamless that the entire process appears rehearsed to people who are not familiar with the process. In most cyphers, the person who takes the turn from someone else will reference the previous person's lines and begin rapping immediately after the previous person finishes. In these types of scenarios, the rhythm from handclaps or ambient noise produced by other participants continues without stopping and serves as a backdrop to more fluid exchanges among participants. In cyphers, rappers mix memorized lyrics, completely impromptu rhymes, fantasy, and descriptions of their realities to exchange lyrics and create the ideal amount of exchanges among their peers. In these cyphers, there are equal turns at talk, head nods by people who are present who aren't rappers, cheers by participants when the rapper who is currently at the helm of the cypher says something profound, and a person or group of people providing the background music for the cypher. Although these examples come from the rap cypher, many of these norms and rules of engagement remain consistent in other types of hip-hop cyphers, such as dancing and deejaying.

LESSONS FROM THE CYPHER

To gain the most insight into improving instruction from the cypher, there needs to be a particular focus on the fact that participants in cyphers are most often gathered in a circle. In these circles, they have mutual turns at talk, give quick responses to peers that indicate approval, and engage in various practices that ultimately function to improve the current cypher and upcoming ones. Particular appreciation is given to rappers who are inventive and can reference phenomena that are in their surroundings in their raps, while those who do not enact this practice are still commended for their efforts. These attributes of the cypher are honed in cogenerative dialogues with four to six students, providing much information about how to improve the urban science classroom.

The first lesson from the cypher that I will discuss addresses the physical structure of the classroom. It is based on the fact that the cypher dictates that participants should be organized in a way that facilitates eye contact and has participants positioned just about equidistant from each other. Therefore, the ideal classroom should be structured in a way that allows students to be in close proximity to each other and to the teacher. The cypher teaches educators that in order to facilitate exchange among participants, the classroom has to be organized in a circle, and the teacher has to be positioned in a way that includes him or her as part of the classroom structure and not at the helm of the classroom. The cypher also informs educators about the need to structure the class in such a way that any student, at any given time, can have the floor while engaging in different activities that support the smooth functioning of the classroom. For example, there has to be the space within the classroom for a student to be working on a classroom assignment while another one is conducting a lab and another is doing research. This setup would be analogous to the cypher where a person is rapping, another is creating the beat that is being rapped to, and another is actively watching and providing subtle verbal or gestural supportive feedback to the rapper.

Another significant lesson for teaching that comes from the cypher is based on studies of rappers in cyphers. By studying the ways that rappers in cyphers interact with their peers and understanding the distinct use of language within the cypher, teachers can gain much information about how to interact with students and orchestrate communication among them. In cyphers, the rapper at the helm at any given time can be compared to the teacher. This person, at the moment when he or she is leading the cypher during a rap performance, often draws analogies from the immediate surroundings. In addition, the rapper consistently ensures that the general emotion during the cypher is positive by making references to the words and actions of other members of the cypher during his or her rap.

Finally, the pace and volume of the rap is rarely consistent. In order to draw cypher participants into the rap, the use of voice is significant, and the voice emphasis on lines that the rapper perceives to be memorable is distinct. Usually, a more animated voice indicates to listeners that they should pay closer attention to a particular part of a rap during a verse. In urban science classrooms, when the entire class must be structured in a way that maximizes the talents of all students in the classroom, it is useful for the teacher to engage in a similarly complex use of inflection and volume during a lesson.

APPROACHING GENUINE ARGUMENTATION FOR URBAN YOUTH: CONSIDERING REALITY PEDAGOGY

Unfortunately, in many urban schools that predominantly serve students of color, teachers rarely implement the types of instruction described above that foster argumentation and consider artifacts of hip-hop such as the cypher. In my research in these schools, the general perception of student participation and the type of practices that a "good student" should enact is skewed (Emdin, 2010). Teachers of hip-hop youth perceive students to be actively involved, constructively participating, and behaving appropriately when they enact behaviors that, under normal circumstances in students' out-of-school worlds, would indicate a lack of interest. For example, my ethnographic studies in urban classrooms show that in traditional urban science classes, students are commended for blindly following instructions outlined by the teacher, sitting quietly, and getting prescribed results to lab assignments. In other instances, students who do not talk much in the class and who spend the entire class period copying notes are generally considered by teachers to be well behaved while those who indicate a need or desire to be engaged (by using a lot of gestures and speaking loudly) are considered to be a distraction and thus reprimanded. I argue that viewing actions that normally indicate disinterest as active involvement or communication creates a terrible confusion for both the student and the teacher and limits the student's ability to be fully involved in science. Students begin to perceive that the expected behavior in the classroom is to not question, to be quiet, and to be passive. Consequently, students and teachers rarely get to the point where fluid communication and argumentation becomes a classroom norm. With the absence of communication and argumentation, the achievement gaps in science will persist because students never get to the point where the subject matter becomes important enough to engage with in the same ways that they engage with information being delivered in rap music.

For students in urban science classrooms who are, for the most part, largely influenced by or immersed in hip-hop, the separation between their out-of-school and in-school worlds persists only because educators fail to recognize the con-nections between students' cultural understandings and science. When the rela-tionship between students and their teacher mirrors that of the power-wielders and the powerless, and when teachers position students' experience-based under-standings outside of science, students cannot be expected to have an interest in the discipline. Furthermore, when the rule-by-force ideology that dominates urban science teaching and the current ethos of "doing science work" dominates talk-ing science and argumentation, a passion for science cannot be developed among urban youth. The work in this chapter provides avenues through which educators can begin implementing the new approaches to science education discussed above and finding new pathways though which science can be connected to hip-hop by exploring hip-hop youth realities.

Hip-hop, like science, understands that a factual reality exists, and that "sci-ence, though often in an obtuse and erratic manner, can learn about it" (Gould, 1981, p. 54). One of the strengths of hip-hop is its seemingly obtuse and erratic approach to describing the realities of those who endure urban settings. With hip-hop and science, what is perceived to be incoherent and completely out of the norm can emerge to become widely accepted because of its closeness to what is needed or what makes sense when evidence is presented that supports its validity. Approaches to science teaching and learning that utilize hip-hop culture may be perceived as unconventional, inappropriate, and even unrealistic, but they are the key to connecting youth who have been marginalized from academic success to the world of science. If science education is to satisfy the passions and interests of the hip-hop generation, educators must be willing to withstand the pressure to maintain approaches to instruction that historically have not met the needs of urban youth. Instead, educators must explore new hip-hop based approaches that are more true to student realities. Furthermore, educators who are aware of the value of hip-hop must be willing to move beyond the established notions of what hip-hop can be used for in classrooms and push the field of study into new dimen-sions that more fully encompass the aesthetics and cultural logic of hip-hop and their potential to transform teaching and learning.

REFERENCES

Appiah, K. A. (2006). *Cosmopolitanism: Ethics in a world of strangers*. New York: W. W. Norton

Brown, B. (2006). "It isn't no slang that can be said about this stuff": Language, identity, and appropriating science discourse. *Journal of Research in Science Teaching, 43*(1), 96–126.

Burbules, N., & Berk, R. (1999). Critical thinking and critical pedagogy: Relations, differ-ences, and limits. In T. Popkewitz & L. Fendler (Eds.), *Critical theories in education: Changing terrains of knowledge and politics* (pp. 46–66). New York: Routledge.

Clay, A. (2003). Keepin' it real: Black youth, hip-hop culture, and Black identity. *American Behavioral Scientist, 46*(10), 1346–1358.

Council for Graduate Schools. (2008). Ph.D. Completion Rates Differ by Student Demographics. Retrieved from http://www.cgsnet.org/portals/0/pdf/N_pr_PhDC_bookII.pdf

Dewey, J. (1902). *The child and the curriculum.* Chicago: University of Chicago Press.

Driver, R., Newton, P., & Osborne, J. (2000). Establishing the norms of scientific argumentation in classrooms. *Science Education, 84,* 287–312.

Emdin, C. (2007). Exploring the contexts of urban science classrooms. Part 2: The emergence of rituals in the learning of science. *Cultural Studies of Science Education, 2*(2), 351–373.

Emdin, C. (2009). Reality pedagogy: Hip-hop culture and the urban science classroom. In W. M. Roth (Ed.), *Science education from people for people: Taking a stand(point)* (pp. 72–90). New York: Routledge Publishers.

Emdin, C. (2010). Affiliation and alienation: Hip-hop, rap, and urban science education. *Journal of Curriculum Studies, 42,* 1–25.

Emdin, C. (2012). Reality pedagogy and urban science education: Toward a comprehensive understanding the urban science classroom. In B. J. Frazier, K. Tobin, & C. J. McRobbie (Eds.), *Second international handbook of science education* (pp. 59–68). New York: Springer.

Emdin, C., & Lehner, E. (2008). Moving towards research collaboration in urban schools: Forging team alliances, building solidarity, and navigating challenges. In S. M. Ritchie (Ed.), *Research collaborations: Relationships and praxis* (pp. 83–98). Rotterdam, The Netherlands: Sense Publishers.

Evans, J. A., & Reimer, J. (2009) Open access and global participation in science. *Science, 323*(5917), 1025.

Freire, P. (1970). *Pedagogy of the oppressed.* New York: Continuum.

Ginwright, S. (2004). *Black in school: Afrocentric reform, urban youth, and the promise of hip-hop culture.* New York: Teachers College Press.

Gould, S. J. (1981). *The mismeasure of man.* New York: W.W. Norton & Co.

Ladson-Billings, G. (1994). *The dreamkeepers: Successful teachers of African American children.* San Francisco: Jossey-Bass.

Ladson-Billings, G. (1995). Toward a theory of culturally relevant pedagogy. *American Educational Research Journal, 32,* 465–491.

Laudan, L. (1986). *Science and values: An essay on the aims of science and their role in scientific debate.* Berkeley, CA: University of California Press.

Morrell, E., & Duncan-Andrade, J. M. R. (2002). Promoting academic literacy with urban youth through engaging hip-hop culture. *English Journal, 91*(6), 88–92.

National Center for Education Statistics (NCES). (2006). *Nation's report card 2005 assessment results.* Washington DC: U.S. Department of Education.

National Research Council. (1996). *National science education standards.* Washington, D.C.: National Academy of Sciences.

Norman, O., Ault, C. R., Bentz, B., & Meskimen, L. (2001). The Black–White "achievement gap" as a perennial challenge of urban science education: A sociocultural and historical overview with implications for research and practice. *Journal of Research in Science Teaching, 38,* 1101–1114.

Obama, B. (2009). Remarks by the president at the National Academy of Sciences. Washington, DC.

Rivard, L. P., & Straw, S. B. (2000). The effect of talk and writing on learning science: An exploratory study. *Science Education, 84*, 566–593.

Roth, W. M. (Ed.) (2009). *Science education from people for people: Taking a standpoint.* New York: Routledge.

Samuels, D. (1992). The rap on rap. In J. G Nachbar & K. Lausé (Eds.), *Popular culture: An introductory text* (pp. 353–365). Bowling Green, OH: Bowling Green State University Popular Press.

Tobin, K., & Gallagher, J. J. (1987). The role of target students in the science classroom. *Journal of Research in Science Teaching, 24(1)*, 61–75.

Tobin, K., Zurbano, R., Ford, A., & Carambo, C. (2003). Learning to teach through coteaching and cogenerative dialogue. *Cybernetics & Human Knowing, 10*(2), 51–73.

CHAPTER 2

"I Feel What He Was Doin'"

Urban Teacher Development, Hip-Hop Aesthetics, and Justice-Oriented Teaching

Emery Petchauer

For over a decade and at increasing rates, educators have used hip-hop as an educational resource for a variety of purposes, particularly in urban settings and among students of color (Petchauer, 2009). Often framed as an aspect of culturally responsive (Gay, 2000) or critical pedagogy (Freire, 1970), these efforts range from individual teachers using rap songs to develop critical literacies and empower students (e.g., Ginwright, 2004; Morrell, 2004; Morrell & Duncan-Andrade, 2002; Stovall, 2006) and teaching academic content (e.g., Alexander-Smith, 2004; Wakefield, 2006) to charter schools in urban districts such as Philadelphia and New York utilizing hip-hop as entire course curricula (e.g., Irby, 2006).

Currently, the utility of hip-hop to education extends beyond the K–12 classroom and these kinds of uses. The most recent iteration of hip-hop based education (HHBE) focuses on the aesthetic forms, ways of doing, or cultural logic produced by hip-hop culture and how they can help develop new ways of teaching and learning. In other words, instead of looking at hip-hop as content or a product to be utilized for an educational purpose, educators and theorists look at hip-hop as a cultural form that produces organic ideas, epistemologies, and dilemmas that can inform teaching and learning. Pennycook (2007) summarizes this perspective concisely:

> Hip-hop produces and is produced by a cultural context that often thinks differently about questions of language, writing, identity, and ownership from the mainstream discourses of the academy. (p. 150)

Against this backdrop, this chapter has two interrelated purposes. The first is to illustrate the nature of a set of learning activities designed from two hip-hop aesthetics. The specific goal of these learning activities was to enable a class of African American college students who were recent graduates of urban schools and preservice teachers to respond to justice-oriented teaching and democratic curriculum (e.g., Schultz, 2008). The second purpose is to explore the utility of such learning exercises with this specific cohort of students. This second purpose was guided by the following questions: What do these learning activities enable students to learn about justice-oriented teaching, and what challenges arise as they are used? Overall, this chapter illustrates that these learning activities are useful for these purposes, but they also create new obstacles and potential barriers to student learning.

URBAN TEACHER DEVELOPMENT AND HIP-HOP AESTHETICS

There are important and existing connections among urban graduates who are preservice teachers, democratic and justice-oriented teaching, and hip-hop aesthetics. These connections not only ground the learning activities I describe below in a rich cultural context but also make them appropriate for *these* specific students and *these* specific educational purposes. First, these learning activities are important for these students specifically because of the current emphasis on recruiting graduates from urban schools to return as teachers in urban schools. This "grow your own" model emphasized as early as middle school often appears through education-focused charter schools or themed academies. This model requires that urban graduates engage with and respond to a variety of pedagogical approaches (many of which they never experienced as K–12 students) while in undergraduate teacher development programs. Second, it is important to respond to social justice practices specifically because of their increased use, their capacity to empower students, and their contested meanings in education (North, 2006). Finally, hip-hop is a valuable resource to use for this purpose and population because of its existing connections to urban contexts (Chang, 2005), social justice and protest (e.g., Bynoe, 2004; Chang, 2005), and related uses in education (e.g., Stovall, this volume). Although the broad umbrella of hip-hop includes a wide variety of images, values, and discourses—some of which are deeply problematic— the more progressive and empowering strands that have endured since hip-hop's inception are well suited for justice-oriented purposes.

One important distinction to make with respect to these learning activities described below is between the content of hip-hop and its aesthetic forms (Petchauer, 2009). This distinction is made in regard to the "elements" that make up the core of hip-hop practices: rapping (i.e., *emceeing*), playing and manually manipulating vinyl records (i.e., *DJing* or *turntablism*), graffiti or aerosol art, and forms of dance such as breakdancing (i.e., *b-boying/b-girling*). Within these creative practices, for example, content refers to what a rapper says in a song, but aesthetic form refers to the Black linguistic and stylistic practices according to which it is said (see Alim, 2006; Smitherman, 1997). Content is what records a hip-hop DJ plays; aesthetic form is how they are played: fading or cutting from one record to another, building tension through manually rearranging different parts of the song with multiple copies of a record. Content is what a body looks like while dancing; aesthetic form is the cultural logic in hip-hop by which bodies compete (i.e., *battle*) against one another in the social space called a *cypher* (see Schloss, 2009). Content is the moniker that a graffiti artist paints or draws, but aesthetic form includes the politics of space and rubrics of appraisal that dictate who can paint where and according to what sanctions.

Allowing hip-hop aesthetics to guide educational practice can look many different ways, and some theoretical examples exist in educational research. For example, Rice (2003) examined the hip-hop aesthetic of sampling (Schloss, 2004) in order to depict how hip-hop can produce new ways of teaching argumentation by sampling and juxtaposing events or artifacts against one another and then looking at how these artifacts produce new meaning. Christen (2003) illustrated that there are distinct processes of mentoring, collaboration, citizenship, and apprenticeship within hip-hop graffiti crews according to which new members develop new skills and are socialized into the group. Although these are theoretical examples, the challenge for educators has been moving from such theory to practice. Moving toward practice, Petchauer (2012) has applied the aesthetic of sampling as a way for students to learn from their urban schooling experiences, and in this volume, Emdin used the aesthetics of battling and the cypher to enhance teaching practices in urban science classroom.

The two hip-hop aesthetics that create the learning activities in this chapter are *autonomy/distance* (Shusterman, 2000) and *kinetic consumption* (Kline, 2007). Autonomy/distance refers to the characteristics of hip-hop that resist compartmentalization and problematize modernist dichotomies. In other words, hip-hop is seldom "either/or" but more often "both/and." Shusterman points to hip-hop luminary KRS-ONE and his concurrent status as emcee, teacher, activist, and philosopher as one example of this aesthetic. This characteristic is also commonly illustrated by the limitations of hip-hop musical subgenres to accurately capture hip-hop music. Subgenres such as conscious, gangsta, reality, hard core, or party rap are commonly used in an attempt to describe different artists, but these are largely insufficient because many artists at different periods in their careers (or even within a single album) can accurately be classified into any number of these categories simultaneously. The same applies to judgments about the moral value of much hip-hop music, wherein a single song can be constructed as a cautionary tale of street violence or as a glorification of that same topic (Potter, 1995).

Kinetic consumption (Kline, 2007) refers to the fact that "hip-hop is meant to be felt and not just seen and/or heard" (p. 55). A key feature of authenticity and appreciation in any hip-hop activity is when the audience or participants experience a deep affective resonation illustrated through some kinetic response. This aesthetic is often suggested through the common phrase in hip-hop communities, *I feel you*. Response could be verbal such as shouts of appreciation, call and response, or singing/rapping along. Bodily responses include head nodding and forms of hip-hop dance such as breaking. Nonphysical responses could include an affective reaction or agreement with an idea or experience. Some cultural observers point to the kinetic associations of the verb *hop* in the term *hip-hop* as an implicit indicator of hip-hop's kinetic and dynamic characteristics.

Kinetic consumption (Kline, 2007) is further elucidated by a focus on an African-centered epistemology that is based on affect. According to this system of knowing, affective or emotional experiences are valid and crucial ways of knowing the world and building knowledge (Akbar, 1984; Asante, 1988). These contrast a Eurocentric, Enlightenment epistemology that privileges reason and rationality as the primary and valid ways of knowing. Since emotional and affective experiences are often the first kinds of experiences individuals have with a phenomenon, this way of knowing is seen as an important balance to Eurocentric rationality (Akbar, 1984).

LEARNING THROUGH HIP-HOP AESTHETICS: STUDENTS AND CONTEXT

The learning activities described below took place over the course of 2 semesters. The course in which these learning activities took place, Education and Society, is an introductory education class consisting of 24 African American students (15 women and 9 men) at a historically Black university in the Northeast. Consistent with the university demographics, the majority of students in the course graduated from urban school districts such as Philadelphia, Pittsburgh, New York, and Newark, New Jersey. Education and Society is a core-curriculum class designed to provide students from urban schools with a foundational understanding of their schooling experiences—how they have been shaped and conditioned in both desirable and undesirable ways—as a necessary platform for learning at the university level and preparation as teachers.

The set of learning activities based upon the hip-hop aesthetics of autonomy/distance (Shusterman, 2000) and kinetic consumption (Kline, 2007) was organized around one of the course texts, *Spectacular Things Happen Along the Way* by Brian D. Schultz (2008). The text gives the account of "room 405" as Schultz and his 5th-grade class on the South Side of Chicago co-constructed a democratic curriculum called Project Citizen, and Schultz utilized related social justice–oriented teaching. During the school year, the 5th-grade students designed a year-long project around what they saw as one of the most pressing needs in their lives: a new school building. The rich descriptions and photographs of the school facilities (e.g., bullet holes in windows, broken toilets and bathroom faucets) make clear why the 5th-grade students chose this focus. During the school year, the 5th-grade students designed ways to garner support from local, state, and national politicians and access various resources. A consistent element of the text also involves the dilemmas that Schultz faces as the teacher/facilitator of the democratic project, such as deciding whether to step in and exercise power when he sees that the children might be misrepresented and manipulated by media outlets. Overall, the text provides a rich and realistic example of a democratic and social justice approach, including the tensions that both students and teachers must navigate.

Student Assignments

Given the demographics of Education and Society and the focus of the class, *Spectacular Things* (as we called the book in class) was an appropriate text through which to explore the nature and use of hip-hop aesthetics. These subsequent learning activities provided two main sources of data. In the culminating learning activity with this book, using autonomy/distance (Shusterman, 2000), students were to discuss in written form which educational aspects and practices of room 405 could be considered both good and bad or helpful and harmful to the 5th-graders in the text. In this way, students were led to resist binary and compartmentalized thinking when evaluating educational practices in the text. Also, based upon kinetic consumption (Kline, 2007), the project required students to discuss which classroom practices and occurrences they "felt" and explain why. A clear distinction was made here between practices students felt and practices that they felt were of a certain quality (such as effective), wherein this second use of the term can be understood as a substitute for a different process such as belief or thought. These final written projects submitted by students totaled 81 pages of double-spaced text.

As an ongoing assignment that prepared students for this final project, students also completed eight reflective journals through the semester (between 250 and 300 words each). In these journals, students were directed to write about practices they felt, discuss practices that were surprising, pinpoint similar or dissimilar experiences from their own schooling experiences, discuss practices they agreed or disagreed with, or explain connections to other class readings. These journals served a variety of functions. They increased the likelihood that students would read the chapters, allowed me to monitor progress, and created a resource of emerging reflections that students could use in the final project. I collected, read, and returned journals throughout the semester, but I intentionally did not include them in data analysis. Instead, the final project described above, constructed in part by these journals, was the central pool of data I analyzed. Finally, these primary data sources were triangulated by observations and conversational interviews (Patton, 2001) with students over the course of both semesters and field notes based upon classroom interactions and discussions.

Kinetic Consumption

I used a variety of qualitative data analysis techniques to understand the utility of these learning activities. I used constant comparative coding (Strauss & Corbin, 1998) to analyze data from students' final projects and understand what kinetic consumption (Kline, 2007) allowed them to identify. Coding data through this process produced three categories: events, student or teacher qualities, and curriculum. I also used classical content analysis to identify the number of items coded into each of these categories.

In order to understand the utility of kinetic consumption (Kline, 2007) and not just what it allowed students to identify, I also coded data into three tiers based upon how clear students made the basis (i.e., epistemology) of kinetic consumption. I used constant comparative coding (Strauss & Corbin, 1998) as well as key-words-in-context (i.e., paying attention to the context of important words such as *felt*). Tiers one and two constitute correct applications of kinetic consumption but are separated by how clearly students made their reasons for feeling different items they identified. In other words, responses coded into tier one make clear upon what kinetic consumption was based. In tier two, the basis for kinetic consumption is unclear. Tier three constitutes what I judged as misuses and misapplications of the approach. In many instances, my coding of responses into this tier hinged on students' correct use of the term *felt*. For example, if a student reported that she "felt a certain practice was empowering to students," I judged that as an incorrect use of kinetic consumption since the key term to kinetic consumption, *felt*, in such an instance is interchangeable with terms such as *thought* or *believed*. However, if the student reported that she "felt a certain practice because it was empowering to students," I judged this as a correct use of kinetic consumption.

This distinction based upon such a fine linguistic detail could indeed seem like simple semantics, word choice, or writing voice and thus not constitutive of a fundamental difference in meaning making. However, I make this fine distinction and analytical move based upon two assumptions. The first of these is that word choices are not arbitrary but are emblematic of cognitive and affective processes. Although people's vocabularies would certainly set the boundaries within which they could express themselves or describe their cognitive and affective processes, I judge that illustrating the parameters and meanings of kinetic consumption in class gave students enough background knowledge to warrant my judgment. Second, I make this distinction based upon its existence in hip-hop aesthetics and Hip-Hop Nation Language (Alim, 2006) created by local hip-hop and Black speech communities. As a whole, hip-hop aesthetics and language support this distinction, and failing to make such a fine distinction would be incongruent with the theoretical basis of this exploration and learning activities.

Autonomy/Distance

I also used constant comparative coding (Strauss & Corbin, 1998) to analyze the practices that autonomy/distance allowed students to identify as both helpful and harmful as well as why. I used classical content analysis to calculate the frequency with which students identified items. An analysis to produce tiers, as described in the previous section, was not necessary for autonomy/distance because there were fewer opportunities for students to misuse it compared to kinetic consumption.

EVALUATING JUSTICE-ORIENTED TEACHING: KINETIC CONSUMPTION

The students in the class felt different aspects of the democratic project that I coded into events, student or teacher qualities, and curriculum, with some overlap in a few instances. The categories, frequency with which students identified items in these categories, and examples of the items are summarized in Table 2.1. The data illustrate that kinetic consumption allowed students to identify a variety of important practices in the text. Overwhelmingly, though, students felt events that took place in the classroom and various aspects of the democratic curriculum rather than student and teacher qualities. Excluded from Table 2.1 are instances in which students seemed to misunderstand or misuse kinetic consumption, which will be discussed below.

A closer analysis of student responses illustrates some of the more specific ways that kinetic consumption worked in this learning exercise and the different levels of success that students had with it. As described above, I divided these levels of success into three tiers based upon how clearly students made the epistemological application of kinetic consumption. Below, I share some specific examples from each of these tiers to illustrate in more detail students' uses and misuses of kinetic consumption.

Tier One

The 13 student responses classified into tier one demonstrated clear applications of kinetic consumption as well as why students felt the coordinating items

Table 2.1. Categories of Kinetic Consumption, Frequencies, and Examples

Category	Frequency	Example
Student quality	4	Gratefulness of students for project
Teacher quality	2	Schultz's use of negative criticism
Event	17	Students helping themselves by giving speeches and writing letters
Curriculum	22	Problem-based focus of Project Citizen

in Schultz's (2008) text. Candace (a pseudonym, as are all student names) made her use of kinetic consumption very clear by stating, "Instances and practices that I felt throughout the book were not only things I liked, they were things I understood and could relate too [sic]." One of the practices that Candace felt was when the 5th-grade students identified the problems in the school facilities and environment that affected their lives. Candace relayed that she felt these because she could relate to them due to the fact that most of the problems identified by the students in the text also existed at her high school:

> For example the missing water fountains, the backed up toilets, bullet holes in windows, and the problem with the heat. I understood how those issues can prevent one from learning, [and] that was why I really felt what these kids were going through.

Candace also felt the problem-based nature of Project Citizen because, again, it was similar to an experience she had in high school. Her experience was a curricular unit called Project Change that she described as teaching students "to overcome whatever disadvantages they had and to use those disadvantages to make something positive." Even though she remembered Project Change as less successful than Project Citizen in the text, the similar experience still enabled her to feel that element of the text.

Shamika was also clear about why she felt the successful and sustained collaborative work among the students in the classroom based upon her belief that "it is a task to get young people to work together, especially if it does not involve a television set or video game."

> At first I thought, "Well, these kids are doing well now but it's only going to be a matter of time before they give up." I will be the first to admit that I was wrong, and they kept being persistent with their project.

In this instance, it seems that she felt the students' sustained collaboration because it contrasted with a negative (mis)conception that she held about adolescents, namely that they have difficulty working together, particularly when the work is not mediated by technology.

Having similar experiences of their own allowed students to feel certain classroom practices in the text, but recognizing a disconnect between their own experiences and those of the 5th-graders in the text also allowed them to feel practices. Stephanie illustrated this clearly by discussing why she felt the fact that the students could discuss and identify not only the school conditions and related effects but also the related conditions of the surrounding community:

> I did not have this luxury of discussion at an early age, not at school anyway. So, this really got my attention during the reading and made me wish that

my fifth grade teacher took such an interest about what my class thought about what was going on in our world.

Overall, students' responses in tier one made correct usages of kinetic consumption and also made clear why they felt these particular practices.

Tier Two

The three responses classified into tier two constitute instances when students felt particular practices, but the reasons for doing so were not made as clear as in tier one. Kareem explained that he felt the aspect of the curriculum that was based upon the 5th-grade students' ideas with a focus on tangible results:

For example, to "get the word out," the children having input and being excited about the subject matter and goals of the project demonstrate[s] that they want to study something that will have tangible results. The children are also attain[ing] different skills, experiences, and exposure to different things through the curriculum. The children are speaking publicly, interviewing officials, writing up plans, and executing them within a real life setting.

Despite the fact that Kareem felt this aspect of the curriculum, it was unclear specifically why he felt this aspect or upon what he based kinetic consumption. It could be based upon a belief that learning activities in schools normally do not have such a practical, tangible focus. It also could have been based upon a variety of personal experiences that positioned him to make a meaningful transaction with the text. Despite these possibilities, Kareem failed to mention these or other reasons for why he felt this curricular aspect. Thus, without appropriate details, the source of kinetic consumption in this instance is unclear.

Amanda pointed out a variety of Schultz's student-centered practices in line with the democratic curriculum that she felt. These included allowing students to generate their own ideas, lead their own discussions, formulate interview questions, write support letters, and even learn from their failures. Her explanation of these practices demonstrated that she understood the benefit of such practices:

Often times we see teachers in classrooms shoot down their students' ideas or take charge of the discussion. This teacher in particular sat back and watched as his students let their creativity build. His students were always involved and always aware of what was going on because it was their project. It was their school and they wanted to take all necessary steps in rebuilding it.

Although Amanda demonstrated a clear understanding of the practices, it remains unclear precisely why she felt these practices. It is possible that she felt these practices because they contrasted with what she believed teachers often do or because learning activities often position students in passive rather than active roles. However, without such details, the basis of kinetic consumption in this example is unknown.

Tier Three

The third tier of student responses contains seven instances in which students did respond to the democratic practices, but they did so by misusing kinetic consumption. Briana illustrates the most common misuse through her discussion of Schultz's perspective of his students:

One particular incident that I *felt was good* [emphasis added] was that the teacher was great in realizing the strong potential of the students. He wanted to take away the scripted lesson plan and let the students develop their own unique interests.

Other student responses mirrored this form. In doing so, they did not necessarily feel practices were "good" as Briana did, but they felt practices had other qualities, such as being "interesting," "helpful," "surprising," and "effective." In such responses, students' uses of "feeling" can be seen as synonymous with "thinking" or "believing." In other words, in the example above, it would be accurate to read the response to mean "I [thought] it was good." The term *feeling*, as it is used here, is not clearly an instance of kinetic consumption or an affective response to the material in the text.

Although some students misused kinetic consumption, this does not necessarily mean that the learning activity was entirely fruitless. Instead of using feeling as the main method of response, some students responded to the text by discussing what they agreed with or what surprised them. Darren illustrated this response clearly when he talked about how the students garnered media support for their efforts toward a new school building:

I thought to myself, "How could these students be prepared with the intelligence to hold a [sic] interview with someone and receive the accurate information that they need?" . . . It makes me think that the students were highly intelligent but were being stereotyped because of the surrounding school.

Darren clearly did not incorporate the aspect of kinetic consumption into his response. However, in his attempt to do so, he gathered an important point about how stereotypes often function to limit the perceived capabilities of adolescents in some urban schools.

Summary

Kinetic consumption allowed students to identify a variety of items from Schultz (2008) that are related to democratic curriculum and justice-oriented teaching. These items can be classified as student or teacher qualities, events, or curricular aspects. Students' responses can be grouped into three tiers based upon their accurate use of the hip-hop aesthetic and how clear they made their reasons for feeling different items. The basis for students feeling different practices included having similar or different experiences as well as recognizing that the behaviors and accomplishments of the 5th-graders in Schultz's classroom contrasted negative stereotypes about urban adolescents.

EVALUATING JUSTICE-ORIENTED TEACHING: AUTONOMY/DISTANCE

In addition to the kinetic consumption activities above, students in Education and Society also responded to democratic curriculum and justice-oriented teaching by using the hip-hop aesthetic of autonomy/distance (Shusterman, 2000). Students were to cite and explain which educational practices associated with Project Citizen could have been both helpful and harmful to the 5th-grade students in the text. Table 2.2 summarizes the seven identified items, frequencies, and reasons why students thought they could be both helpful and harmful.

As with kinetic consumption, this part of the learning activity enabled the students to identify a variety of classroom practices from the text and think divergently to consider ways that they can be both helpful and harmful to the 5th-grade students. Compared to kinetic consumption, however, there were fewer opportunities for students to misuse or fail at using autonomy/distance.

Looking at the frequency of identified items, the two items students recognized most often as being both helpful and harmful were *students learned by doing/nondirective teacher* and *contact with "outsiders."* It is also worth noting that *students learning by doing* is closely related to *teachers and students co-constructing the curriculum*, which was cited five times. To provide more insight into these two main items, I share narrative data from student responses below.

Students Learn by Doing/Nondirectiveness of Teacher

Throughout Schultz's (2008) account of Project Citizen, his 5th-grade students learned by doing. This included students delegating responsibilities among themselves, creating and distributing surveys, analyzing data together, creating press packets, giving presentations, and other activities. Michael described some of the benefits of this approach:

Table 2.2. Identified Practices via Autonomy/Distance and Reasons Why They Are Helpful and Harmful

Practice	Frequency	Helpful	Harmful
Students learned by doing/nondirective teacher	10	Engaged students in learning activities; empowered students	Students not successful in a teacher-centered classroom; missed reading, writing, and math; errors went uncorrected
Dependency on Internet	1	Supplied them with important information	Caused them to overlook other relevant resources
Contact with "outsiders" (e.g., reporters, politicians)	10	Publicized their efforts and solicited help	Possible misrepresentation; negative perceptions of Project; police brutality
Use of culturally relevant texts (e.g., Martin Luther King Jr.; Malcolm X)	1	Taught students about political rights and was useful for language arts	Students might "go to extreme" and boycott or resort to violence
Teacher addressing racial differences between himself and students	1	Can learn from one another	Students could reject him due to racial differences
Teacher and students co-constructing curriculum	5	Kept student interest, made curriculum relevant	Students chose topics unrelated to state tests; unprepared for future
Students' high expectations for results from project	2	If successful, reinforcement of positive, democratic values	If not successful, sense of failure and rejection of democratic values

The students were in charge of Project Citizen. This was good because the students had to teach and learn from each other. It was helpful because they learned the basic fundamentals of how to be productive and how to work as one.

Other students echoed similar benefits. They also pointed out that the 5th-grade students felt ownership of their learning, were more motivated, and transferred these skills to local activism even after the school year had finished.

Michael also clearly articulated some of the potential drawbacks of the learn-by-doing focus of Project Citizen. These drawbacks were based upon the traditional academic skills that were not at the center of learning in Project Citizen.

> The bad part of the classroom practices [was that] the children missed out on the major focus of learning. The educational aspect of school such as reading, writing, and math were barely a focus for the teacher in the classroom. I feel that these [errors] are reflected throughout the book, for example the way the students talked and wrote.

In referencing errors "reflected throughout the book," Michael was referring to quotations from 5th-grade students and excerpts from their writing, which contained some grammatical errors or were printed according to their African American Vernacular speech. Schultz opted not to edit materials that his students created (e.g., press packets) or make them speak so-called Standard English. Echoing Michael's assessment, J'nai also highlighted the absence of reading, writing, and math instruction, but framed the potential disadvantages in terms of the following school year:

> I believe that because when [the students] move on further in education, they are going to be missing out on some important information because they were working on the project. This could hurt the students later on in time because their curriculum was based on Project Citizen, and they didn't have a normal [5th-] grade education.

Through examples such as these, Michael and J'nai demonstrate a clear recognition that Project Citizen is atypical in public education. Though it may be empowering to the students of room 405 during this particular school year, there are potential risks for these students as they move beyond Schultz's classroom.

Contact with "Outsiders"

One of the main ways Schultz's students garnered support for their cause was by soliciting attention from reporters and local, state, and national politicians, many of whom visited the class and were given tours of the school. The benefits of this attention were clear throughout the text, as summarized by Kareem: "The radio shows, interviews, and visits to the school brought much renown to the efforts, brilliance, and determination that these children put forth." However, students also recognized some of the potential dangers that arise when one solicits help from outsiders. Kareem also summarized some of these: "The negatives [could have been] cruel criticism. For instance if some shock jock got on the radio negatively responding to their efforts, [this] could have been very hurtful to the children."[1]

Students also recognized that despite the apparent good intentions of reporters and outsiders who visited the school, the representations that they created of the 5th-grade students, the school, and Project Citizen were outside of the control of Schultz and the 5th-grade students. Consequently, the participants of Project Citizen were made vulnerable by letting outsiders into their classroom community. Ashley made this vulnerability clear by speaking about an article written about the class and Project Citizen:

> This experience could have also been harmful, because of what might have been reported once the new article was released. If the news article reported of all negative things such as [Project Citizen] being a waste of time, [it] could have been discouraging to the 5th-graders. If this would have happened, these students may have wanted to give up all of their hard work and efforts and feel like they wasted their time.

Other students supported this position, highlighting that reports could have focused on negative behaviors or school conditions outside of room 405 or "twisted [students'] words all up and made the 5th-grade [students] seem unintelligent and incompetent, which not only embarrasses them as kids, but also [has] a huge effect on their self-esteem."

Summary

The hip-hop aesthetic of autonomy/distance allowed students to identify a variety of justice-oriented and democratic practices from room 405 that could be both helpful and harmful to the 5th-grade students. Identified most often were two items: that students learn by doing/nondirective teacher and contact with "outsiders." With these two items, students recognized the clear benefits, but also understood that outside of room 405, these characteristics of Project Citizen could harm the 5th-grade students in two ways. First, since Project Citizen was a stark contrast to other classes, the students of room 405 might miss out on important skills, information, and modes of learning that will be necessary for their success in later grades. Second, welcoming outsiders into room 405 made the 5th-grade students vulnerable to misrepresentation and manipulation in media outlets.

CRITIQUING AND IMPROVING HIP-HOP AESTHETIC LEARNING ACTIVITIES

The results of this inquiry illustrated how hip-hop aesthetics can be used to create learning activities that enable students to respond to democratic and justice-oriented teaching practices. Although these activities were successful at the most general level, it is necessary to critically evaluate their intended and unintended implications. In other words, it is important to recognize that although some of the intended goals were met, activities and pedagogies in HHBE often "produce new cultural margins and, thus, new forms of marginalization" (Hill, 2009, p. 64). This was the case with both kinetic consumption and autonomy/distance because the new opportunities they created for student learning were not without new obstacles as well.

Kinetic Consumption

Kinetic consumption as a guiding aesthetic allowed students a greater margin of error compared with autonomy/distance. This was evident through tier three of the responses in which students misused kinetic consumption. That there was such a margin of error and subsequent responses from students illustrates an important point about HHBE as a component of culturally responsive pedagogy (Gay, 2000; Ladson-Billings, 1994) for African American students or as a form of cultural modeling (Lee, 1995). This point is that learning activities based upon hip-hop aesthetics are not automatically effective for all African American students. In other words, according to how they were utilized in the work in this chapter, the learning activities were not inherently culturally responsive for these African American students and thus not inherently effective.

This room for error brings up the larger question about what enables someone to feel something—to connect though affect—and thus experience kinetic consumption. The students' responses based upon kinetic consumption that fit into tier one were based upon having similar experiences to those of the 5th-grade students in the text, lacking yet desiring similar experiences, or times when occurrences in the text contrasted with stereotypes about urban adolescents. This suggests that students who might have had more experiences in urban schools and contexts were more likely to be successful with kinetic consumption when used in tandem with Schultz (2008). Conversely, students without experiences similar to those of the 5th-grade students in the text experienced more barriers when it came to kinetic consumption. Though the results above suggest this is the case, descriptive data about the more detailed urban schooling experiences of students in Education and Society could further support or refute this claim.

These shortcomings of kinetic consumption suggest that it should be used in instances when students have had experiences related to the topic at hand. Whereas a process such as analysis, which normally entails a degree of affective detachment, might have fewer barriers to success when students have not had personal or affective experience with a subject, kinetic consumption might be more effective when students have had such affective and personal experiences. Using it in instances such as this would create fewer opportunities for students to misuse it or fail when using it.

The misuses and shortcomings of kinetic consumption also suggest that there is room to improve its use in classrooms. One clear instance in which this could take place is through the reflective journal activities that preceded the culminating learning activity. In addition to their various functions outlined earlier, these on-going exercises could also be venues for students to refine their understanding and use of kinetic consumption through feedback provided by the instructor. Adding this element to these assignments would likely decrease the instances in which students would misuse and misapply kinetic consumption, make the learning activities more rewarding, and ultimately improve the use of kinetic consumption as a culturally responsive approach.

Autonomy/Distance

One downfall of autonomy/distance is the degree to which it allowed students to see potentially harmful consequences that were beyond what Schultz could foresee and explain in the text. Students identified important ways that the classroom practices could be simultaneously helpful and harmful, but the ones that students recognized most frequently (i.e., students learn by doing/nondirective teacher and contact with "outsiders") were duplications of what Schultz also recognized or had to navigate in the text. Although it was indeed accurate and acceptable for students to identify some of these items that Schultz also identified, autonomy/distance would facilitate a more beneficial learning process if students were directed to explore helpful and harmful effects that were not explicitly covered by Schultz in the text. Additionally, autonomy/distance as it was used did not enable students to engage with the different meanings of social justice education and consider the subsequent implications. For example, one important distinction exists between the concept of justice as equal distribution of goods and resources, and justice as the relationships between groups in particular settings (Young, 1990). As there are a variety of meanings of the term *social justice* in education (McDonald, 2007; North, 2006), these meaning(s), who creates them, and the implications thereof are important dilemmas to engage.

These shortcomings of autonomy/distance suggest that in future uses, students would benefit from having more analytical distance from Schultz as a narrator. In a sense, students' responses to the democratic practices would be enhanced if they critiqued Schultz as a positioned narrator instead of reading him more as an omniscient one. To be sure, Schultz often acknowledges that his perspectives are limited because his social experiences are different from those of his 5th-grade students. However, this acknowledgment alone was not sufficient to enable students to recognize his positionality and incorporate subsequent implication into their analyses. This shift would seem not only to enable students to see beyond Schultz's perspective but also to interrogate the implicit definition(s) of social justice upon which the practices are based.

In order for students to have more critical-analytical distance from both Schultz as a narrator and the social justice practices in the text, there need to be modifications to the learning exercises. One of these modifications would be to present students with different dimensions and aspects of social justice education outside of the account that Schultz (2008) gives (e.g., Ayers, Quinn, & Stovall, 2008; McDonald, 2007) as they engage that text. Such an addition might give students a broader lexicon and more precise critical vision to see beyond the insights that Schultz presents.

CONCLUSION

This chapter contributes to the area of hip-hop aesthetics in education by illustrating and putting into practice a set of learning activities based upon kinetic consumption (Kline, 2007) and autonomy/distance (Shusterman, 2000). This chapter has demonstrated that these are fruitful learning activities when used among urban graduates and preservice teachers for the purpose of enabling them to respond to democratic and justice-oriented teaching. However, the chapter also illustrated that just as learning exercises create new opportunities to learn, they also create new opportunities for failure. Beyond kinetic consumption and autonomy/distance, there are other hip-hop aesthetics and practices with related uses that teachers can create. These include sampling and appropriation (Petchauer, 2012; Schloss, 2004; Shusterman, 2000), battling (Emdin this volume; Schloss, 2009, flow (Pennycook, 2007), and others (see Chang, 2006). The applications and implications of these hip-hop aesthetics extend beyond democratic curricula and justice-oriented teaching. As this is the newest burgeoning area of HHBE, there is much room for researchers and practitioners to explore the uses of these other hip-hop aesthetics in teaching, learning, and curriculum.

NOTE

1. Kareem's example here is most likely a reference to the now-infamous Don Imus incident in which the radio personality made racist and sexist remarks about the Rutgers University women's basketball team in light of their appearance in the NCAA Final Four.

REFERENCES

Akbar, N. (1984). Afrocentric social science for human liberation. *Journal of Black Studies, 14*, 395–414.

Alexander-Smith, A. C. (2004). Feeling the rhythm of the critically conscious mind. *English Journal, 93*(3), 58–63.

Alim, H. S. (2006). *Roc the mic right: The language of hip-hop culture*. New York: Routledge.

Asante. M. K. (1988). *Afrocentricity*. Trenton, NJ: Africa World.

Ayers, W., Quinn, T., & Stovall, D. (2008). *Handbook of social justice in education*. New York: Routledge.

Bynoe, Y. (2004). *Stand and deliver: Political activism, leadership, and hip-hop culture*. Brooklyn, NY: Soft Skull Press.

Chang, J. (2005). *Can't stop, won't stop: A history of the hip-hop generation*. New York: St. Martin's Press.

Chang, J. (2006). *Total chaos: The art and aesthetics of hip-hop*. New York: Basic Books.

Christen, R. S. (2003). Hip-hop learning: Graffiti as an educator of urban teenagers. *Educational Foundations, 17*(4), 57–82.

Freire, P. (1970). *Pedagogy of the oppressed*. New York: Continuum.

Gay, G. (2000). *Culturally responsive teaching: Theory, research, and practice*. New York: Teachers College Press.

Ginwright, S. (2004). *Black in school: Afrocentric reform, urban youth, and the promise of hip-hop culture*. New York: Teachers College Press.

Hill, M. L. (2009). *Beats, rhymes, and classroom life: Hip-hop, pedagogy, and the politics of identity*. New York: Teachers College Press.

Irby, D. (2006). *Do the knowledge: A standards based hip-hop learning and activity guide*. Retrieved from http://artsanctuary.org/wp-content/uploads/2011/12/Do-The-Knowledge-A-Standards-Based-Hip-Hop-Learning-Guide-Updated-11-06.pdf

Kline, C. (2007). *Represent!: Hip-hop and the self-aesthetic relation* (Unpublished doctoral dissertation). Bloomington, IN: Indiana University.

Ladson-Billings, G. (1994). *The dreamkeepers: Successful teachers of African American children*. San Francisco: Jossey-Bass.

Lee, C. (1995). The use of signifying as a scaffold for literary interpretation. *Journal of Black Psychology, 21*(4), 357–381.

McDonald, M. A. (2007). The joint exercise of social justice and teacher education. *Teachers College Record, 109*(8), 2047–2081.

Morrell, E. (2004). *Linking literacy and popular culture: Finding connections for lifelong learning*. Norwood, MA: Christopher-Gordon.

Morrell, E., & Duncan-Andrade, J. M. R. (2002). Promoting academic literacy with urban youth through engaging hip-hop culture. *English Journal, 91*(6), 88–92.

North, C. (2006). More than words? Delving into the substantive meaning(s) of "social justice" in education. *Review of Educational Research, 76*(4), 507–535.

Patton, M. Q. (2001). *Qualitative research and evaluation methods* (3rd ed.). Thousand Oaks, CA: Sage Publications.

Pennycook, A. (2007). *Global Englishes and transcultural flows*. London: Routledge.

Petchauer, E. (2009). Framing and reviewing hip-hop educational research. *Review of Educational Research, 79*, 946–978.

Petchauer, E. (2012). Sampling memories: Using hip-hop aesthetics to learn from urban schooling experiences. *Educational Studies, 48*, 137–155.

Potter, R. A. (1995). *Spectacular vernaculars: Hip-hop and the politics of postmodernism*. Albany: State University of New York.

Rice, J. (2003). The 1963 hip-hop machine: Hip-hop pedagogy as composition. *College Composition and Communication, 54*(3), 453–471.

Schloss, J. G. (2004). *Making beats: The art of sample-based hip-hop.* Hanover, CT: Wesleyan University Press.

Schloss, J. G. (2009). *Foundation: B-boys, b-girls, and hip-hop culture in New York.* New York: Oxford University Press.

Schultz, B. D. (2008). *Spectacular things happen along the way: Lessons from an urban classroom.* New York: Teachers College Press.

Shusterman, R. (2000). *Pragmatist aesthetics: Living beauty, rethinking art* (2nd ed.). Lanham, MD: Rowman & Littlefield.

Smitherman, G. (1997). "The chain remains the same": Communicative practices in the hip-hop nation. *Journal of Black Studies, 28*(1), 3–25.

Stovall, D. (2006). We can relate: Hip-hop culture, critical pedagogy, and the secondary classroom. *Urban Education, 41*(6), 585–602.

Strauss, A., & Corbin J. (1998). *Basics of qualitative research: Techniques and procedures for developing grounded theory.* Thousand Oaks, CA: Sage.

Wakefield, S. R. (2006). Using music sampling to teach research skills. *Teaching English in the Two-Year College, 33*(4), 357–360.

Young, I. M. (1990). *Social justice and the politics of difference.* Princeton, NJ: Princeton University Press.

CHAPTER 3

Rewriting the Remix

College Composition and the Educational Elements of Hip-Hop

James Braxton Peterson

Composition courses at universities tend to employ a wide range of thematic content that is often dependent upon who is teaching them. As scholars of Hip Hop culture continue to enter into and thrive within the academy, the advent of formal innovations of composition courses that reflect the scholarly interests of this growing group of composition pedagogues continues steadily. In this context, the emergence of Hip Hop themed composition courses has been inevitable. Hip Hop composition is not, in this chapter, about composing or performing rap lyrics as a means of learning how to compose descriptive, argumentative, analytical, persuasive, or research-based papers. Instead, Hip Hop composition explores various aspects of Hip Hop culture in order to engage the learning processes involved in becoming strong(er) writers and continuous critical thinkers.

This chapter establishes pedagogical and theoretical foundations for the thematic utility of Hip Hop culture in composition courses. These pedagogical foundations rest upon the aesthetic utility of specific elements of Hip Hop culture (such as MCing or DJing) and the intuitive relationships that these elements have with education generally as well as with certain writing/composition techniques specifically (e.g., brainstorming or authorship itself). Hip Hop culture's educational potential and its pedagogical potential in the composition classroom rely heavily on rap music's obsession with language, wordplay, and various linguistic interactions. Many scholars employ the West African term *nommo* to capture this emphasis on the power of the word (Meachum, 2003; Smitherman, 1997). However, the crux of the pedagogical argument is that Hip Hop culture presents numerous opportunities for teachers to leverage popular culture in order to make instructive interventions in the composition classroom.

Hip Hop scholars and, in fact, one of the culture's founding figures, Afrika Bambaataa, argue that the "fifth element" of Hip Hop culture is knowledge. This assertion is predicated on a range of epistemic considerations that are generated through Hip Hop discourses that articulate the artistry and aesthetics in the foundational elements as well as the knowledge that underpins our best comprehension of the culture's history, its relationship to politics, and its emergence in certain socioeconomic circumstances. In this chapter, the fifth element is situated atop the list of what I am referring to as Hip Hop's educational elements: *knowledge, consciousness, search and discovery*, and *participation*.

THE EDUCATIONAL ELEMENTS OF HIP HOP CULTURE

Hip Hop culture as a whole consists of four main expressive elements. Since the early/mid-1970s, these elements have been MCing/rapping, DJing, b-boying/b-girling, and writing graffiti. Although there is direct educational capacity in the literal elements of Hip Hop, less attention has been paid to how education is implicitly framed through Hip Hop culture, or what I call the educational elements of Hip Hop. These four educational elements consist of the following: 1) knowledge, 2) consciousness, 3) search and discovery, and 4) participation. Together with the foundational elements of Hip Hop, the educational elements underwrite many initiatives that bring Hip Hop culture into classrooms at different levels of schooling and across various disciplines. Importantly, these educational elements are not disconnected from the traditional four elements of Hip Hop. Rather, the educational elements derive from the sensibilities, mindsets, and approaches embedded in the four main expressive Hip Hop elements, or what Petchauer (2009) calls "hip-hop aesthetic forms" (p. 961).

Knowledge

Knowledge in (or of) Hip Hop is one of the authenticating principles of the culture's constituents. Much as in jazz or other forms of Black musical culture, the denizens of Hip Hop pride themselves on an ability to reproduce the facts, information, and/or what is known about the culture. This practice has been buttressed by an array of other cultural/social practices such as Hip Hop's overall competitiveness, an infusion of influences from certain philosophical entities such as the 5% Nation of Gods and Earths, and an abiding protectiveness of the culture from exploitation and external appropriation.[1] The knowledge educational element of Hip Hop culture also assumes its traditional meaning of skills and information cultivated (and learned) through education and experience. Thus, the concept of mastery, exemplified via monikers such as "Grand Master," pervades each of the foundational elements. The artisans and organic historians of the culture demonstrate the wealth of knowledge generated through the practice of any of the foundational elements as well the history that shapes the development of the culture overall. Moreover (and in addition to), this elemental-based knowledge is complemented by the experiential content that Hip Hop music proffers to its constituents.

One of the most widely known verbal purveyors of (experiential content-based) knowledge in Hip Hop culture, Carlton Ridenhour (Chuck D) of Public Enemy, once famously quipped that rap music was Black folk's CNN. This oft-quoted analogy between rap music and the first 24-hour cable news network suggests a number of important parallels about the kind of knowledge particular to Hip Hop. First, it suggests the continuous transferal of information among enclaves of Hip Hop culture the world over. Chuck D was suggesting that the multimedia developments of the information age, in conjunction with Hip Hop culture's explosive popularity, were formulating an international network of informational exchange through various media platforms (e.g., Internet, TV, radio, CDs, and DVDs). Second, a central aspect of Chuck D's equation of Hip Hop with a Black CNN is that Hip Hop was (and in some ways still is) an information source for Black folk. Golden era Hip Hop narratives of power relationships, inner-city poverty, gang violence, and police brutality provided intricate insights into the lived experiences of Black folk across the United States. Still today, the music of the culture is a source of information on the experiences of Black folk around the world in the late 20th and early 21st centuries. Within this parallel is the vital point that knowledge within Hip Hop is most frequently a counternarrative to the mainstream news media. That is, Hip Hop is not simply a rich news/information source; it also often challenges the dominant and hegemonic mainstream media platforms.

This educational element has implications for classrooms in general, but it also has precise implications for composition classrooms. One of the ways in which we cultivate critical thinking in the composition classroom is through substantive discussions about current events. Twenty-first-century college students can often be encouraged to engage in continuous critical thinking when they are challenged to interrogate the various media with which they regularly interface. Music is one such form among many, and Hip Hop music proffers a litany of examples to work with in terms of experiential content that, in turn, invites critical thinking on relevant and/or important issues. For almost any topical issue that affects the communities from which Hip Hop culture derives, an artist will craft lyrics that address the issue and/or inform the listeners about the issue. Some examples of songs that do just this are Jay-Z's (2006) "Minority Report" and Lil Wayne's (2006) "Georgia Bush," which address the political aspects of Hurricane Katrina's impact on New Orleans.

One can only imagine how often the Trayvon Martin case came up in college classrooms during the spring 2012 semester. Issues/cases such as these are opportunities to bring Hip Hop directly into the composition classroom in order to facilitate critical discussions on relevant issues. In my own Hip Hop Culture and Composition courses I regularly bring in lyrics, play songs, or show music videos as points of entry into complex discussions. Although there are too many songs/tributes made specifically to address the Martin case to list here, one selection that I used was Reef the Lost Cauze's 2012 "The Prey (For Trayvon & My Son)," a bleak reimagining of the final minutes of Trayvon Martin's life. Reef the Lost Cauze is an "underground" Philadelphia rapper whose music often chronicles local inner-city life. While his rap moniker alone is enough consideration for an engaging discussion around Hip Hop culture, nihilism, and urban life, his lyrics in "The Prey" recount a version of the events leading up to Trayvon Martin's death, make allusions to historical racism, and outline the practices of institutional racism and police brutality. The epilogue to the song quotes (i.e., samples or excerpts) comments made by Charles Dutton's character in the now-classic Hughes brothers' 1993 film *Menace II Society*. In a cautionary conversation with several of the film's protagonists, young Black men who are inherently seen as society's menace, Dutton's character states the following: "The hunt is on. And you're the prey." The use of this quote in "The Prey" is an important opportunity for composition students to learn and appreciate the value of a well-researched and well-placed quote in terms of developing (or in this case, initiating) their arguments or compositional discussions. It also serves the purpose of opening up a discussion about the vilification of inner-city youth and the institutional challenges that continue to afflict young Black men in America—all of which requires knowledge of these institutions and practices, the film that is quoted here, and some of the reporting on the case itself.

Some of the most common counternarratives that Hip Hop offers deal with the reporting of violence in urban communities and, in the case above, a gated middle-class community. These counternarratives matter because too often the most prevalent reports of violence in urban communities center on various pathologies and deficit explanations for people of color. The knowledge conveyed through Hip Hop often renders a more sophisticated view of violence, including an acknowledgment of social inequalities, an engagement with historical racial violence, and the social toxins that help sustain violence in the present. This type of knowledge from Hip Hop ultimately results in knowledge of self. That is, exposure to the counternarratives and information from Hip Hop (regardless of one's racial identification) feeds and shapes one's understanding of self with relationship to systems of power and oppression in the world.

Consciousness

Directly related to knowledge is consciousness. In this way, consciousness is knowledge of self, one's surroundings, as well the social and/or historical forces at play in one's existence. For Hip Hop, an important aspect of the educational element of consciousness resides at the heart of the continuing debates about the content of the music. The rampant misogyny, consumerism, and violence in most popular manifestations of the culture are often critiqued based upon the assumption that a certain level of consciousness about social conditions is central to Hip Hop culture. This old school (1970s to mid-1980s) or golden era (mid-1980s to mid-1990s) bias sometimes obscures the rich corpus of underground/grassroots Hip Hop not readily available on mainstream platforms for the music (Peterson, 2006). That said, consciousness is an important element for educators interested in employing Hip Hop in the classroom because it flies so forcefully in the face of the anti-intellectual nature of popular culture in general and mainstream representations of Hip Hop specifically.

A tremendous amount of Hip Hop artistry is dedicated to articulating place and space. Forman's (2002) *The 'Hood Comes First* is a scholarly monograph dedicated to this phenomenon in the music. At its core, the consciousness educational element of Hip Hop culture requires awareness of one's immediate surroundings, but consciousness also features other relevant issues and learning opportunities beyond the space/place awareness factor. This element, more so than any other educational element, implies a commitment to social justice. In fact, consciousness in most Hip Hop "circles" suggests knowledge of institutional and historical forms of oppression as well as a dedicated interest in addressing and reforming the societies that continue to support forms of oppression. Although there are, again, a litany of examples from which an instructor may choose songs that wrestle with consciousness from a Hip Hop perspective, one of the more light-hearted means of tapping into the potential in this particular educational element, I find, comes from Aaron McGruder's *The Boondocks*.

The Boondocks is an animated series and a serialized, nationally syndicated comic strip. The strip and the series are equal parts urban/Hip Hop humor and sociopolitical commentary via satire and, more often than not, direct attacks on some of the more egregious purveyors of Black pathology in the eyes of McGruder—like R. Kelly or Black Entertainment Television (BET). However, the series offers some productive opportunities for the composition classroom, student writing, and critical thinking. The title of the strip and series gestures directly toward the consciousness of place so prevalent in Hip Hop discourses—artistic and in everyday language. The "boondocks" refers to a place far away from the 'hood or inner-city existence. The distance is geopolitical in the sense that the "boondocks" is further away from the urban world in class or station than it is in plain geography. The main characters of *The Boondocks*, Huey and Riley, are brothers who (together) essentially reflect a sort of 21st-century Hip Hop double consciousness. Riley exudes a thug mentality, he is antisociety, and he devises violent means to steal material items so often lauded in Hip Hop music. Huey (like his founding Black Panther party member namesake, Huey P. Newton) is sociopolitically conscious. Both brothers are voiced by actress Regina King, and their repartee forms the substance of the strip and the animated series. *The Boondocks* provides exceptional subject matter for comparative analysis composition assignments. It can function as the workshop/in-class example or as the subject for the assignment itself, but it features a wide range of comparative-analytical opportunities: the boondocks and the 'hood; Huey and Riley; and/or DuBoisian double consciousness and that proffered by McGruder through his characters. Ultimately, the consciousness element of Hip Hop culture does not require Hip Hop "texts" to make the point or to shape the lesson. Young people who consider themselves constituents of a Hip Hop generation will likely be invested in the sociopolitical issues of the day, especially as they are chronicled by and through the music of the culture. The ultimate question for educators is if we are prepared to seek these chronicles out so that we might better discover the educational potential of youth culture in the composition classroom.

Search and Discovery

Search and discovery is that rarely realized educational element of Hip Hop culture that beckons young people to locate themselves in the music and experiences of Hip Hop that speak directly to their own lives. Neate (2004) speaks to this element and its central role throughout Hip Hop:

> When people say that Hip Hop is dead it just shows they're not in touch. People talk about the elements of Hip Hop culture but . . . in any period of Hip Hop, the best stuff had to be searched for. That's why . . . *search and discovery* [emphasis added] is the most neglected element of Hip Hop. (p. 58)

Search and discovery encourages students influenced by Hip Hop culture to seek further knowledge and to prepare themselves for the ongoing benefits of intellectual discovery. The strongest sense of search extends beyond simply comprehending the lyrics of Hip Hop music. The traditional methods of Hip Hop music composition use "samples" from previous recorded music to create new music (Schloss, 2004). One representative example is Jay-Z's 1998 song "Hard Knock Life," which samples "The Hard Knock Life" from the Broadway classic *Annie*. Often misunderstood as simply copying previous music, the practice of sampling is often so sophisticated that cultural-outsiders cannot recognize when it is taking place. People deeply familiar with Hip Hop and its norms not only easily recognize sample-based music, but they are in tune with the aesthetic and thus expect it. This sensibility and the collage-text can then instigate the listener's search for its historic musicological origins.

This kind of search, however, is not limited to musical sources and origins. Search and discovery also carries over into a search for other important information. One way to situate this element is within the composition unit that features or requires students to visit the library and familiarize themselves with the various databases and research resources available to them. That said, the spirit of search and discovery is an important element for effectively introducing to students of the Hip Hop composition classroom. Many of these students will be familiar with a wide variety of search engines and Internet-based search tools. The challenge is to impress upon them the meaning of "discovery" that challenges students to view writing and writing courses/assignments as something other than an academic requirement.

Participation

Perhaps most significant among the educational elements is the mandate to participate in Hip Hop culture. For those teachers and scholars who wonder how Hip Hop culture transformed from an inner-city New York, local phenomenon into an international mainstay of popular youth culture, the origins of the b-boying/b-girling are instructive (see Schloss, 2009). The b-boy's role as dancer quickly developed into one of the earliest points of entry for a generation of young people who were invited to participate in the frustrated, angst-ridden, and brazenly responsive culture of the era. Participation is the central impulse that the various initiatives to implement Hip Hop culture into the classroom will employ. According to KRS ONE (2003), the legendary artist and self-professed Teacher of Hip Hop, the culture is driven by being:

"Hiphop is the mental activity of oppressed creativity. Hiphop is not a theory and you cannot do Hiphop. Oppressed urban youth living in the ghettos of America are Hiphop. Rap is something you do; Hiphop is something you live" (KRS ONE, 2003, p. 211).

From this perspective, Hip Hop is fundamentally a participatory culture. There is no such thing as being part of Hip Hop yet not participating in some way. Even those who watch, applaud, and cheer for those b-girls whose kinesthetic abilities inspire awe, are fundamentally participating in the culture (Schloss, 2009). This mandate of participation extends beyond the specific element of b-boying and b-girling, too. The cipher,[2] the key unit of participation in Hip Hop activities, is itself a form of participation (Johnson, 2009). Given the centrality of participation, this educational element leads teachers and scholars to reconceptualize the ways that participation can function in different classroom contexts (see, for example, Emdin, this volume). In the composition classroom, participation is required in each aspect of the course, but it is most important in classroom discussions. The Hip Hop culture composition classroom (like any composition classroom) thrives on the day-to-day in-class discussions that allow students to hone their critical thinking skills and develop their knowledge of composition vis-à-vis a range of topical considerations—current and historical. All humanities class-rooms can thrive off of robust intellectual discourse (i.e., class participation). The Hip Hop composition classroom simply requires active participation.

REMIXING IS REWRITING

Although the four educational elements of Hip Hop have specific implications for classrooms in general and composition classrooms specifically, there is a key connection between the notion of remix in Hip Hop and composition classrooms. The theoretical underpinnings of this discussion stem from a synthesis of Law-rence Lessig's (2008) *Remix: Making Art and Commerce Thrive in the Hybrid Econ-omy* with ideas detailed in Joseph Harris's (2006) composition primer, *Rewriting: How to do Things with Text*. Each of these scholars negligibly acknowledges the import of Hip Hop culture in the development of their own scholarly work on composition, mostly because neither is a scholar of Hip Hop culture. Thus, Lessig and Harris tend to skirt the issue of Hip Hop culture's emergence and its inherent capacity to formally embrace the rewriting and/or remixing of music, culture, his-tory, and politics.

The theoretical synthesis of Lessig and Harris's work concerns the areas of Read Only (RO) and Write/Read (WR) cultures, two opposing concepts in com-position that deal with artistic and commercial engagement with media. Accord-ing to Lessig (2008), advancements in technology, especially the Internet, and the exponential growth in memory/space capacity of computers has facilitated the emergence of a WR culture that uses "tokens" of RO culture in order to produce new artistic texts. Lessig's formulation considers how countless computer users excerpt, sample, or quote from previously produced images, films, or music (con-tent easily found online) in order to revise, remake, or remix these RO tokens into completely different artistic texts. Although Lessig is largely concerned with the limitations of current copyright law to account for the potential creativity inher-ent in 21st-century WR culture, he also provides a solid operational definition of remix, which bears repeating here: "remix is collage; it comes from combining ele-ments of Read Only culture; it succeeds by leveraging the meaning created by the reference to build something new" (Lessig, 2008, p. 76).

Hip Hop culture has been engaged in WR culture (e.g., sampling tokens of RO culture) since its inception in the mid-1970s. With a long and storied presence in Hip Hop culture, the musical remix provides one of the clearest examples of this engagement. The remix is a retooled or revised and updated version of a song. Some might argue that rap music's first prominent and popularly received single, the Sugar Hill Gang's 1979 "Rapper's Delight," is a lyrical remix of Chic's "Good Times," a disco single that sports the original beat sampled/replayed in the Sugar Hill Gang's breakout song. Remixes have taken various forms. They can feature additional artists/lyricists, new or distinct lyrics, new sample-based productions, and/or extended versions of the original. Often in contemporary Hip Hop music, the most popular or successful rap songs are revisited and remixed by adding other lyricists to the production. Remixing in Hip Hop culture further underscores the extent to which the culture itself relies on collage and the reuse of other texts, especially previously recorded sound in order to produce new texts, new records, and new styles. Here again, Hip Hop culture is a heuristic device. For all of Lessig's (2008) astute theorization of the relationship between WR and RO cultures, Hip Hop is historically and in current practice already there. Remix is a fundamental component of the compositional aspects of Hip Hop culture; thus, it models Lessig's sophisticated discussion of remix culture.

This sense of the remix also lends itself directly to Harris's (2006) thesis in *Rewriting* and my own sense of the interstitial relationships among Hip Hop culture, Harris's approach to composition, and Lessig's (2008) conceptualization of RO/WR cultures. For Harris (2006), the kind of intellectual writing most often "done" in composition classrooms takes certain qualities:

> [It is] bound up inextricably with the books we are reading, the movies we are watching, the music we are listening to, and the ideas of the people we are talking with. Our creativity thus has its roots in the work of others—in response, reuse, and rewriting (p. 2).

Harris goes on to define rewriting as a "social practice" so that he can develop his emphasis on the "how" of composition in the 21st century; he hopes to respond to this how prompt by delineating key moves that rewriters make. At issue here is rewriting as social practice, a concept with direct ties to the aesthetic forms of remix and revision within Hip Hop culture. His book's subtitle, *How to Do Things with Texts,* is a not-so-subtle remix of John L. Austin's (1965) book title *How To Do Things With Words.* Harris insists that this remix, rather than attempting to repeat with texts what Austin attempts with words (i.e., capture the performative nature of language), is his way of transforming the dialogue about composition from something that is static into something much more dynamic.

Throughout *Rewriting*, Harris (2006) develops five rewriting moves: (1) *coming to terms*, which he defines as "re-presenting the work of others in ways that are both fair and useful" in your own writing; (2) *forwarding*, which is the practice by which writers forward other texts, concepts, and so on with their own framework or commentary; (3) *countering*, which is the process by which the "rewriter" rethinks or qualifies a position or argument; (4) *taking an approach*, which is drawing upon a distinctive style or mode; and (5) *revising*, which is combining the previous four moves in efforts to revisit and rework your own writing. These five moves formulate a writing template for the Hip Hop culture and composition classroom. Here again, the aesthetic forms of Hip Hop culture function heuristically as a means to attain the learning outcomes of the traditional composition course. Each element of Hip Hop culture (DJing, graffiti artistry, breaking/b-boying, and MCing) relies on various rewriting moves. Moreover, writing about Hip Hop culture invites students to assess the rewriting and remixing elements of Hip Hop's aesthetic forms utilizing the tools of rewriting and remixing in their compositional efforts. For example, quoting another scholar or writer in order to develop an argument is both a rewriting move (either forwarding, countering, and/or taking an approach) as well as an implementation of the aesthetic form in Hip Hop most commonly referred to as sampling (Schloss, 2004).[3]

Each of the rewriting moves has its advantages (and disadvantages), but the notion of forwarding, because it relies on an email analogy and because it specifically requires the reuse of other texts and concepts, makes a striking connection with Lessig's ideas about Write/Read culture and challenges us to rethink this particular move as a model of composition students. Over the last 10 years, email forwarding has degenerated into an endless succession of prayer chains, banking scams, and the occasionally inappropriate attempt at humor. As an analogy for a move that students might make/take in the processes of writing or composition, forwarding will ring stale among current students, as many of them automatically delete any and all forwards. In fact, many of us likely do the same or simply ignore them altogether (as I do). Forwarding, then, is probably not the best metaphor for Harris's attempt to explicate a move that is essential to the Hip Hop culture and composition classroom. He clarifies that "a writer forwards the views of another when he or she takes terms and concepts from one text and applies them to a reading of other texts or situations" (Harris, 2006 p. 6). And here is where the confluence of Lessig's (2008) and Harris's concepts is productive. While Harris signals the import of considering newer technologies and media in the composition classroom, Lessig is ready and willing to minimize traditional notions of composition and enhance the concept with the kind of democratized participatory processes that result in the proliferation of sample-based digital compositions found on various media sites (e.g., YouTube).

Harris's (2006) *Rewriting* and Lessig's (2008) *Remix* are certainly not either/or propositions for the Hip Hop composition classroom. Instead, they offer distinct, sometimes overlapping, sometimes contested approaches to crafting compositions that are formally and aesthetically consistent with various aspects of Hip Hop culture. Note well here that Hip Hop culture developed parallel to the Information Age. The Hip Hop Generation, those born between 1964 and 1985, have witnessed an extraordinarily fast pace in technological advancement (Kitwana, 2002). Consider the shift in musical platforms from the eight-track, to vinyl, to the cassette, to CDs, to digital formats such as MP3s. Harris argues that the reuse of texts in this moment or climate is completely natural and should be cultivated in the composition classroom, while Lessig strongly suggests that technology now allows us to use other texts to create original compositions—something that the artisans of Hip Hop have been doing since the mid-1970s. Although these theories or pedagogical approaches put into bold relief the formal aesthetic potential of Hip Hop in the classroom, many in the academy (and beyond) remain unconvinced or even hostile to the idea that Hip Hop should even be in a classroom. According to Kermit Campbell (2005),

> instead of reaching out to youth in communities and schools by drawing on their potential for critical consciousness through rap and hip-hop, politicians, parents, and media pundits censure such creative expression, turning a deaf ear to a generation increasingly shaped by the digitally mixed and sampled rhetoric of hip-hop. (p. 329)

The best of Hip Hop scholarship seeks to reverse the trajectory of this quote. What follows are brief sketches of the Hip Hop culture and composition courses that I have proffered in this effort to leverage the intellectual interests of "a generation increasingly shaped by the digitally mixed and sampled rhetoric of hip-hop."

HIP HOP COMPOSITION

The first Hip Hop and Composition course that I taught was entitled "Writing About Hip Hop Culture." I offered this course as a part of the Writing Across the University program at the University of Pennsylvania during the spring of 1997. Arguably one of the earlier attempts to connect Hip Hop and composition at the post-secondary level, this course reached capacity immediately and was one of the most diverse groups of students that I had ever had while teaching at the University of Pennsylvania. As this course took place in 1997, most of these students were born in the late 1970s and thus fit squarely within Kitwana's (2002) Hip Hop Generation timeframe. At this time, much of the scholarship on Hip Hop culture, remix culture, and the shifting sense of revision and rewriting in the Information Age such as that of Harris (2006) and Lessig (2008) either did not yet exist or was otherwise unavailable to me at this early stage of my career as an instructor. There were few critical texts centered on Hip Hop studies, so this early iteration of the Hip Hop and composition course was very much grounded in the aesthetic sensibilities of Hip Hop.

Students in this course were particularly concerned with the aesthetic forms of Hip Hop and how they connected to composition. Their commitment to these specific cultural and/or aesthetic principles challenged them to engage in practices related to the classroom but indicative of their own relationships to Hip Hop culture. The students in this class, for example, generated a bevy of cultural products and compositions that underscored their critical engagement with Hip Hop culture beyond the classroom. Several students organized a journalistic publication entitled H2O. This publication focused on the local Hip Hop scene and the artistry of the students in the course. Other students established a weekly open-mic performance event in Philadelphia called "The Gathering," open to all artisans of Hip Hop culture. Since its inception, the event has been maintained by many different community members in Philadelphia (including Emery Petchauer, one of this volume's editors) and still operates as one of the longest running all-ages Hip Hop community events in the United States. Some of the students in this course have gone on to film school, the fashion industry, the academy, and the music industry.[4] In fact, Dr. H. Samy Alim, a pioneer of Hip Hop sociolinguistics, was an undergraduate student in this course. In each of these cases, Hip Hop culture has been a common presence in the subsequent careers of these former students.

For many reasons, this initial composition course does not present a replicable model. In fact, most of my own Hip Hop composition courses after this initial one were essentially different in both form and function. Yet there are still important points about course design and classroom practice from this first course that I continue to employ in a variety of Hip Hop courses—composition and others. These points serve as the basis for practical applications in Hip Hop composition courses.

The Design of Hip Hop Composition

In over 15 years of teaching various incarnations/iterations of the Hip Hop culture and composition course, I often distill the educational elements within the mix of the traditional composition course and its requisite "outcome" expectations. The ways that I have done this, however, have changed over the years. These changes illustrate some of the quintessential characteristics of Hip Hop composition courses. An introduction to one of my early course syllabi is an important starting point to illustrate these changes:

> This course is designed to enhance and develop your writing skills for the challenges, experiences, and assignments that you will face and/or be required to execute as an undergraduate. In general this course uses various aspects and/or artistic manifestations of Hip Hop culture as the impetus to think critically, articulate accurately, and to write clear and compelling prose. The goal of English 15 is to enhance students' writing by sensitizing them to their composing processes and familiarizing them with the features of effective and persuasive prose. Students will learn to think critically, observe closely, and assess rhetorical situations accurately in order to respond confidently and flexibly to various audiences, aims, subjects, and forms.

In this course overview, Hip Hop culture is the impetus for writing. Students are asked to engage the culture more as observers than as actual participants, participant-observers, or constituents of the culture. Thus, in this initial iteration of the course, the educational element of participation is less then salient. Of course, students were expected to participate in the class in various ways, as they are in every course, but the types of participation that are central to Hip Hop were not infused in the class (a point I will return to below).

Note also that in this first course, the aesthetic forms of the culture are not necessarily held out as models for composition or engagement. The course description implies that Hip Hop is an object about which students will write, respond, articulate, and think critically. The description largely ignores that Hip Hop operates according to sensibilities, habits, mindsets, and so forth. It is important to keep in mind that during this early period, there were few documented connections between Hip Hop and formal school settings. Without a doubt, this was a burgeoning time for Hip Hop scholarship more broadly, with the seminal publications of Rose's *Black Noise* in 1994 and Perkin's *Droppin' Science* in 1996. Additionally, Hip Hop educational activities were taking place undocumented by scholarly disciplines during this time. But specific educational and pedagogical connections in scholarly communities were yet to develop.

A more recent introduction to one of these course syllabi reflects some important changes based upon the developments within Hip Hop and education since my first composition course in 1997. Attention is still given to the traditional aims of the composition classroom, but my approach shifts generally to understanding Hip Hop as a discursive and compositional model. This shift is based upon a tacit recognition that Hip Hop is not simply an object but a culture with aesthetic forms. The description that guided the course reads as follows:

This course is designed to explore the numerous ways in which Hip Hop culture functions as a discourse in the public sphere, including but not limited to the study of: poetry, cultural criticism, journalism, literature, drama, film, and sociopolitical movements. These various exploratory approaches to Hip Hop reveal the complexities of a culture, once labeled a "fad" that has since become ubiquitous on the American popular landscape. The course uses film, literature, music, music video and scholarly-cultural criticism to investigate Hip Hop and the various discourses that attend it. We will explore the origins and various eras (Old School, Golden Age, and Current) of Hip Hop and we will compare, and contrast the critical and creative literature that derives from rap music and Hip Hop culture. We will take up the debates of authenticity and identity, and through close readings, hearings, and viewings of the texts of Hip Hop, we will construct well-informed positions on how writers, rappers, and regular folks use texts and contexts to achieve "authentic" identities. A key goal of the course is to explore and develop scholarly ways of engaging Hip Hop culture.

Subtle changes in the second course overview above shifts the compositional focus in a few key ways. First, there is a move away from Hip Hop as an object and toward Hip Hop as a discursive model. In this way, the course centers on the notion that various manifestations of Hip Hop possess argumentation, debate, persuasive logic, and emic ways of making truth claims. These manifestations then become useful tools for the composition student when they are the subject of rigorous study.

A second key change is a shift in participation. Students study the critical discourses on Hip Hop culture, debates of authenticity and identity, and other discursive aspects of Hip Hop, but students are also invited to participate in this very discourse. Unlike in the earlier iteration of the course, students are not simply writing *about* Hip Hop. By studying the ways that Hip Hop makes claims and then using those same modes to make claims about Hip Hop, composition students are engaging in a deeper type of participation unique to Hip Hop. Forman (2002) makes the important point that scholarly, journalistic, and social commentary literature that engages Hip Hop is actually a critical part of Hip Hop culture. This is evidenced by the longstanding tradition within Hip Hop of independently collecting cultural documents such as flyers, tapes, records, video and television footage, newspaper clippings, personalized and time-period clothes, interviews, and more into personal archives. From this perspective, writing about Hip Hop through studying the discursive models of Hip Hop is a form of participation in the culture.

Hip Hop Composition in Practice

Beyond these ways of conceptualizing Hip Hop in composition courses in general, the scholarly ways of engaging Hip Hop in the composition classroom specifically take on a variety of forms and/or approaches. With each of these approaches, the general aesthetics of Hip Hop serve as the bases for classroom composition techniques.

Creative Revision. Creative revision is an excellent approach to writing in the composition classroom. Of course, students have to document all of their sources accurately, but in the spirited sense with which Harris (2006) positions rewriting, I have encouraged my students by helping them understand that their work is in collaboration with hundreds of other scholars who have spoken and written before them. Thus, "saying something new" is a matter of "how" rather than "what." From the perspectives of Lessig's (2008) remix theory and Harris's (2006) rewriting approaches, we have only begun to institute the means of defamiliarizing texts and manipulating them in composition environments (paper, online, audiovisual, and so on). Much of the language about compositional citation focuses on the consequences of poor documentation or misdocumentation, rather than acknowledging the central problem in 1st-year composition courses: How do students write something new, insightful, and interesting to themselves and their intended audience? The answer has been defamiliarization: representing a text in such a way that it appears in a new light to your audience. Defamiliarization requires various aspects of Harris's rewriting moves, including coming to terms, forwarding, and countering. And at its best, it also allows students to incorporate multimedia resources into their research as well as their actual compositions. A useful assignment for the application of creative revision is the album review assignment. This assignment requires students to choose a popular album and research the reviews written about the album. When composing their review, they must cite and otherwise situate themselves within the published discourse on the album. However, as part of their argument/discussion, they must establish a reading/listening of the album that cuts against the grain of the conventional reviews. Students will almost always rely on the texts of the album itself or music videos made from specific songs in order to present a less familiar take on the album under consideration.

Cutting and Quoting. A viable way of defamiliarizing a text aesthetically/formally consistent with Hip Hop culture is through the use of the cut. The cut defamiliarizes the text from which it is borrowed. According to late literary critic James A. Snead (1984), "James Brown is an example of a brilliant American practitioner of the cut whose skill is readily admired by African as well as American musicians" (p. 69). Snead suggests that in Brown's performance, the ruptures (i.e., cuts) strengthen the rhythm rather than weaken it. Furthermore, Snead argues, "black music sets up expectations and disturbs them at irregular intervals: that it will do this, however, is itself an expectation" (p. 69).

Two important pedagogical opportunities derive from this section of Snead's discussion. First, current and practical examples of cut and repetition are located in Hip Hop culture. Taking Brown as the example, the rap group EPMD samples (i.e., cuts from and repeats) James Brown's song "The Payback" (from Brown's 1973 album of the same name). On EPMD's song entitled "I'm Mad" from their 1990 album, *Business as Usual*, the group uses the line "I'm mad" from Brown's "The Payback" as the refrain or quote. Their use of this cut demonstrates their own acknowledgment of Brown's authenticity and the respect that he garners in African and American communities. In some ways, a James Brown cut supports and authenticates a rap lyric while it reinscribes the musical genius of Brown. If his lines are quotable in rap music, then he is "down with" the Hip Hop generation. If his lines are quoted in rap music, then rap music is connected to the success, social acceptance, and cultural iconography of James Brown. In EPMD's "The Big Payback" (from their 1989 album entitled *Unfinished Business*), the group signified off of Brown's "The Payback" again. This time, they sample the line/refrain, "the payback," and modify the title of the original

("The *Big* Payback") so that at the same time that they are referencing Brown's musical authenticity, they are submitting their own virtuosity in relation to his.

This kind of cutting in Hip Hop functions as a heuristic device for the composition classroom. Through a fairly common use of sampling and cutting, EPMD demonstrates the value of the principles of Harris's rewriting and the formal properties of Lessig's notion of remix culture. EPMD quotes/samples James Brown and in doing so, they defamiliarize Brown's text, authenticate their own, and in the process also craft an original composition. This is a classic model for the work that writers strive to do in the composition classroom. The musical interactions between EPMD, Brown, and the cut reflect the connections between composition writers, texts, and the quote. Intertextual quotes should not only authenticate and/or exemplify the composition, they should, by virtue of being a part of the text in some new and interesting way, posit the original text in an unfamiliar light. The relationship between the quote and the essay should be similar to the recursive relationship between EPMD's "I'm Mad" and "The Big Payback," and James Brown's "The Payback."

Freestyling and Brainstorming. As another example, brainstorming is a vital component in all composition processes and of special import in the Hip Hop culture and composition classroom. Brainstorming is still one of the most effective prewriting strategies available to students who are learning how to write. No matter what form it takes from listing, clustering, and/or tree diagrams, the brainstorm is a central step in the composition process. For the Hip Hop composition classroom, the ritualistic pastime known popularly as freestyling is an important cultural counterpart to brainstorming. When explored and employed as a writing strategy, freestyling sparks student creativity and other important writing tools such as structural and spatial order, chronology, and improvisation. Freestyling or freestyle sessions are when groups of MCs/rappers form a cipher and improvise rhymes/lyrics in turns. In many cases, a freestyle rhyme functions much like an improvised jazz riff in that it derives from the author/MC/musician but crystallizes in the performance.

The freestyle prewriting exercise is designed to function in much the same way. Groups of students are challenged to freestyle (not necessarily in verse) their ideas, theses, or topics in small groups. They all have a turn to verbally freestyle while another person within the small group takes notes on their content. In the best-case scenario, each student-writer can freestyle his or her ideas and take notes on someone else's. Students then share/compare results. Usually, students realize that freestyle is actually not that free at all, but it is an opportunity to verbalize ideas in a setting conducive to creativity. This freestyle exercise actually adds a subtle competitive aspect to traditional brainstorming activities. Fortunately, there are various DVDs and YouTube clips that demonstrate freestyle performances so that while students might learn about this specifically Hip Hop form of brainstorming, they can also come to appreciate the competitive nature of on-the-spot composition. By positing brainstorming as a form of free-styling or vice versa, students are invited to approach this prewriting exercise via an aesthetic form particular to Hip Hop culture and valuable to those developing writers for whom traditional structures might seem limiting or impertinent to their own writing processes.

CONCLUSIONS: RESISTING PRESCRIPTIONS

Alongside the guidelines and strategies in this chapter, my intention has not been to prescribe rigid ways of implementing Hip Hop culture and/or rap music into composition courses. Instead, my intention has been to share some themes, approaches, examples, successes, and challenges that I have encountered on my journey to integrate my own culture (such as Hip Hop) into specific academic and pedagogical practices. I have to acknowledge also that although I tend to argue for a constructivist, culturally pertinent appeal of Hip Hop culture in a wide variety of classrooms (high school and college), there are clear limitations to integrating Hip Hop music and lyrics into the composition classroom. The central limitation bears revelation here. The *nommo* or word power of rap music and Hip Hop culture derives primarily from the African American oral and folk traditions. As such, rap music, much like the blues or a Black Baptist sermon, tends to thrive in oral-aural contexts and can appear to be flat and/or stale on the printed page. Any of the examples described herein will certainly bear this out when compared with listening or viewing the recorded performances of Hip Hop. This particular challenge is one with which Hip Hop scholars and teachers are regularly confronted.

Despite these challenges, the composition classroom proffers a lesson that can be drawn from this problem of context. That is, every composition has a particular and appropriate context. This particular oral-literal dichotomy only serves to underscore this fact and in turn provide Hip Hop composition instructors with an inaugural lesson about writing. To wit: The situation (i.e., the assignment, the audience, and the platform) shapes the reception of the composition. "The purpose and audience for each text define writing tasks. Because tasks are not uniform, students need to have the ability to write in multiple genres, formats, and styles" (Copeland, Mitchler, & Hesse, 2005, p. 3). If, as scholars and teachers, we can come to appreciate and understand the Hip Hop Generation's preference for technological composition and Hip Hop as a viable economy of expression, then the potential of our composition classrooms increases exponentially.

> This thing called hip-hop, this inner-city, youth-driven artistic and cultural movement has accomplished in our society what embattled multiculturalism has been powerless to accomplish—that is, to make the inhabitants of America's inner cities relatable and indeed lovable (Campbell, 2005, p. 328).

NOTES

1. The 5% Nation of Gods and Earths, founded by Clarence 13X in the early 1970s, is a philosophical offshoot of the Nation of Islam. Five percenters (as they are often called) believe that 85% of the human population is "dumb, deaf, and blind," 10% is enlightened but they tend to exploit the 85%, and 5% are the poor righteous teachers who challenge the corrupt 10% for the minds of the 85%.

2. The vernacular use of the term *cipher* in Hip Hop culture does not just linguistically appear out of language limbo, and it does not directly derive itself from "Standard English." Instead, it flows into the everyday language of Hip Hop from and through the 5% Nation of Gods and Earths, from the minds and mouths of those poor righteous teachers who view the cipher as encompassing 360 degrees of daily lived experiences.

3. In a scholarly work central to Hip Hop studies, *Making Beats: The Art of Sample-based Hip Hop*, Joseph G. Schloss (2004) catalogs numerous repetitive processes and initiatives in the production of Hip Hop music. Some of these include: looping, or repeating a sampled excerpt of music; sampling itself, which might be characterized as a form of allusion; chopping—cutting or partitioning a portion of previously recorded music or vocals; digging, which is the process by/through which DJs sometimes feverishly search for previously recorded material to loop/chop/sample; and locking up (i.e., achieving the desired effect of a beat/musical production), an aesthetic result whereby the beat or musical production achieves a certain and sublime combinatory praxis.

4. Yaminah McKessey is currently at USC film school and is working on a documentary that studies Old School Hip Hop; Aaron Jones is an MC in Dujeous, a live Hip Hop band from New York City, and he is a buyer for Dr. Jays, a Hip Hop–oriented urban clothing store; H. Samy Alim is an associate professor at Stanford University who has already published several books on Hip Hop culture and education; and Ted Chung is a music industry executive who has worked with a "who's who" of Hip Hop artists.

REFERENCES

Austin, J. L. (1965). *How to do things with words*. Oxford, UK: Oxford University Press.
Brown, J. (1973). "The payback." On *The payback*. New York: Polydor.
Campbell, K. (2005). *Getting our groove on: Rhetoric, language and literacy for the Hip Hop generation*. Detroit: Wayne State University Press.
Copeland, M., Mitchler, S., & Hesse, D. (2005). Good writing instruction is what's needed: NCTE task force on SAT and ACT writing releases report. *The council chronicle: The National Council of Teachers of English*, 15(1). Retrieved from http://www.ncte.org/magazine/archives/GoodWriting
EPMD. (1989). "The big payback." On *Unfinished business*. New York: Def Jam.
EPMD. (1990). "I'm mad." On *Business as usual*. New York: Def Jam.
Forman, M. (2002). *The 'hood comes first: Race, space, and place in rap and Hip Hop*. Middleton, CT: Wesleyan University Press.
Harris, J. (2006). *Rewriting: How to do things with texts*. Logan, UT: Utah State University Press.

Jay-Z. (1998). "Hard knock life." On *Vol 2 . . . Hard knock life.* New York: Def Jam.

Jay-Z. (2006). "Minority report." On *Kingdome come.* New York: Def Jam.

Johnson, I. K. (2009). *Dark matter in b-boying cyphers: Race and global connection in hip-hop* (Unpublished doctoral dissertation). University of Southern California, Los Angeles, CA.

Lil Wayne. (2006). "Georgia Bush." On *Dedication 2.* 101 Distribution.

Kitwana, B. (2002). *The hip hop generation: Young Blacks and the crisis in African American culture.* New York: Basic Civitas.

KRS ONE. (2003). *Ruminations.* New York: Welcome Rain Publishers.

Lessig, L. (2008). *Remix: Making art and commerce thrive in the hybrid economy.* New York: Penguin Press.

Meachum, S. (2003). Nommo, hip-hop, and the classroom [workshop]. Philadelphia: Art Sanctuary.

Neate, P. (2004). *Where you're at: Notes from the frontline of a hip hop planet.* New York: Riverhead Books.

Petchauer, E. (2009). Framing and reviewing hip-hop educational research. *Review of Educational Research, 79*(2), 946–978.

Peterson, J. (2006). The elements and eras of Hip Hop culture. In S. Steinberg, P. Parmar, & B. Richard (Eds.), *Contemporary youth culture* (pp. 357–364). Westport, CT: Greenwood Press.

Reef the Lost Cauze. (2012). "The prey (For Trayvon & my son)." United States: Author.

Schloss, J. G. (2004). *Making beats: The art of sample-based hip-hop.* Hanover, CT: Wesleyan University Press.

Schloss, J. G. (2009). *Foundation: B-boys, b-girls, and hip-hop culture in New York.* New York: Oxford University Press.

Smitherman, G. (1997). "The chain remains the same:" Communicative practices in the Hip Hop Nation." *Journal of Black Studies, 28*(1), 3–25.

Snead, J. (1984). Repetition as a figure of Black culture. In H. L. Gates (Ed.), *Black literature and literary theory* (pp. 59–80). New York: Routledge.

CHAPTER 4

The MC in Y-O-U

Leadership Pedagogy and Southern Hip-Hop in the HBCU Classroom

Joycelyn A. Wilson

Hip-hop can save the world one leader at a time. I made this claim to students each semester when they enrolled in my leadership course titled "Hip-Hop: The Black Aesthetic." Many interested students saw the term *hip-hop* on the registrar's list and assumed it would more or less be a breeze class to augment heavier course loads.

For example, a freshman registered once and dropped shortly thereafter because he, like others, walked in the first day with thoughts of living out dormant dreams of being a rapper, only to realize later that rapping as a practice would make up only a small portion of the major assignments. "I *am* hip-hop," he claimed, with emphasis on the *am*. "*Sure* you are," I thought to myself, with emphasis on the *sure*. He, like some others, expected discussions of the GOAT (Greatest of All Time) to dominate the seminars. "Professor Wilson," he would ask, "is it Tupac or Biggie? Nas or Jay-Z? Lil Wayne or Andre 3000?" I graciously ignored his outbursts. He, like other students, thought this was a course focused on bashing southern hip-hop and framing it as the poster child of all things gone wrong with the culture rather than critically engaging the politics of OutKast, TI, and Young Jeezy, or the complex social paranoia in the narratives of UGK and The Geto Boys, or the spirituality of David Banner and Big KRIT. While many students hoped for a class featuring an interrogation of lyrics laced with *bitch* this or *nigga* that—topics with which they were no doubt already familiar—my purpose for the class was quite different, as I aimed to introduce them to the intersection of critical theory with African-centered philosophies using an intensive writing routine and boundary-pushing exercises. These practices, coupled with a heavy load of reading, which they also did not expect in a "hip-hop class," would help position these college students—all of whom were on the verge of full adulthood—to practice *authentic hip-hop leadership,* or what the HipHop2020 Curriculum Project (HipHop2020) refers to as *leadership that keeps it real* (Wilson, 2010).

Established in 2006 as a social engagement program for K–12 educators, HipHop2020 has grown into a repository of instructional activities that triangulate popular media, social network technologies, and hip-hop epistemologies in order to develop the leadership capacities of youth and youth influencers. The primary methodological tool HipHop2020 uses for exploring leadership narratives of the hip-hop/millennium generation is called Hip-Pop Leadership Pedagogy (HPLP).[1] If Kitwana (2002, 2005) defines the *hip-hop generation* as low-income African American, African Caribbean, and Latin youth born between 1965 and 1984, then the *post-hip-hop/millennial generation* extends to more diverse ethnic groups who come from a variety of socioeconomic backgrounds and were born between 1985 and 2004 (Asante, Jr., 2008). I refer to this latter generational cohort as the millennial *hip-pop generation* because hip-hop culture, all forms of popular music and art, and the social media technologies operate as 21st-century culture-making tools. Additionally, as this generation's socialization remains under the heavy influence of global media and technology, clearer interpretations about their worldviews are revealed through intersections of popular art, culture, and digital media.

The overall aim of HipHop2020 is to nurture the authentic leadership capacities of pre-college and college students, and train teachers, educators, and parents on techniques that support their development. At the collegiate level specifically, HipHop2020 engages learners in an educational process that complicates hip-hop's cultural nuances—therefore cultivating its paralinguistic sensibilities—as a method for achieving specific learning outcomes determined by the teacher/instructor/parent/youth influencer. Said differently, the HipHop2020 initiative focuses on the use of stories and narratives to encourage self-identity and teach students strategies for how to *keep it real at the intersection where worlds collide* (Fluker, 2009; Wilson, 2010). The ultimate desire is to co-construct meaning among youth, youth influencers, and young adults on how these cultural sensibilities can positively inform life choices, thereby reinforcing progressive decision-making and the necessary approaches for addressing personal challenges and social enigmas of race, class, and gender politics.

For example, in "The Kid Cudi Lesson: The HipHop2020 Curriculum Project and Authentic Leadership," published in the Spring/Summer 2010 volume of the *International Journal of Africana Studies,* I explained the art of authentic hip-hop leadership in relation to the hip-hop aesthetic, and described the research, teaching, and outreach mission of HipHop2020 by reporting findings from an activity called "The Kid Cudi Lesson" (Wilson, 2010). If "The Kid Cudi Lesson" discussed *the what,* in this chapter I articulate in much more detail *the how.* I unpack the concept of authentic leadership and how hip-hop arrives at this type of leadership through its aesthetics of sampling. I also detail the specific activities that pedagogues and campus personnel can use to explore leadership and other topics in their respective classrooms, even when these groups do not firmly locate themselves within the hip-hop community of practice. As a whole, this chapter expands the relevance of Hip Hop Based Education (HHBE) into the college classroom as a strategy to develop leadership qualities in young adults.

THE STUDENTS AND THE COURSE

The work in this chapter draws significantly from my aforementioned course entitled "Hip-Hop: The Black Aesthetic." I taught it at a predominantly African American all-male liberal arts college located in the American Southeast. The basic mission of this HBCU (Historically Black College and University) is the leadership enhancement of its all-male student body across disciplines. The location of this college allows for cross-registration with other area institutions, and so the enrollment is often higher each semester, with an average total of 30 students including those from adjoining colleges and universities. Five students represented the area's all-female college. Three students represented the area's co-ed university. Cross-registration increases gender diversity in the class, as well as age diversity. For the spring 2011 semester, which is the focus of this chapter, the population was majority male complemented by six female students. One student was a sophomore. Two were juniors, and the remaining students were seniors—graduating seniors and 5th-year seniors.

The course design was based on using the aesthetic practices of hip-hop to enhance the critical and creative leadership capacities of college students. To do this, I frame hip-hop as a community of practice where the focus of inquiry is situated on what hip-hop participants "do"—that is, how they practice hip-hop in their day-to-day lives. For example, some of the students who enrolled in this course were surprised to see that their participation in the activities relied on whether or not they got to class on time—especially since I locked the door one minute before we were scheduled to start. As for dress code, some students were uncomfortable with my dismissal of anyone wearing jeans or pants that began mid-thigh. I did not allow men to wear hats, fitted caps, do-rags, scraggly beards, poorly groomed hairstyles, or grills (i.e., metal-fronted plates inserted in the mouth). The ladies who cross-registered from neighboring colleges could not wear too-short skirts or midriff-baring tops as bare body parts are unwelcoming to an intellectual space. "Leaders are well dressed," I constantly reminded them. "Err on the side of caution when you come in here!"

From this perspective, my interests lie in exploring and examining how students use elements of the culture—particularly the philosophy of realness—to create meaning and draw further understandings of themselves and their communities (Wilson, 2007, 2010). Deducing these aesthetic forms, kinship norms, language styles, and epistemologies of authenticity offers contemporary critiques of generational narratives about Blackness, as well as contemporary ideas about identity, race, class, and gender. As well, a course such as this offers a space to debunk the misconceptions of hip-hop maintained by both students in the course and critics of HHBE.

When I teach "Hip-Hop: The Black Aesthetic," I divide the course into four lessons. The flow of this chapter mirrors my classroom approach. Each section of this chapter thus represents a class unit or lesson. The two lessons presented represent standard units that occur each semester. Lesson One is called the "Story of the Sample," and focuses on the history of hip-hop within the tradition of the Black Aesthetic. At the beginning of each class session, students take part in an activity called "The Jump Off." The purpose of "The Jump Off" is to get students thinking about the ways in which hip-hop samples and pulls from elder cultural traditions, musical forms, lifestyles, and ways of being (Keyes, 2004; Ramsey, 2003; Schloss, 2004). As I will explain below, it is this sampling practice in hip-hop that produces *authentic hip-hop leadership,* or *leadership that keeps it real.* In the section called "Ma'atic Hip-Hop: Towards a Hip-Hop Philosophy of Education," I present a clearly defined rubric to argue that the future of hip-hop pedagogy must rely on a set of standards in order for it to be taken as a serious instructional strategy.

Lesson Two extends this theory of cultural and epistemological sampling to highlight examples of the cultural politics of hip-hop—with close attention given to narratives of the South. Although we also use narratives from the East and West coasts, we pay particular attention to southern rap, its history, and aesthetic forms for two reasons. First, the course takes place in Atlanta, Georgia, a primary production center of film, television, and hip-hop music. Second, Atlanta is the bed of the civil rights movement, and the college where the course takes place offers access to resources, perspectives, and archives that are unavailable elsewhere. A goal of HipHop2020 is to elevate southern aesthetic forms into the body of knowledge used to employ Hip Hop Based Education. In this lesson, I will provide a brief description of the southern hip-hop community of practice while pointing to some of the tensions that resulted in southern hip-hop finding a place in the overall culture. I also provide examples of unique linguistic norms that speak to the network's perspectives of authenticity, race, class, and politics and how it *schools on* these issues.

Lesson Three introduces students to the HPLP critical studies approach in order to prepare them for the biweekly critical synthesis essays they must submit. The writing rubric follows a five-point scale based on six traits of writing: ideas and content, organization, voice, word choice, sentence fluency, and grammatical conventions. In this section of the chapter, I will explain how students engage in the analysis of these narratives, how they present their findings to the class through discussions and presentations, and how they organize these findings in one-page critical synthesis essays for final submission to me, their instructor.

Lesson Four presents conclusions and implications for further research in the field of hip-hop studies and leadership pedagogy.

LESSON ONE: THE STORY OF HIP-HOP IS THE STORY OF THE SAMPLE

Teaching leadership through a hip-hop aesthetic begins with students gaining a clear understanding of hip-hop's sampling tradition. Schloss (2004) illustrates how the musical practice of sampling dates back to hip-hop's earliest years. In *Rap Music and Street Consciousness*, Keyes (2004) situates this idea of musical sampling within an African historical linguistic context of *cultural reversioning* where rappers—through rhythm—operate within *nommo*, "the power of the word," a concept that permeates Black poetic speech throughout the African Diaspora. *Nommo* "generates the energy to deal with life's twists and turns" therefore providing the "verbal recognition of self-worth and personal attributes" (Baber, 1987, p. 83). Analyzing from this perspective of *nommo*, Keyes grounds the rapper/MC in the West African tradition of the *bard* and the *naamu-sayer* as it relates to performance and storytelling. The *bard* in traditional African societies was the storyteller-singer whose main purpose was to document the nation's history and transmit cultural norms and values through performance. The *naamu-sayer* was considered the *bard's* apprentice or the affirmer of the *bard's* words. In the section called "African Nexus," Keyes (2004) writes: "While performing, a *bard* makes use of formulaic expressions, poetic abstractions, and rhythmic speech—all recited in a chant-like fashion that prefigures rap" (p. 20). She continues:

> The effectiveness of a bard's performance is achieved through the use of the imagery that is created through the bard's words. . . . Because of the masterful use of words, a bard is revered and highly respected in a community, a role claimed later in the diaspora by the most adept MCs. (p. 20)

Concerning the role of the *naamu-sayer*, Keyes notes, "A bard may also be accompanied by an apprentice, the naamu-sayer, who responds by singing 'naamu' in affirmation of the bard's words, adding an active interchange between the bard and the naamu-sayer, who represents the voice of the listener" (p. 20). We illustrate and extend this duality of the *bard* and *naamu-sayer* into the realm of the rapper and the DJ; the rapper and his hype-man; the rapper and a featured artist; the duo, where each member is both the *bard* and the *naamu-sayer* at any given time; and the rapper and his audience.[2]

The objective of Lesson One, then, is threefold: 1) to understand the history of hip-hop as one predicated on sampling; 2) to situate the musical and linguistic elements of hip-hop within an African-centered tradition of performance and philosophy, and 3) to provide the foundation that locates hip-hop's epistemology of realness within an African-centered pedagogy traditionally known as Ma'at (Asante, 1986; Hilliard III, 1986, 1995, 1997, 2002; Wilson, 2007, 2010). We reach these objectives of the lesson through a variety of activities that help students understand the concepts of *cultural reversioning, nommo*, the role of the *bard/naamu-sayer* relationship, and the concept of Ma'at as they all relate to the contemporary practice of hip-hop as a leadership practice. When students finish this lesson, they are much better positioned to consider their internal *bard/naamu-sayer* relationship within the context of their day-to-day activities and decisions.

Schoolifying Hip-Hop: Sampling "School" and the Genesis of HipHop2020

Hip-hop culture is obsessed with *doing school* in a myriad of ways that represent the overall hip-hop community and its regionally specific networks. In an article titled "The Case of Democratic Schooling," published by the *Harvard Educational Review* in 1986, Henry Giroux and Peter McLaren defined schooling as a practice situated in the "idea of a politics and a project of possibility" (p. 221). Concerned about Reaganomics-fueled public school reform, these two preeminent scholars of education and cultural studies grounded their notion of schooling within philosopher Ernst Bloch's basic principle of natural law, a theory insisting that a world wrought with oppression and exploitation will always be under the gaze of an ideological revolutionary force, and that the critique of such a society should begin from the standpoint of the victims of that society. From this perspective, Giroux and McLaren conclude that schooling based primarily on meeting the needs to sustain American capitalism should be subordinate to "a democratic vision where citizenship and the politics of possibility are given serious consideration" (p. 221). Giroux and McLaren argue that schools should be sites for determining "which struggles should be waged in the name of developing a more just, humane, and equitable social order both within and outside of schools" (p. 221) and places where "classrooms are seen as active sites of public intervention and social struggle." In practice, school should promote teachers' growth as "transformative intellectuals" that encourage their students to be "critical agents" (p. 215) who question what they read, the values that they uphold, and the way they utilize knowledge.

Schooling from such a Deweyan point of view should empower students with the cognitive and technical resources to succeed in addition to the social and political capital to "redefine the nature of critical learning and practice outside of the imperatives of the corporate marketplace" (Giroux & McLaren, 1986, p. 221). Extending Giroux and McLaren's position, critical researchers argue that school as a place, practice, and process should also encourage a pedagogical authenticity designed around a series of high-order critical thinking activities that 1) sharpen students' decision-making skills (e.g., Pardue, 2008), 2) teach conflict resolution strategies (e.g., Hill, 2009), 3) frame students' roles in social justice activism (e.g.,

Cermak, 2012; Land & Stovall, 2009), and 4) enhance cultural sensibilities that awaken the natural leadership capacities of students at the secondary and post-secondary level (Petchauer, 2012; Wilson, 2010).

With these goals in mind, HipHop2020 extends Giroux and McLaren's conceptualization of schooling into the realm of hip-hop and its schooling of leadership. During the initial phase of HipHop2020's development, its focus was on understanding the *language of schooling* in hip-hop and how school is described in the narratives of the post-*Brown v. Board of Education* hip-hop generation (Wilson, 2007). The current phase of the curriculum focuses on the type of leadership that is created through hip-hop aesthetics. This begs the question, what is the *language of leadership* in hip-hop, and what equity does this schooling fetish hold when working with students enrolled in this HBCU humanities course where the objective is to frame and facilitate authentic hip-hop leadership?

I define hip-hop culture as a community of practice where the concentration is on what participants do, how participants learn, how participants co-construct meaning, and where participants practice their hip-hop sensibilities (Lave & Wenger, 1991; Wenger 1998; Wenger, McDermott, & Snyder, 2002). From the perspective of the hip-hop community of practice, the expectation is to learn something when participants engage in any hip-hop activity—especially rap music—at community, national, and global levels (Wilson, 2007, 2010). Therefore, a hip-hop community of practice framework lends itself to questions such as, how does hip-hop "do" school? How does hip-hop *school on* leadership?

The African Oral Tradition as embodied by the practice of signification helps address these questions. For example, to *signify on* someone or something is to take a particular word, visual, or motif and create another meaning for the benefit of the "signifier." Describing the dualities of interpretation between literary traditions, Henry Louis Gates Jr. (1988) argues in *The Signifying Monkey* that when understanding the literary tool of signifying, the ultimate task is to "echo and re-name". He writes,

> Our task is not to reinvent our traditions as if they bore no relation to that tradition created and borne, in the main, by white men. Our writers used that impressive tradition to define themselves, both with and against their concept of received order. We must do the same, with or against the Western critical canon. To name our tradition is to rename each of its antecedents, no matter how pale they might seem. To rename is to revise, and to revise is to Signify. (p. xxiii)

Applying this theory to the hip-hop aesthetic, I take for example the name OutKast formed by the Atlanta-based rap duo consisting of Andre Benjamin (Andre 3000) and Antwan Patton (Big Boi). Patton and Benjamin *signify on* the adjective in two ways. First, they rename and revise by replacing a "k" for the "c" in the conventional spelling of the word, which describes someone who is unaccepted or marginalized to the peripheries of society. However, OutKast takes this meaning further by signifying *and* schooling. I call it *schoolifying*. To schoolify is to craft new lenses through which to view these words, images, and motifs of hip-hop. Using metaphor, metonym, and other techniques, rappers press the meanings of words in order to create new significances and construct new word associations in the minds of their listeners. In so doing, they are able to quickly and effectively educate their listeners on who they are and what their expression(s) represents. They are able to provide instructions as to how their subsequent utterings should be interpreted. To be clear, I argue that Patton and Benjamin use their group name to begin schoolifying their audience. They echo and rename, they change the spelling, but moreover they create an acronym—Operating Under The Krooked American System Too-long—in order to *school on* a new meaning of the word as it relates to their worldview and experiences (see OutKast, 1994).

OutKast is one of many examples of how *schoolifying* happens in the hip-hop community of practice given its obsession with teaching, learning, and signifying on norms, values, traditions, and a variety of social issues. The Atlanta-based group The GOODie MOb further illustrates this point. Some media outlets write the group's name in all capital letters. For my illustration, I rely on the spelling used on album covers for *Soul Food* (1995) and *Still Standing* (1998). The first word, *GOODIE*, brings two words together as one—*Good* and *Die*—as *MOb* takes on a different personality for this rap group. While they embrace the common definition of a mob being a group or crowd of people, in two ways they resist the notion that this crowd is known for violence and crime. First, leading with *GOODIE* implies that they are a group (or mob) that has come together to represent the common good (pun intended) of all people—particularly those navigating society's institutional margins. Second, they make the "M" and "O" capital, resulting in a reverse acronym that means The GOOD Die Mostly Over bullshit. Notice they refuse to capitalize the "b" in *bullshit*. Robert "T-Mo" Barnett, a member of the four-man group, explains their choice to subordinate the "b" as a decision made when they were going through possible group names. "We settled on GOODie MOb and didn't want to highlight the 'b' because we didn't want to highlight what it stands for: *bullshit*. You know? Small mess." He continues, "Kids were dying over shoes, money, and things that were small and unnecessary. They were dying over nothing. So we always make the 'b' small because bullshit is small" (Personal communication, August 2, 2012).

These ideological perspectives offer insight to the epistemological complexities of what hip-hop believes participants should know. Returning to the examples above, what does it mean to be an OutKast? What narrative examples on The GOODie MOb's album support their claim that those who serve the common good typically fall victim to an unwarranted physical or spiritual death? How does each group leverage its lyrical prowess to explore self-identity, racial and gender politics, war, poverty, and other frustrations born out of the complexities of the social system? And finally, why should the way these hip-hop artists *schoolify* matter in relation to the practice of authentic hip-hop leadership and pedagogy in the post-secondary classroom?

In this regard, it is important to understand hip-hop's fascination with packaging its epistemological perspectives into separate "schools of thought" and ways of being. These are communicated through a variety of paralinguistic behaviors. In other words, hip-hop has the unique ability to create cultural sensibilities and new ways of looking at the world by recycling words, sounds, ideas, traditions, lifestyle choices, and leadership styles. "If hip hop is about nothing else," explains Todd Boyd, author of *The New HNIC: The Death of Civil Rights and the Reign of Hip-Hop* (2002), "it is about the redefinition of language . . . these cultural improvisations on English [that] alter the language in new and interesting ways" (p. 72). For the voices of the hip-hop community of practice, all linguistic and paralinguistic behaviors, "all images, sounds, ideas, and icons are ripe for recontextualization, pun, mockery, and celebration" (Rose, 1994, p. 3).

Take for example its obsessive recontextualization of "school" as metaphor and tension across generations. There is the golden era of hip-hop—the early 1980s through the mid-to-late 1990s—which is referred to as "middle school" or "old school" hip-hop. Songs like The Furious Five's "The Message" (1982) signaled a proliferation of social commentary about family, church, spirituality, media consumption, the prison industrial complex, and the public school system. Go-to songs that represent the old school include Afrika Bambaataa's "Planet Rock" (1982) and Public Enemy's "Brothers Gonna Work It Out" (1990), both of which schooled in their own creative ways about Afrocentricity, knowledge of self, global unity and peace, love of Black women, complexities of Black masculinity, community violence, and the persistent challenges of nonviolence, urban sprawl, and staying in school. When teaching a hip-hop leadership course, it is important to isolate this time period in order to identify hip-hop's elder generation and compare its thoughts, music-making styles, behaviors, and practices to more contemporary "schools" of hip-hop.

People's associations with each "school of thought" create what sociolinguists call a register-dependent conversation that helps construct, establish, interpret, and complicate cultural identity—especially when we look at ideas across generations (Le Page & Tabouret-Keller 1985). An example of this is the work of Sonja L. Lanehart. In her book *Sista Speak* (2002), she used the narratives of five African American women who represent three generations of her family as a means for probing themes of "language, literacy, identity, ideologies, education, and . . . issues that touch all of our lives" (p. 2). By taking this approach, Lanehart concluded that the stories of the African American women are not unique to her chosen subset, but are shared with other disenfranchised community members. She argues that "their stories are reflections of ourselves and glaring reminders of our educational and social needs as a nation and community" (p. 224). So by examining language texts closely—be they family narratives or rap lyrics—we are better able to draw conclusions and implications about its speakers and about their connections with others.

In the next two sections, I expand upon the HipHop2020 pedagogical perspective by articulating the relationship between hip-hop based education and HipHop2020's theory of authentic leadership. In order to professionalize (and therefore standardize) the pedagogy, it is important to locate hip-hop pedagogy within a larger educational context. I argue that a hip-hop pedagogy functions within Keyes's theory of cultural reversioning, and that to understand how, we must take a deeper look at its philosophy of schooling and authenticity within an African tradition of universal values referred to as Ma'at.

Authentic Hip-Hop Leadership: Schoolin' on Leadership That Keeps It Real

Authentic leadership is "a process that draws from both positive psychological capacities and a highly developed organizational context, which results in both greater self-awareness and self-regulated positive [behaviors] on the part of leaders and associates, fostering positive self-development" (Luthans & Avolio, 2003, p. 249). A leadership model that primarily exists in the business industry, authentic leadership makes the claim that highly structured organizations (and the desire to exist within intensely hierarchical spaces like colleges and universities) are where many leaders lose a sense of self and developing leaders struggle with their self-identity. The result is often poor decision-making and an increased focus on short-term gratifications (George, 2003). Leaders, as argued by Fluker (2009), "who are not awake" or "aware of the interiority of experience . . . can endanger the mission of a team, organization and, as we have witnessed too many times to ignore, very large numbers of people" (p. vii). They can also risk harm to themselves and others if they neglect to "exhibit a subconscious insomnia where character is developed and supported by a sense of socioenvironmental identity, awareness, and purpose" (Wilson, 2010, p. 159).

Rather than a hierarchical top-down style of leadership that filters to subordinate levels, authentic hip-hop leadership, which I will use interchangeably with *leadership that keeps it real*, is an organic style that assumes everyone has the capacity to lead by virtue of pursuing their life-purpose and contribution to society. Rather than accountability flowing to one power player, in authentic hip-hop leadership, the accountability is to self, others, and societies, be they local, national, or global. In other words, the vocational path one chooses must engender personal fulfillment as well as benefit the sustainability of families, neighborhoods, and the institutions that work on behalf of these communities. The task of the authentic hip-hop leader, then, is to locate one's purpose in life. Along this vein, *leadership that keeps it real* "self regulates according to a set of principles rather than self-interested preferences" (Wilson, 2010, p. 160). Its innovation lies in the aesthetic use of hip-hop culture and digital social media as applicable ways to acquire, nurture, and sustain these authentic leadership sensibilities. The practice of *leadership that keeps it real* therefore begins with the individual following a set of principles (i.e., rules of engagement) that guide the construction of self- and community awareness that the hip-hop community refers to as "knowledge of self."[3]

Knowledge of self is achieved by adherence to a code of ethics that is inextricably tied to hip-hop's ideal of realness. The challenge to achieving knowledge of self lies in concretizing the "keep it real" mantra that has haunted hip-hop culture since its 1970s beginnings. The contemporary view of keeping it real has caused great tragedy and its essential meaning has suffered a slow, self-annihilating death that has resulted in tremendous acts of violence and misogyny—paired with hegemonic masculinity, emphasized femininity, and excessive materialism in the name of a quasi-street loyalty—because hip-hop culture has struggled with a clear and definitive rubric for realness. In a HipHop2020 class, students critique these ideals with guiding questions such as "What does it mean to be authentically human and practice an awareness that is humane at its core?"

In the next section, I describe the rubric that gives rise to how students pursue these questions as they work at locating an authentic hip-hop leadership practice suitable to their overall personal and professional development. I rely on the sampling research carried out in the ethnomusicological work of Keyes (2004) and Schloss (2004) to argue that hip-hop's realness principle has its beginnings in the African epistemology of Ma'at, similar to how rap music locates its nucleus in the West African tradition of orality, performance, and musical production.

Ma'atic Hip-Hop: Toward a Hip-Hop Philosophy of Education

Authentic hip-hop leadership purports that leadership and self-awareness are codependent attributes. The main objective of teaching this type of leadership is to demystify the relationship between leadership and self-awareness by using a seven-point rubric that facilitates better critiques of the values, norms, and ideas contained within hip-hop aesthetic forms and practices. Leadership that keeps it real is therefore action-oriented and achieved by the consistent practice of seven characteristics: truth, balance, order, justice, reciprocity, harmony, and righteousness. I call it Ma'atic Hip-Hop because these seven universal values are referred to as Ma'at (phonetically pronounced *mah-ot* or *may-ot*). Ma'at has its roots in ancient Kemetic society as a code of conduct for how human beings should live and govern themselves. These seven principles later spread throughout the African continent in a variety of languages under different names (Hilliard III, 1997) and can be considered the basic tenets of varied spiritual practices around the world.

Ma'at is understood in at least three distinct ways: as an ethical theory based on a set of fundamental values; as spiritual ideology; and as a vision for education (Asante, 1986; Delpit & White-Bradley, 2003; Hilliard III, 1986, 1995, 1997,

2002). These three arms of Ma'at are interconnected and integral to traditional African beliefs about what it means to be *human* and *humane*, as described in Asa G. Hilliard III's "Pedagogy in Ancient Kemet" (1986) and *SBA: The Reawakening of the African Mind* (1997). To gain an understanding of Ma'atic Hip-Hop and its role in the development of a theoretical frame that guides hip-hop pedagogy, it is important to gain a deeper understanding of the tradition of African education.

In his research, Hilliard describes how the Ma'at pedagogical system served as the central organ for the education of students (or apprentices, as they were called) in ancient Kemetic traditions. The fundamental stance of education was twofold: to develop the spirit and character of the student, and to use this encouragement of self-identity to help students cultivate a technical skill. It was believed that human beings had the potential to personify divinity through acts of righteous balance, order, and harmony in all areas of physical and natural existence. In the Ma'at-centered classroom, the ultimate aim was to teach the consistent practice of truth, justice, and morality so that they were "reflected in the intimate and harmonious ties between and among education, politics, economics, religion, and so forth" (Hilliard III, 1995, p. 91). The ultimate goals were to achieve unity of person and unity of nature. Apprentices were taught that social responsibility and spiritual correctness were mutually inclusive and tied to their vocational training. In other words, the purpose of technology was "to develop a greater understanding of man's relationship to nature and mankind's place in nature" (Hilliard III, 1995, p. 91). It was believed that when a person's character was intact, his or her technical contributions to society were more meaningful and aligned with the Ma'at order. The process of self-knowledge was thus carried out through methods of participation and observation whereby the apprentice was confronted with problems of the conscience through the heavy use of proverbs, songs, and stories. Hilliard (1995) opines, "It was the fundamental belief in the unity or interconnectedness of all things that made the use of analogies such a powerful pedagogical tool" because it led to critical thinking and "the development of a sense of responsibility and judgment" (p. 91).

In the case of authentic hip-hop leadership development, leaders must complicate what it means to be human, what it means to be humane, and therefore what it means to be real. These three essential questions are addressed through the interrogation of hip-hop narratives filtered through the seven characteristics listed above. In order to apply these principles, students pose questions of the narrative such as:

- Where is the transparency in the narrative?
- What is true about the story?
- How can order be described in the story?
- What are the dilemmas in the narrative?
- Who and what is the narrative about?
- Where is the conflict in the narrative?

- Where is the quest for (and question of) fairness or lack thereof (particularly as it relates to race, economics, war, and gender?
- Where is the duality of humanity in the story?
- Where is the reconciliation of humanity in the narrative?
- What evidence of ethics and morality or lack thereof is in the narrative?
- How does the story end?
- What is the moral of the story?

In traditional African thought, Ma'at was the guiding epistemology to bring about equilibrium in societies and communities threatened by personal and social chaos brought on by the coexistence of diverse populations with diverse axiological pursuits. The highest aim of a Ma'at-centered education was for a student to understand their *Neter*, or "how God is revealed in the person".[4] So, the principles of Ma'at are basic, fundamental, and universal—applicable across ethnicity, religious or spiritual affiliation, gender, and age. Ma'at also reveals itself as a key element of the early practice of hip-hop. Its principles appeal to hip-hop's transnational flexibilities, and remain applicable to how one navigates his or her way through personal desires, tragedies, and challenges faced on a day-to-day basis. Members and participants of the hip-hop community are encouraged, if not ordered, to practice their authenticity by seeking knowledge of self (i.e., to keep it real)—a practice that ultimately resolves to authentic leadership. Regardless of the subject area, I argue that HHBE as a developing field is and must continue to be grounded in the concept of Ma'atic Hip-Hop pedagogy in order for the field to develop into a sustainable area of study for the next generation of hip-hop scholars.

Lisa Delpit and Paula White-Bradley's "Educating or Imprisoning the Spirit: Lessons from Ancient Egypt" (2003) provides an exemplar of how Ma'at is applied in programs designed to raise the test scores of children who live in low-income communities. Through their work they conclude that a culturally responsive pedagogy integrated with principles of Ma'at humanizes the experiences of these students in a way that affirms their abilities to think clearly and focus more in the classroom setting. A dearth of literature exists that focuses on the use of Ma'at in the post-secondary classroom—particularly the post-secondary hip-hop studies classroom. In the next section, I describe how Ma'atic Hip-Hop—as a theoretical framework for contextualizing hip-hop's philosophy of education—informs Hip-Pop Leadership Pedagogy when southern hip-hop culture is used as the database of narratives in my hip-hop studies course on leadership development.

LESSON TWO: "THE SOUTH GOT SUMTHIN' T' SAY"

As it stands, HHBE and hip-hop studies more generally revolve around East and West coast artists or communities (Hill, 2009; Petchauer, 2009). Focusing primarily on hip-hop practices of New York or Los Angeles adds fuel to the high art/low art debate that has found its way into how we understand rap music (Hill, 2009), but more importantly it disconnects HHBE from the rich cultural legacy of the southern hip-hop community of practice—particularly when we understand the contributions southern music and culture made to the overall sound and aesthetic of hip-hop's golden era. Herein lies another reason I started HipHop2020: to give HHBE a space in southern hip-hop and to use the lived experiences of southerners as told through southern hip-hop for educational purposes. In this section, I give a brief description of the southern network, its language norms, and their significance to the overall hip-hop community of practice.

Southern School in Session: A Description of Hip-Hop in the South

Almost every form of music popular in New York City, particularly hip-hop music, gets its roots from the South. Jazz, blues, soul, and funk were carried right along with the migration of African Americans who escaped to northern and midwestern states for the benefits that a Jim Crowed South did not offer. In the early 1970s, hip-hop culture was formed around these musical styles but with a creative twist that linked elements of style, dress, and talk with a worldview considered rebellious and militant to peripheral onlookers. Because hip-hop culture gelled in the South Bronx, New York, it is historicized as a culture created in New York, and with this has come a regional arrogance that continues to rear its ugly head. Even in the scholarship, New York is credited as the birthplace of such a dynamic culture. Lacking is the recognition that hip-hop culture samples its elements from southern-born expressions that currently dominate the overall hip-hop community of practice.

Southern hip-hop is hip-hop produced in the U.S. South, with Atlanta, Miami, Houston, New Orleans, and Memphis serving as its main production centers. Over the last decade, Atlanta and Miami have risen as major cities not only for hip-hop culture and rap music but also for film and television. Although there is overlap in these sites, each has its unique contribution to the overall culture. What I refer to as pre-southern hip-hop began in the late 1970s and early 1980s when cities like Atlanta and Miami began to create their own signature style to fill the existing regional voids while simultaneously being influenced by the elements of up-North innovations. For example, down-South hip-hoppers wore hip-hop fashion styles: Kangol hats, Adidas jogging suits, and fat-laced tennis shoes were trends just as they were for up-North hip-hoppers, and graffiti art made its way to the sides of Atlanta's MARTA trains and freeway overpasses. As dance groups showcased their talents in southern breakdancing, popping, and locking in school variety shows, Atlanta modified the dance style with the inclusion of a one-two, side-to-side hustle and called it yeek dancing, or simply *yeeking*.[5] Southern hip-hop contributed not only to the dance element of the culture; in many ways, it changed the way hip-hop talked, how hip-hop led, how it dressed, packaged its music, even how it schooled its listeners.

With the rise of hip-hop in the South came further complications of what authenticity and realness meant in the overall practice of the culture. The South—its lifestyles, views of the world, linguistic norms, and perspectives of race, class, and gender—is the last U.S. region to gain commercial notoriety in the rap industry, and the first U.S. region to catch holy hell for what everyone outside the South thought were ignorant call-and-response lyrics sprinkled with a gang of incomprehensible southern slang about nothing other than "bitches, hos, and ig'nant negroes." "Hip-Hop Is Dead" was recorded in 2006 by New York–born rapper Nasir "Nas" Jones, who has made Atlanta a home base and was a resident at times during the making of the song. Albeit OutKast's Andre "3000" Benjamin declared hip-hop was dead on 2001's "Funkin Around" from their album *Big Boi and Dre Present . . . OutKast*, Jones's claim added fuel to a burning fire that had begun 5 years earlier when Houston, Texas–based rapper Chad "Pimp C" Butler from the group UGK (Underground Kingz) authoritatively represented hip-hop in the South "as country rap tunes" rather than "muthafuckin' hip-hop records" on their classic song "Let Me See It" from the album *Dirty Money*. Atlanta-based rapper Chris "Ludacris" Bridges responded to Jones by wearing a T-shirt printed with the words "Hip-Hop Ain't Dead, It Lives in the South." Quoted in an MTV News interview, Ludacris responded to Nas directly and Pimp C indirectly, saying:

> I don't feel that hip-hop is dead. . . . I feel like the South is keeping it alive. What we do is hip-hop. Some people may not feel that way. You gotta respect some people's opinion, but hey. You gotta stay to your opinion in the game . . . because the South is dominating it right now, [so] saying that hip-hop is dead is like saying the South is dead too. They may not like some of the music going on in the South. But everybody in the South is saying, "We are keeping it alive." . . . At the end of the day, hip-hop is what you make it. What we do in the South isn't hip-hop—that's what some people think. We think it is. Some people say it's country-rap tunes. Hip-hop is what you make it.[6]

The South began to claim their commercial space in hip-hop's cultural landscape in the mid-1990s when the focus shifted from Death Row Records, Bad Boy Records, 2 Live Crew, and even Master P and his No Limit soldiers to a new organic sound of soul, funk, and live instrumentation ushered in by Arrested Development but taken higher by a production crew that went by the name of Organized Noize Productions.

First on their label was the aforementioned duo, OutKast. During the 1995 *Source* Magazine Awards ceremony—amidst a rambunctious audience consumed by what was known as the East Coast/West Coast war[7]—Patton and Benjamin won the award for Best New Rap Group for their album titled

Southernplayalisticadillacmuzik (1994). Salt-n-Pepa, rap music's first female duo to reach commercial notoriety, presented the nominees. Upon opening the envelope, to their own arrogant dismay, the ladies begrudgingly announced "And the winner is . . ." They paused, and in unison their elevated voices said "OutKast?" They might as well have said, "Who tha hell is OutKast? Is that those country ass niggaz from Atlanta? Oh hell no!" The camera panned the audience. Everyone was stunned. The audience's taunts were followed by boos and, perhaps, some coastal intimidation because on that August evening in New York's Madison Square Garden the tide of hip-hop's geopolitics turned. Benjamin stood with Patton, his rap partner/*naamu-sayer*, and stepped to the microphone to turn his bittersweet acceptance speech into a southern-fried injunction, informing reluctant admirers, "I'm gon' tell y'all sumthin'. Tha South got sumthin' t'say!"[8]

What is the view of the world from the Southside? The history and acceptance of southern hip-hop in the larger music industry parallels that of hip-hop based education. The HipHop2020 Curriculum Project has made it a point to find out what the story of southern hip-hop is in the grand novel of hip-hop and understand how these stories can be used as applicable material to the lives of all youth and youth influencers—especially at the post-secondary level. If hip-hop is obsessed with teaching, learning, and leading, in what ways does southern hip-hop remix values, traditions, and morals so that the next generation of leaders has the necessary capacities to enjoy life's experiences and seek a life of balance while following a solid value system? How might they stay committed to justice while leading with their heart, or speak the truth while remaining aware of their purpose? What's the significance of understanding that relationships are established and nurtured through actions of reciprocity (balanced give and receive), and that the moral rightness of life is demonstrated through what is said and done (Fluker, 2009; George, 2003; Wilson, 2010)?

The Language of Southern Hip-Hop

Many of the messages found in southern hip-hop are linguistically cryptic and phonologically obscure. More often than they should be, the points of view that emerge from southern narratives are mistaken as lacking relevant commentary and authenticity aligned with the ideals of hip-hop's forefathers and foremothers. Most of the time these aesthetics are co-opted, commodified, exploited, and marketed to the mainstream for mass distribution and profit generation for cultural capitalists. The results are repackaged images sold using stereotypical strategies that provoke tension within the African American community and among the hip-hop community of practice. What goes unnoticed are the number of southern songs that challenge traditional notions of hip-hop and confront consequences of poverty, prison, drug culture, and inefficient social institutions, such as schools, churches, and families. Studying the language use—the way it sounds and the contextual meanings—reveals many of the messages inherent in hip-hop culture, and in southern hip-hop specifically.

For example, when the southern rap group Trillville (2004) uses the *bitch-nigga* combination to rhythmically signify "Bitch nigga you can neva eva . . . get on my level ho!" they are not loose in their verbal attack as many hip-hop practitioners who live outside the southern hip-hop region may have thought when Jonathon Smith, aka Lil Jon/The King of Crunk, produced this youth-inspired ode. Instead, the three African American males who make up Trillville, two of whom are college-educated, were extremely calculated about whom they are referring to as a *bitch-nigga* (and *ho*). In fact, they schoolify about the pejorative function of the three terms. In an interview I conducted for the May 2003 issue of *XXL* magazine, one of the group's members schooled me. "Actually," he started, "when we wrote the hook, we was thinkin' 'bout people like [George W.] Bush. That's a bitch nigga!" (Wilson, 2003, p. 60) They continued to explain to me that anyone who attempts to work against them—be it an uncaring teacher, police officer, or politician—that person falls under the B-N-H category and is dealt with in a particular fashion. While Trillville's coded yet direct language is extremely profane, referring to former president Bush as a *bitch nigga* is a modern take on an ancient means by which to prioritize the subordinate voice (Rose, 1994) and allows Trillville to school on someone who, in their eyes, is insensitive to the needs of others.

Because culture is semiotic (Denzin, 1992; Geertz, 1973), looking at the phonology and the meaning behind words like *bitch* in hip-hop narratives further adds to understanding the culture's language, speakers, beliefs, expectations, and values (Wilson, 2007). The question, then, is where does the educational significance lie in the deconstruction of words like *bitch* and *nigga*, or in OutKast's and The GOODie MOb's commandment to pay attention to what they and others in the South have to say? Why does it matter? What currency does it have in authentic hip-hop leadership development? Aside from opening the conversation to dialogue about the social implications of George W. Bush's presidency and why three African American males consider his actions morally reprehensible, the cultural and pedagogical value lies in examining how this kind of knowledge is produced, transmitted, and used to advance what is known about social and cultural realities. It is also a window of opportunity to explore authentic hip-hop leadership—asking questions and critiquing whether or not Bush kept it real according to the principles above.

LESSON THREE: "IT'S HIM AND I/AQUEMINI," "THE OUTKAST LESSON"

"The OutKast Lesson" is an activity that follows Lesson One, "The Story of Hip-Hop is the Story of the Sample," and Lesson Two, "The South Got Sumthin T' Say." By the time students engage in artist-named lessons such as "The Kid Cudi

Lesson" or "The OutKast Lesson," they have a good theoretical understanding of hip-hop's relationship to sampling and cultural reversioning. They have been introduced to hip-hop as an outgrowth of the Black Aesthetic and to Ma'atic Hip-Hop as a philosophy of education, authenticity, and leadership.

In this section, I articulate the elements of Hip-Pop Leadership Pedagogy, how students deconstruct the narratives, and how they present their ideas through discussion, presentation, and writing. I will refer to a video housed on the HipHop2020 website (www.hiphop2020.org). In this lesson, HipHop2020 students were asked to analyze "Aquemini," a song from OutKast's third studio album of the same title. They were asked to filter the song through the principles of Ma'at as articulated in Molefi Asante's "The Egyptian Origin of Rhetoric and Oratory" (1986). The objective of this assignment was for students to critique the lyrical narratives in the song and explain authenticity—or the lack thereof—in the song according to the theory of Ma'atic Hip-Hop and the role of the orator. Students were asked to take the objectives a step further by writing an essay in which they were to explain whether or not the ideas in the song are relevant to their personal lives and, if so, they were charged with using one example to explain how. Students were required to use at least three to five references from class readings to substantiate their arguments.

Preparing for the Essay: The Ins and Outs of Hip-Pop Leadership Pedagogy

Hip-Pop Leadership Pedagogy is a narrative-based instructional approach. Its pedagogical imperative is both a spiritual one and a technical one in that its aim is to transform the self and the spirit while enhancing students' cognitive skills and encouraging self-identity. The purpose of HPLP is to teach authentic leadership skills to youth and youth influencers in a way that engages them in exercises of personal awareness and growth, exposes them to contemporary community challenges, and equips them with the tools and strategies to nonviolently address these challenges. As stated above, the philosophical orientation of HPLP is rooted in the theory of Ma'atic Hip-Hop. Its analytical approach is inspired by James Spradley's (1979) domain analysis whereby the students inductively interrogate the seven principles of truth, justice, order, balance, harmony, reciprocity, and righteousness as they are contained in the narratives, practices, and aesthetic forms of the hip-hop community (Asante, 1986; Hilliard III, 1986, 1995, 1997, 2002; Wilson, 2010). The goal is to use the hip-hop aesthetic as a means for helping the next generation determine their sociocivic contributions while becoming "better moral reasoners, ethical reasoners, critical thinkers, resolvers of conflict, and consumers of culture" (Wilson, 2010, p. 163). How is this done? The objective is to teach students to be student-researchers: to show them how to generate questions, reach a substantive grounded theory based on these questions, and effectively communicate their findings according to an assignment given to them by their instructor.

Hip-Pop Leadership Pedagogy is inspired by Spradley's *domain analysis* as it is articulated in his book *The Ethnographic Interview* (1979). He describes the process as a four-step ethnographic analysis technique based on the constant pursuit of locating the meaning participants make in their lives according to their use of significant words, behaviors, lifestyle norms, practices, and other nonverbal cues. The first step is the selection of a semantic relationship. Spradley describes nine semantic relationships to choose from but suggests beginning with *strict-inclusion* (X is a kind of Y) or *means-end* (X is a way to do Y). For the purposes of operationalizing HPLP, I created two new semantic relationships: 1) *tell-tale* (X is a way to describe Y) and 2) *deficient-of* (X is a lack of Y).[9]

The second step requires a selection of data that fit the selected semantic relationship in order to begin this search for meaning. I assign the semantic relationship and the data until students become comfortable with the analysis. For example, the semantic relationship for this exercise is *tell-tale* and the primary data is the hook/chorus from "Aquemini" (see Table 4.1).

In their groups, students conduct a preliminary search of data—in our case lyrics, interviews, and videos—to determine what words are used repeatedly or to determine if specific names are given to particular things. These repeated words and phrases are called *domains*. Domains are a collection of shared categories that have a certain kind of relationship to one another. Sometimes students select phrases from verses that represent song titles or repeated words. These words and phrases can contribute to the primary domain or they can become supporting domains. The third step is to locate a domain and its shared categories by creating a list. Whatever word or noun is used most frequently in relation to the data is perhaps a good cover term (X) to start the domain. The cover term can be an invariable recurrent category or the blend of overlapping categories.

In the OutKast song, the word *Aquemini* (an amalgamation of Patton's and Benjamin's zodiac signs, Aquarius and Gemini) is used repeatedly, often at the end of the song's chorus, and thus, it is a good cover term. In the ways that it is used, the word becomes an implicit metaphor for the duo and both their individual and collective representation of Blackness. This can be the case in the song's chorus in Table 4.1 and in the following verse excerpt:

Is every nigga with dreads for the cause?
Is every nigga with golds for the fall?
Naw. So don't get caught up in appearance.
It's OutKast. Aquemini. Another Black experience.

The variable terms (X) belong to the category and contribute to the creation of the semantic relationship. In the case of HPLP, we have our variable terms. They are the seven authentic hip-hop leadership principles listed above. In Table 4.1, we take "justice" as an example of a variable term (Y). It is crucial to the

Table 4.1. Taxonomy of Kinds of Justice in OutKast's "Aquemini"

Cover Term (X)	Variable Term (Y)	Excerpt	Semantic Relationship/Memo
Aquemini	Justice, Balance, Harmony, Order, Reciprocity, Truth	[Chorus] "Even the sun goes down. Heroes eventually die. Horoscopes often lie. And sometimes 'y.' Nothin' is for sure. Nothin' is for certain. Nothin' lasts forever. But until they close the curtain. It's him and I. Aquemini"	X describes Y: • Aquemini is a way to describe the relationships between balance, harmony, order, and justice. At the beginning of the hook they describe natural order. That the sun must go down so that it can rise again. History shows that the ultimate sacrifice of a hero is often death in the name of a cause, and that in grammar we must sometimes use the letter "y" as a vowel. Not all the time but sometimes. • The chorus implies that life and its situations exist within a balanced harmony (e.g., reciprocity) or duality of good and bad, up and down, right and wrong. • Justice implies equity. Injustice happens when the natural order of things is out of balance. In regard to personal justice, Patton and Benjamin see themselves as equals who balance out one another until the natural order of this balance comes to an end. • The truth of this is that nothing in life is 100% certain, that nothing lasts forever, and that everything has its proper time and cycle.

process that students understand the interplay between the principles. For example, rarely do we find justice existing without order, balance, or harmony. It only adds to the building of the domain when supporting principles are included in the analysis. After selecting the semantic relationship and the data, followed by the creation of the domain or "the symbolic category that includes other categories" (Spradley, 1979, p. 100), students can then begin to ask questions of the data. Casting "Aquemini" as a concept for understanding balance, harmony, order, and justice rather than simply a song title, students can ask questions such as, "In what other ways can 'Aquemini' be described in the song?" or "How can I describe 'Aquemini' as it relates to my personal experiences?" Answering questions such as these leads students to the final step of domain analysis: the creation of what grounded theorists call the memo (Charmaz, 2002; Creswell, 1998; McCann & Clark, 2003a, 2003b, 2003c).

Instead of approaching research with an explanation to test, grounded theorists inductively manipulate these guidelines to generate themes and patterns such that theoretical explanations emerge directly from the data (Denzin, 1992; Dey, 1999). Memo-writing is the link between the theory and the methodology. It is where students—who by now are operating as critical researchers—distill their thoughts about the analysis of the data and the semantic relationship. The abstractions that result from memo-writing become the thoughts and theories shared in group presentations and in the final essay.

Spradley's (1979) techniques, while seemingly tedious, offer a way to consistently compare the material. Although primarily used by scholars to analyze interviews, this ethnographic typology can be used by students to interpret lyrics, explore an artist's linguistic productions, and consider the meanings inherent in music videos, and even the analysis of interviews. Hip-Pop Leadership Pedagogy is both a research methodology and pedagogical strategy. The innovation of the approach is founded upon the use of ethnographic research methods as a basis for instruction, and students become student-researchers, learning to question what they read, say, and listen to. Hip-Pop Leadership Pedagogy triangulates data collection and analysis methods with popular media, hip-hop culture, and social network technologies as an instructional approach for helping young leaders acquire a fundamental definition of leadership. Digging into the narratives can help them more efficiently apply both the definition and approach to the challenges that face them personally, as well as the problems that plague their communities.

LESSON FOUR: WHERE DO WE GO FROM HERE?

Ethnomusicologists Cheryl Keyes (2004) and Joe Schloss (2004) argue that rap and hip-hop's musical, stylistic, and production forms operate within an act of cultural reversioning where the roots of rap are located in West African traditions of the *bard, naamu-sayer,* and *nommo*. Keyes argues that these fundamental language and metalinguistic practices interacted with the geopolitics of the slave trade, ultimately producing African American oral traditions found in both the secular and spiritual aesthetic domain. From Keyes's perspective, it is logical to argue that African pedagogical traditions underwent a similar process of cultural transmission and reversioning through space and time.

In this final section, I address implications for further research for educators and researchers interested in using the HPLP methodology. I also present implications for the field as its validity and reliability in the classroom rests on substantiating the pedagogy within a hip-hop theoretical framework or philosophy of education that I call Ma'atic Hip-Hop.

Implications for a Standard Hip-Hop Philosophy of Education

As the study of hip-hop culture continues to grow into a viable field for academic research, it will become increasingly important to use a methodology that opens the culture to ways of understanding its complexities, contradictions, sensibilities, aesthetic forms, and practices. This is crucial because of hip-hop's global influence—an influence that arranges the community around common practices of rapping, deejaying, graffiti art, and breaking coupled with specific articulations based on location-sensitive nuances. Because space is political, racialized, gendered, and class-specific, how youth and youth influencers interact in spaces, both using and creating spaces, constitutes the content of human experience and therefore how the world is viewed, how knowledge is produced, and how education is acquired.

"Keepin' it real" is the overarching, contradictory, complex-natured, African-centered, socially aware, politically astute concept in hip-hop culture. In hip-hop culture, the ideology is a normative imperative that demands hip-hop members and participants express their social and emotional vulnerabilities honestly and openly. Imani Perry (2004) calls the idea a "rallying cry" that includes "celebrations of the social effects of urban decay and poverty . . . assertions of a paranoid vigilance in protecting one's dignity" (pp. 86–87). In addition to what could be a self-destructive application, realness also taps into the spirit of hip-hop, challenging it to strive toward an existential peace that could literally change lives, thoughts, actions, perspectives, behaviors, teaching methods, and learning practices. This perspective, albeit controversial and complex, is the decision-making filter for many of the culture's members, and it is therefore crucial to the growing canon of hip-hop scholarship. I call this hip-hop philosophy of education Ma'atic Hip-Hop because it utilizes African traditions of education that teach to the self, spirit, and society of students. As hip-hop scholars push toward the professionalization of HHBE, we must rely on a hip-hop theory of education such as Ma'atic Hip-Hop in order to sustain the hip-hop studies field into the future of what is known about progressive teaching and learning.

Implications for Educators, Researchers, and Other Youth Influencers

Teachers, educators, parents, and other youth influencers often ask me how to use hip-hop as an instructional method. Many of them find the technique intimidating and, for a variety of reasons, many youth influencers shy away from employing a hip-hop pedagogy in formal school environments and in afterschool activities. Perhaps it is because of the ongoing misconception that hip-hop single-handedly promotes community violence, violence against women, and material gluttony. Or, maybe it is because educators think they must listen to rap music and be a participant in the culture in order to integrate a hip-hop pedagogy in standards-based curriculum. Hip-hop no doubt has its challenges, as do all forms of expressive art. I—along with a host of other education researchers—would argue, however, that the constructive value inherent in hip-hop's aesthetic forms far outweighs the negative (Duncan-Andrade & Morrell, 2008; Low, 2011), and while a level of literacy in hip-hop will help in a classroom setting, it is not necessarily the case that an educator must be able to recite the lyrics of Nas or Jay-Z from memory in order to participate in HHBE.

Herein lies another reason why I started HipHop2020. When I started the curriculum project in 2006, my goal was to develop a standard pedagogy contextualized in a hip-hop philosophy of education that equipped teachers and educators with the necessary resources for applying pop culture pedagogy in formal and informal educational spaces. A main purpose of the project was—and still is—to pen activities and lessons that would curb educator anxieties and increase student engagement, performance, and motivation. So a focus of HipHop2020 is teacher training and preparation in hip-hop based pedagogical strategies. It is also crucial that hip-hop pedagogues commit to capacity-building in a way that ensures the future sustainability of the field. A commitment such as this can alleviate the anxieties of youth influencers who want to use the technique but are threatened by the content and the idea that they do not identify with the hip-hop or millennial generation.

NOTES

1. HipHop2020 was originally established in 2006 under the direction of Joycelyn Wilson. The purpose of HipHop2020 is to promote the essence of the hip-hop practice in a way that both challenges and nurtures research, scholarship, knowledge production, and knowledge acquisition in the field of hip-hop studies, pedagogy, and technology. The Curriculum Project is one of the flagship programs of HipHop2020. Its purpose is to triangulate hip-hop aesthetic forms, pop culture, and digital media in order to develop the leadership capacities of youth and youth influencers.

2. Examples of how MCs—whether consciously or unconsciously—sample from this musical tradition can be found in the mutuality of Eric B. and Rakim or DJ Jazzy Jeff and the Fresh Prince, where the DJ (*naamu-sayer*) provides the beat for the MC (*bard*) to rhyme (or talk in rhythm) to the song provided by his DJ. "Amazing" by Kanye West is another example because it features rapper/MC Young Jeezy over a tribal production, where he—through chopped and screwed fusions of "yeah" and "let's go"—functions as West's *naamu-sayer* (or hype-man/feature). Atlanta duo OutKast and New York hip-hop pioneers

Run-DMC are two great examples of the *bard/naamu-sayer* relationship in rap music as Andre 3000 and Big Boi operate in a back-and-forth style of storytelling and historicizing through a southern language vernacular. Run and DMC also skirt the traditions of the *bard/naamu-sayer* continuum, with the support of their DJ Jam Master Jay.

3. See the music of artists such as KRS-One, Queen Latifah, Poor Righteous Teachers, The GOODie MOb, Ice Cube, Arrested Development, and Nas.

4. See James (1954). In Greek philosophy, the challenge was "man, know thyself." In the Judeo-Christian philosophy, the challenge is to "seek ye first the Kingdom of God." See also Carruthers (1986, 1995).

5. See videos such as OutKast's "Bombs over Baghdad" and Ciara's "1-2 Step" for various forms of yeek dancing.

6. Ludacris' response appears in an interview here: http://www.mtv.com/bands/m/mixtape_monday/121806/

7. The East Coast–West Coast hip-hop beef is considered the most controversial coastal battle in hip-hop history. The feud began in the 1990s between both artists and fans of rap music; however, the root of the war was between Christopher "The Notorious BIG" Wallace and Tupac "2Pac" Shakur who were signed to Bad Boy Records (East) and Death Row Records (West), respectively, and ultimately murdered as an outcome of the conflict. The 1995 *Source* Awards was a tipping point of the feud. Suge Knight, the CEO of Death Row Records, mocked Sean Combs, the CEO of Bad Boy Records. And although attempts were made to keep peace, the obvious reality was that the war would brew and steep until someone was hurt and/or killed. The South remained neutral during this battle to such a degree that at the *Source* Awards, little to no attention was paid to artists such as OutKast, The GOODie MOb, or Organized Noize Productions.

8. See Sarig, R., 2007.

9. Spradley argued in *The Ethnographic Interview* that data contained at least nine semantic relationships. The most common is Strict inclusion (X is a kind of Y). Others are Spatial (X is a place in Y, X is a part of Y); Cause-effect (X is a result of Y, X is a cause of Y); Rationale (X is a reason for doing Y); Location for action (X is a place for doing Y); Function (X is used for Y); Means-end (X is a way to do Y); Sequence (X is a step or stage in Y); and Attribution (X is an attribute, or characteristic, of Y).

REFERENCES

Asante, M. K. (1986). The Egyptian origin of rhetoric and oratory. In J. Carruthers, M. Karenga, & K. Kuumbisha (Eds.), *Kemet and the African worldview: Research, rescue, and restoration* (pp. 183–188). Los Angeles, CA: University of Sankore Press.

Asante, M. K., Jr. (2008). *It's bigger than hip-hop: The rise of the post-hip-hop generation.* New York: St. Martin's Press.

Baber, C. (1987). The artistry and artifice of black communication. In G. Gay & W. L. Baber (Eds.), *Expressively Black: The cultural basis of ethnic identity* (pp. 75–108). New York: Praeger.

Boyd, T. (2002). *The new HNIC: The death of civil rights and the reign of hip hop.* New York: New York University Press.

Carruthers, J. (1986). The wisdom of governance in Kemet. In J. Carruthers, & M. Karenga (Eds.), *Kemet and the African worldview: Research, rescue, and restoration* (p. 13). Los Angeles: University of Sankore Press.

Carruthers, J. (1995). *Mdw Ntr: Divine speech: A historiographical reflection of African deep thought from the time of the pharaohs to the present.* London: Karnak House.

Cermak, M. J. (2012). Hip-hop, social justice, and environmental education: Towards a critical ecological literacy. *The Journal of Environmental Education, 43*(3), 192–203.

Charmaz, K. (2002). Qualitative interviewing and grounded theory analysis. In J. Gunrium & J. A. Holstein (Eds.), *Handbook of interview research* (pp. 675–694). Thousand Oaks, CA: Sage.

Creswell, J. W. (1998). *Qualitative inquiry and research design: Choosing among five traditions.* Thousand Oaks, CA: Sage.

Delpit, L., & White-Bradley, P. (2003). Educating or imprisoning the spirit: Lessons from ancient Egypt. *Theory Into Practice, 42*(4), 283–288.

Denzin, N. (1992). *Symbolic interactionism and cultural studies: The politics of interpretation.* Cambridge, MA: Blackwell.

Dey, I. (1999). *Grounding grounded theory: Guidelines for qualitative inquiry.* San Diego, CA: Academic Press.

Duncan-Andrade, J. M. R., & Morrell, E. (2008). *The art of the critical pedagogy.* New York: Peter Lang.

Fluker, W. (2009). *Ethical leadership: The quest for character, civility, and community.* Minneapolis, MN: Fortress Press.

Gates, H. L., Jr. (1988). *The signifying monkey.* New York: Oxford University Press.

Geertz, C. (1973). *The interpretation of culture: Selected essays.* New York: Basic Books.

George, W. W. (2003). *Authentic leadership: Rediscovering the secrets to creating lasting value.* San Francisco, CA: Jossey Bass.

Giroux, H. A., & McLaren, P. (1986). Teacher education and politics of engagement: The case for democratic schooling. *Harvard Educational Review, 56*(3), 213–239.

Hill, M. L. (2009). *Beats, rhymes, and classroom life: Hip-Hop pedagogy and the politics of identity.* New York: Teachers College Press.

Hilliard III, A. G. (1986). Pedagogy in ancient Kemet. In M. Karenga & J. Carruthers (Eds.), *Kemet and African world view: Research, rescue, and restoration* (p. 257). Los Angeles, CA: University of Sankore Press.

Hilliard III, A. G. (1995). *The maroon within us: Selected essays on African American socialization.* Baltimore: Black Classic Press.

Hilliard III, A. G. (1997). *SBA: The reawakening of the African mind.* Gainesville, FL: Makare.

Hilliard III, A. G. (2002). *African power: Affirming African indigenous socialization in the face of the culture wars.* Gainesville, FL: Makare.

James, G. G. M. (1954). *Stolen legacy.* Trenton, NJ: African World Press.

Keyes, C. (2004). *Rap music and street consciousness.* Chicago, IL: University of Illinois.

Kitwana, B. (2002). *The hip hop generation: Young blacks and the crisis in African-American culture.* New York: BasicCivitas Books.

Kitwana, B. (2005). *Why white kids love hip-hop: Wankstas, wiggers, wannabes, and the new reality of race in America.* New York: BasicCivitas Books.

Land, R., & Stovall, D. (2009). Hip hop and social justice education: A brief introduction. *Equity and Excellence in Education, 42*(1), 1–5.

Lanehart, S. (2002). *Sista speak: Black women kinfolk talk about language and literacy*. Austin, TX: University of Texas Press.

Lave. J., & Wenger, E. (1991). *Situated learning: Legitimate peripheral participation*. Cambridge, UK: Cambridge University Press.

Le Page, R., & Tabouret-Keller, A. (1985). *Acts of identity*. Cambridge, UK: Cambridge University Press.

Low, B. (2011). *Slam school: Learning through conflict in the hip-hop and spoken word classroom*. Stanford, CA: Stanford University Press.

Luthans, F., & Avolio, B. J. (2003). Authentic leadership development. In K. S. Cameron, J. E. Dutton, & R.E. Quinn (Eds.), *Positive organizational scholarship: Foundations of a new discipline* (pp. 241–258). San Francisco: Berrett-Koehler.

McCann T. V., & Clark, E. (2003a). Grounded theory in nursing research: Part 1—methodology. *Nurse Researcher, 11*(2), 19–28.

McCann T. V., & Clark, E. (2003b). Grounded theory in nursing research: Part 2—critique. *Nurse Researcher, 11*(2), 19–28.

McCann T. V., & Clark, E. (2003c). Grounded theory in nursing research: Part 3—application. *Nurse Researcher, 11*(2), 19–28.

Outkast. (1994). "True dat." On *Southernplayalisticadillacmuzik*. Atlanta: LaFace Records.

Outkast. (1998). "Aquemini." On *Aquemini*. Atlanta: LaFace Records.

Pardue, D. (2008). *Ideologies of marginality in Brazilian hip-hop*. New York: MacMillan.

Perry, I. (2004). *Prophets of the hood: Politics and poetics in hip-hop*. Durham, NC: Duke University Press.

Petchauer, E. (2009). Framing and reviewing hip-hop educational research. *Review of Educational Research, 79*(2), 946–978.

Petchauer, E. (2012). *Hip-hop culture in college students' lives: Elements, embodiment, and higher edutainment*. New York: Routledge.

Ramsey, G. P. (2003). *Race music: Black cultures from bebop to hip-hop*. Berkeley, CA: University of California Press.

Rose, T. (1994). *Black noise: Rap music and black culture in contemporary America*. Middletown, CT: Wesleyan University Press.

Sarig, R. (2007). *Third coast: OutKast, Timbaland, and how hip-hop became a southern thing*. Boston: Da Capo Press.

Schloss, J. G. (2004). *Making beats: The art of sample-based hip-hop*. Middletown, CT: Wesleyan University Press.

Spradley, J. (1979). *The ethnographic interview*. Fort Worth, TX: Harcourt Brace Jovanovich.

Trillville (2004). "Neva Eva." The King of Crunk & BME Recording Present: Trillville & Lil Scrappy. Burbank, CA: Warner Bros.

Wenger, E. (1998). *Communities of practice*. New York: Cambridge University Press.

Wenger, E., McDermott, R., & Snyder, W. M. (2002). *Cultivating communities of practice: A guide to managing knowledge*. Cambridge, MA: Harvard Business School Press.

Wilson, J. (2003, May). Call of the wild. *XXL Magazine*, 60.

Wilson, J. (2007). *Outkast'd and claimin true: The language of schooling and education in the southern hip-hop community of practice* (Unpublished dissertation). University of Georgia, Athens, GA.

Wilson, J. (2010). The Kid Cudi lesson: The HipHop2020 Curriculum Project and authentic leadership. *The International Journal of Africana Studies*, 156–172.

PART II

CURRICULA, COURSES, AND PEDAGOGIES WITH HIP-HOP

One of the most expansive developments in HHBE has been using hip-hop as a framework to organize courses and curricula inside and outside of schools. Similar to the work in the previous section of this volume, chapters under this heading expand beyond using aspects of hip-hop as hooks or prompts to learning. Instead, these efforts include curricula and courses that use multiple dimensions of hip-hop—or the full culture of hip-hop—in more comprehensive, organizing, and structural ways. In some instances, actually doing hip-hop is a key part of these curricula. These types of programs most often operate in community or afterschool settings and focus on important educational goals not addressed in formal state-related schooling.

Many of these classroom and curricular expansions are initiated by educators who are absent in much of the HHBE literature. These groups are (1) hip-hop affiliated educators who do not study their practices through research methods and (2) educators who have a genuine interest in HHBE and other student-centered pedagogies but do not personally affiliate themselves with the culture. Many of these educators have engaged in meaningful dialogue since the fall of 2010 through the Twitter-based #HipHopEd discussion Tuesdays from 9:00 P.M. until 10:00 P.M. (EST). Many of these educators have met like-minded pedagogues through this international, weekly discussion.

As some of the chapters in this section will address, classroom and curricular uses of hip-hop sometimes come at a cost by presenting educators with challenges. These are the kinds of challenges that emerge in many types of progressive, student-centered initiatives, and understanding them helps to refine HHBE and other practices. Often, these challenges revolve around constructs such as realness, womanhood, place, masculinity, and citizenship that are shaped by hip-hop and, consequently, bound to the learning environment via HHBE. Although educators can anticipate some of these challenges, some only emerge in the midst of deep engagement. Interrogating some of these challenges, the chapters in this section help educators to anticipate some of them and constructively deal with the unanticipated ones when they arise.

Chapter 5 begins this section of the volume at the same place where many HHBE course and curricula begin: with the teachers. Decoteau J. Irby and H.

Bernard Hall draw from data collected during HHBE professional development workshops to explore the changing professional and cultural demographics of teachers who are interested in using HHBE at increasing rates. With this focus, the authors directly address the ways that HHBE is expanding beyond hip-hop identified educators and into a variety of schooling contexts. In Chapter 6, Bronwen Low, Eloise Tan, and Jacqueline Celemencki use two hip-hop based afterschool programs focusing on youth writing and documentary filmmaking in Montreal, Canada, to explore how the central tropes of authenticity and realness shape the ways that students engage with these programs. The authors argue that when teachers use rap, both as text and as a creative practice, it should be conceptualized and studied as an aesthetic, cultural, and imaginative production rather than as a mirror of the real. In Chapter 7, Derek Pardue examines the use of hip-hop culture as a state-based political project in São Paulo, Brazil, aimed at creating opportunities for poor and working-class youth to learn about "being Brazilian." Pardue examines how these "Cultural Points" have become alternatives to conventional school classrooms and analyzes ways that organizing hip-hop as a national culture has influenced popular notions of citizenship in Brazil. In Chapter 8, David Stovall describes a college bridge social studies course designed to study the current waves of gentrification and urban "renewal" in Chicago by using the corollary historical context of hip-hop's genesis in New York City in the 1970s. Stovall analyzes the generational obstacles between him and his students (living on opposite ends of the hip-hop generation spectrum) to offer pedagogical insights about how HHBE practices in social studies classes can contribute to education for self-determination and social justice.

Overall, the chapters that comprise Part II of this volume provide concrete examples of HHBE within a wide range of contexts, curricular foci, and teacher/student demographics. Like the chapters in Part I, authors stop short of rigid prescriptions but instead aim to inspire similar educational practice that readers and practitioners can tailor to their own local needs.

Fresh Faces, New Places

Moving Beyond Teacher-Researcher Perspectives in Hip-Hop Based Education Research

Decoteau J. Irby and H. Bernard Hall

Hip-hop based education (HHBE) refers to the use of hip-hop, especially rap songs and lyrics, as curricular and pedagogical resources (Hill, 2009; Petchauer, 2009). The research presented in this chapter strengthens HHBE scholarship and supplements the current literature by identifying lines of inquiry that encourage the field to explore in greater detail "who is using hip-hop in the curriculum, their motivations for doing so, and their prior experiences with hip-hop" (Petchauer, 2009, p. 964). This study makes problematic many tacit assumptions about who is using HHBE and where they are using it by presenting professional demographic, school, and survey response data collected from nonresearching teachers. The educators examined in this study were participants in one of four teacher education workshops called "Schooling Ourselves." The workshops were designed to prepare teachers to incorporate hip-hop into their classroom teaching practices.

Hip-hop based educational research documents and evaluates the effectiveness of HHBE in transmitting disciplinary knowledge, improving student motivation, teaching critical media literacy, and fostering critical consciousness in primarily urban K–12 educational settings (Dimitriadis, 2001; Duncan-Andrade & Morrell, 2005; Emdin, 2008, 2009; Hill, 2009; Pardue, 2004; Stino, 1995). The body of research derives primarily from urban public school teachers or community-based educators who use HHBE as a supplement to existing curricula and/or who work with urban K–12 populations (e.g., Alexander-Smith, 2004; Bitz, 1998; Cooks, 2004; Jeremiah, 1992; Pike, 2000). Consequently, the current body of research is dominated by teacher-researcher accounts. Such studies are typically qualitative and/or ethnographic accounts that explore student responses to HHBE and rely on teacher-researcher reflection as a means of examining teacher identity and researcher positionality, respectively (Hill, 2009).

Despite the richness of the burgeoning HHBE research, the overreliance on teacher-researcher accounts of HHBE practice and theory is wrought with short-comings. Regarding nonresearching teachers, there is little knowledge of who is interested in HHBE, the characteristics of the educational spaces and student populations with whom teachers work, or their motivations for employing HHBE. Findings often fail to consider the demographics of the urban teaching force and the issues of identity that may mitigate the effectiveness of HHBE if and when it is taken up by teachers who do not identify with hip-hop culture. As such, current HHBE practices and theory may not accurately account for many issues that nonresearching teachers may face in implementing HHBE. Understanding what issues may emerge for subaltern nonresearching practitioners is critical given the growth in numbers of research studies, curricula, professional development op-portunities, and conferences that encourage more extensive use of culturally rel-evant teaching generally and of HHBE more specifically.

The teacher-researcher perspective and analytical lens of HHBE research has not kept with the trend of HHBE practice. That is, it has not expanded into tra-ditional K–12 educational spaces with nonresearching teachers or considered the diversity of teachers and places where HHBE possibly occurs. Recent scholarship has encouraged exploration of HHBE possibilities for K–12 teachers in primarily urban educational spaces with nonresearching teachers (e.g., Hill, Perez, & Irby, 2008). The current literature situates HHBE almost exclusively in the urban class-room context, commonly understood as educational spaces that cater to "at-risk" youth. Such a narrow conception of the urban classroom context fails to account for the diversity of places, teachers, student populations, pedagogies, and out-comes that may be associated with HHBE. We are concerned with learning more about practicing K–12 teachers who are interested in HHBE, where they might take up these practices, and how identity and place influence the effectiveness of practices and outcomes of HHBE. Such insights will help academic research-ers strengthen HHBE theory and practice. It will also help teacher educators and hip-hop pedagogues prepare teachers to effectively incorporate HHBE into their teaching and learning practices.

We build a case for addressing the identified lacunae through presenting in-formation about a small sample of teachers who attended a professional devel-opment workshop designed to prepare teachers to effectively incorporate HHBE into their classrooms. Drawing primarily from survey data collected during these workshops, we examine who is interested in using HHBE and explore critical is-sues of relevance to teacher educators and researchers. Our findings push the field by calling for HHBE research to give more critical attention to (1) the diversity of teachers interested in using hip-hop in their classrooms; (2) the need for basic teacher education about hip-hop and critical issues within hip-hop culture; and (3) the variable of educational setting (place) and the place-related constraints that teachers may face in their attempts to adopt HHBE.

TEACHER RESEARCH AND HIP-HOP BASED EDUCATION

Hip-hop, rooted in the inner-city post-industrial experiences of urban youth of color (Rose, 1994), has long been considered a driving force in education for urban youth (Powell, 1991). As early as 1991, educators, realizing hip-hop's potential to educate youth, began tapping into the music and culture as a means of exploring "the values and attitudes of young people" (Powell, 1991, p. 257) as well as a way to teach language arts (Jeremiah, 1992). The first educational arena where hip-hop was recognized as an educational force was the streets (e.g., Macklis, 1989; Powell, 1991; Sullivan, 2003). Powell (1991) recognized that hip-hop was a source of informal education. The ability of hip-hop to educate youth is precisely why it has been adopted by individuals who are part of formal and semiformal educational settings.

Hip-hop based education scholarship results primarily from teacher-researcher accounts or what Baumann and Duffy (2001) refer to as *writing and reporting classroom inquiry* produced by teachers. The notion of "teacher as researcher" emerged most prominently in the early 1990s in reference to a set of professional staff development techniques designed to help teachers improve their own teaching practices by addressing "the perception of a gap between a current state of affairs and a more desirable state" in classroom or school settings (Bracey, 1991, p. 404). Defined as *systematic intentional inquiry*, teacher research varied in the institutional settings where it occured and ranged from a systematic collection of particular information about a class with few expectations that the data would be used to inform future classes to well-carried-out studies, resembling academic research, conducted with the intent of informing future practice. Problems and solutions to problems were purported to exist within the classroom context itself. Teacher as researcher professional development techniques such as keeping logs, analyzing student essays and journals, observing students and self-observation (audio and video recording) are all practices reflected in contemporary teacher-research scholarship (Bracey, 1991).

Teacher research as methodology was established through the work of Cochran-Smith and Lytle (1993, 1998), who offered theoretical and methodological underpinnings to the otherwise professionally oriented set of practices. The authors' work distinguishes research on teaching from teacher research by wrestling with epistemological and methodological issues inherent to teacher research. Baumann and Duffy (2001), in their review of teacher-research methodology, identify four broad themes that comprise teacher research: (1) *General attributes of teacher research* refers to the source from where teachers' research questions and inquiry generates, (2) *process of teacher inquiry* captures the collaborative nature of teacher research and reliance on learning from and with students, (3) *teacher researcher methods* capture the practical processes of both teaching and collecting data, and (4) *writing and reporting classroom inquiry* identifies the forms and structures used to share findings. Of concern within the field of HHBE is the issue of general attributes of teacher-researchers and its alignment with the goals of academia or the "visibility" (i.e., publication) of the teacher research (Bracey, 1991).

Within the HHBE literature, the bulk of what is known about the use of hip-hop pedagogies within traditional K–12, nontraditional K–12, and post-secondary settings derives from the firsthand experiences of teacher-researchers who themselves employ the practices and publish in academic journals (e.g., Abowitz, 1997; Alexander-Smith, 2004; Hill, 2009; Morrell & Duncan-Andrade, 2002; Sundeen, 2003). Teacher-researchers of HHBE have primarily employed qualitative methodologies that locate teacher effectiveness in a "range or continuum of teaching behaviors," specifically teachers' conceptions of the self and other, the structure of social relations in the classroom, and teachers' notions of knowledge (Ladson-Billings, 1995, p. 478).

The attributes of the teacher-researchers, especially those who employ teacher research toward a goal of visibility, and nonresearching teachers must be given due consideration to round out the knowledge within the field. Teacher attributes and the places from where theoretical underpinnings for HHBE derive undoubtedly shape inquiry, methods, and writing and reporting of findings. Many hip-hop based educators/teacher-researchers rely on critical theories of learning and apply them to classroom practices (e.g., Duncan-Andrade & Morrell, 2005; Emdin, 2008, 2009; Morrell & Duncan-Andrade, 2002; Stovall, 2006). Some rely on culturally relevant pedagogy (e.g., Abowitz, 1997; Alexander-Smith, 2004; Hill, 2009), while others use critical pedagogy grounded in the Freirean tradition that represents an "approach to schooling that is committed to the imperatives of empowering students and transforming the larger social order in the interests of justice and equality" (McLaren, 2007, p. xvii). Culturally relevant pedagogy (Ladson-Billings, 1994, 1995) offers both a practice and theory that "not only addresses student achievement but also helps students to accept and affirm their cultural identity while developing critical perspectives that challenge inequalities that schools (and other institutions) perpetuate" (Ladson-Billings, 1995, p. 469).

We assume that hip-hop based educators possess additional knowledge (personal, professional, cultural) about hip-hop. We also assume that teacher-researchers who conduct studies for the purpose of visibility are familiar with recent research and concerns of the larger field and are different from teacher-researchers who seek only to solve their specific classroom or school problems. Separately, these attributes equate to either a teacher who understands hip-hop or a teacher who is well informed. Taken together, additional knowledge *and* familiarity with current literature inform the ability to perceive a gap between a current state of affairs and a more desirable state—that HHBE offers a platform for culturally relevant and critical theories of learning to be made increasingly relevant for today's youth. Although critical and culturally relevant theories are well known to teachers, the connections may not be as clear for educators who lack a knowledge base in hip-hop culture that guides and informs their theoretical understanding of what possibilities HHBE affords in solving everyday problems encountered in classroom settings and of the larger concerns within the field of education (content and context—see Bracey, 1991). This makes HHBE teacher-researchers unique. In regard to nonresearching teachers, their knowledge base is different, as often are their reasons for conducting teacher research. The failure to recognize and wrestle with these dissimilarities is a weakness of the current literature.

The broader understanding of the importance of hip-hop (content) and how it is inextricably connected to the issue of place (context) is recognized in HHBE but remains critically underexplored. Most HHBE research is nested in the urban context—at the city, district, school, and/or classroom level. Too often, it does not look beyond or unpack the meanings or relations of HHBE educational practices and theories to the diversity of educational settings that comprise urban districts. This tendency narrows *urban* so that the term seems to refer to marginalized educational settings, such as underperforming districts and schools, community centers, or educational spaces for "at-risk" youth (e.g., Dimitriadis, 2001; Pardue, 2004; Stephens, Braithwaite, & Taylor, 1998; Stino, 1995). Further complicating the issue of place are the associations of place and people that the term *urban* connotes. *Urban, minority, at-risk*, and other identifiers become conflated, rendering the significance of HHBE to urban educational settings vague and unchartered.

It is often unclear how settings and populations can be characterized. Among the research studies reviewed by Petchauer (2009), nearly all, regardless of educational setting, examine African American or Black youth, ethnically diverse, low-income, and/or poor student populations. The conflation of populations and places and the decontextualized use of the term *urban* may be a push back on deficit-oriented labels that are often afforded to oppressed populations. Instead of labeling students in deficit-oriented ways, students and the educational environments are reduced to "urban." At the other end of the educational spectrum, HHBE has a presence in higher education (e.g., Abowitz, 1997; Anderson, 1993; Baker, 1991; Petchauer, 2012; Rice, 2003; Saunders, 1999). In these ways, what is known about HHBE is gleaned from either K–12 educational spaces that appear to serve urban populations or from higher education settings; however, the variable of place beyond the urban context and as nested within the urban context remain unclear at best.

Teacher-researcher studies of HHBE make important contributions to the field of HHBE regarding curricular strategies and pedagogical interventions in traditional and nontraditional educational environments. However, insufficient attention has been paid to nonresearching teachers working in a variety of K–12 settings and the impact of teacher identity and place on teacher effectiveness. To address the identified gaps in the literature, this research study turns the investigative lens away from teacher-researcher perspectives toward practicing K–12 teachers (i.e., nonresearching). It focuses on teachers who are interested in using HHBE but are not necessarily inclined to document their experiences in the classroom through publishing in scholarly journals.

RESEARCH METHODS, QUESTIONS, AND CONTEXT

The Schooling Ourselves teacher education workshops were designed to encourage and prepare teachers to use HHBE. Workshops are based on the content and methods contained in *Do the Knowledge*, a standards-based hip-hop learning and curriculum guide (Irby, 2006) that explores cultural literacy, critical literacy, and media literacy through hip-hop. The creation of the guide and workshops are the brainchild of a community-based organization with a mission of promoting African American art forms. The organization sought to create a guide that would be teacher-friendly and aligned with Pennsylvania state academic standards for "Reading, Writing, Speaking, and Listening" and "Arts and Humanities." The workshops supplement the learning guide by offering educators the opportunity to learn how to work with the content and methods of the guide. Workshops were offered through the educational component of a local museum. One workshop per semester was held for 2 academic years.

Twenty-seven teachers attended the first workshop. Thirteen teachers attended the second workshop and 18 and 21 attended the final two workshops. Certified teachers who participated in the 3½-hour workshops were offered Act 48 professional development credits for completing the workshop. Act 48 requires all Pennsylvania educators holding Pennsylvania public school certification to participate in ongoing professional education. Under Act 48, educators must obtain six credits of collegiate study; six credits of continuing professional education courses; 180 hours of continuing professional education programs, activities, or learning experiences; or any combination of credits or hours equivalent to 180 hours every 5 years to maintain active status.

We analyze workshop registration forms, pre- and post-surveys, and workshop evaluations collected by the hosting institution to answer the following questions: What are the general characteristics of teachers who participate in Schooling Ourselves? How familiar are participants with hip-hop culture and HHBE, and what is their intent for using HHBE after completing the workshops? What are general characteristics of the places where the teachers work? Finally, what is the relation of the findings to the current aims, theories, and practices of HHBE, and how might these findings contribute to urban teacher preparation?

Data Sources

This research relies on information collected through three primary data sources: workshop registration forms, Likert-scale workshop pre- and post-surveys, and continuing professional education learning experience evaluations. All surveys were collected independently by the institution providing the ACT 48 teacher professional development workshop. Data were provided to the researchers after all personal identifiers were removed. From data gathered, we glean basic information about participants, including school name (or organization), school address, grades taught, number of years teaching, certification status, and zip codes in an effort to understand who participants are and the places where they might employ HHBE.

All participants completed a registration form to participate in the workshop and to obtain Act 48 credits for participation. Because registration forms are mandatory and collected prior to the workshop day, the return rate for this data is the highest of that collected. The forms contain school names and addresses, participant zip codes, certification status, and grade levels from a total of 79 workshop registration forms.

Pre- (n = 29) and post- (n = 45) workshop survey items are included for analysis. The voluntary one-page surveys combine Likert-scale and open-ended items to evaluate the value added from the specific workshop. Photocopies of surveys were mailed to the workshop facilitator after each workshop to offer formative feedback for improving workshop content and delivery. Response rates were 37% and 57% for pre- and post-surveys, respectively. It is unclear why response rates were low; however, of the three data sources analyzed in this study, the pre-survey is the only data source administered both on the day of the workshop and in the morning.

We examine select survey items to understand participants' knowledge of HHBE before the workshop and to learn if the workshop improved their knowledge of HHBE and increased their willingness to use HHBE in their classrooms. Applicable items from pre-surveys include: How much to you know about hip-hop culture? Have you ever used hip-hop in your classroom? Do you feel knowledgeable about using hip-hop to improve literacy and critical thinking? Relevant post-evaluation survey items include: Do you now have a better understanding of the history of hip-hop's development and culture? Do you now feel more knowledgeable about using hip-hop to improve literacy and critical thinking? Do you plan on using any of the information you learned in your classroom?

Certified teachers in attendance to receive Act 48 professional development credits completed continuing professional education learning experience evaluations as required by the Commonwealth of Pennsylvania Department of Education. Sections of the forms related to our research questions include certification data, teacher subject areas, grade levels taught, and open-ended feedback for improving the workshops.

Data Analysis

Using the described data sources, we provide a broad description of workshop participants. Our primary interest is understanding the professional and school characteristics. We examine residential and school zip codes to understand where teachers live and work. To ascertain school characteristics, we supplement primary data by matching National Center for Education Statistics (NCES)

Common Core Data set for public, charter, and private school information with school names and addresses.

Survey data were analyzed using Statistical Package for the Social Sciences (SPSS) data analysis software. Frequencies and crosstabs reveal basic descriptions of workshop participants' professional and school characteristics and summarize survey responses. Racial compositions of schools are collapsed into two variables indicating majority White or majority Black, Hispanic, and Asian (students of color). Geographic data are organized using dichotomous variables based on both residential and school locations (city/suburb). School information and teaching experience are organized using categorical variables based on grade level, school type, years teaching, certification, and urban or suburban locale. The number of pre- and post-surveys available was too few to pursue any reliable comparisons of means.

WHO ARE THE TEACHERS?

Teacher Characteristics

To develop a general profile of the workshop's population, we collected information from the workshop registration forms and professional development evaluation forms. Findings are summarized in Table 5.1. For each item, the table presents a raw number of teacher responses as reflected on the various feedback forms, the percentage based on number of responses, and the overall response rate. The data source(s) are listed in the final column. The findings reveal that teachers who are not represented in HHBE research are interested in using HHBE.

Of the 63 participants for whom certification data are available, 87% of respondents indicate that they are certified in their respective state (Pennsylvania and New Jersey). A relatively high level of certification is expected since the workshop offers Act 48 credits for continuing education of certified teachers. Overwhelmingly, workshop participants report teaching at the K–12 level. A majority works with populations in grades 1–8. Eighty percent work in the primary grades, 11% work in secondary schools, and 10% work in settings that either do not cater to any specific grade or do not work with K–12 populations. Grade levels on pre-workshop surveys reveal a similar pattern and also highlight a tendency for teachers to work with elementary school populations within the primary grades.

Twenty-nine participants complete the workshop pre-survey. Slightly over 50% report having more than 10 years of teaching experience: 31% report having from 11 to 20 years of experience and 21% report having more than 20 years of teaching experience. Among less experienced teachers, 28% have between 2 and 5 years of experience and the remaining respondents have less than 2 years'

Table 5.1. Summary of Teacher Characteristics

Teacher Characteristics (N = 79)	Number (n)	Percent (%)	Response Rate (n/N)	Source (Reg. Eval, Pre-, Post-, NCES)
Certification			.797	Eval.
Yes	55	87		
No	8	13		
Grade Level*			.81/.367	Eval./ Pre-survey
Primary	51/23	80/79		
Elementary	na/14	na/48		
Middle	na/9	na/31		
Secondary	6/3	9/10		
Other	7/3	11/10		
Years Teaching			.367	Pre-survey
Less than 2	2	7		
From 2 to 5	8	28		
From 6 to 10	4	14		
From 11 to 20	9	31		
20 or more	6	21		
Teachers Workplaces by Locale and School Type			.873	Reg.
Urban	35	51		
Public (traditional)	9	26		
Public (charter)	16	48		
Private	5	14		
Other	5	14		
Suburban	34	49		
Public (traditional)	14	41		
Public (charter)	0	0		
Private	16	47		
Other	4	12		
Residential Locale			.810	Reg.
Urban	24	39		
Suburban	40	61		

*Grade-level data were available from two sources: professional development evaluation forms and pre-workshop surveys. Results from both sources are reported in Table 5.1 using Source A/Source B format.

experience. Many report teaching multiple subjects, a consequence undoubtedly related to the large proportion of teachers working in elementary and middle
school settings.

School locations for participants are almost evenly split between the number of participants who report teaching in the local urban school district (defined as schools located inside the School District of Philadelphia) and in the
surrounding suburban school districts. Fifty-one percent of respondents report
teaching in the city of Philadelphia; however, of this 51%, only nine teach in
district public schools, a mere 26%. In other words, most participating teachers who work in the city of Philadelphia teach in private schools or public
charter schools (74%), illustrating that although participants teach within the
geographical boundaries of an urban district, the actual schools in which they
teach may be quite different from traditional public schools. This finding begs
further exploration to understand why more urban public school teachers did
not attend the Schooling Ourselves workshops, while teachers from private and
charter schools attended in higher rates. The differential rates of attendance between traditional public school teachers and private and charter school teachers may reflect issues such as inflexible curriculum or lack of administrative
support that can be common in this current era of accountability. Private and
charter schools, in contrast, may offer more autonomy and support to teachers
who wish to adopt educational practices such as HHBE.

The remaining 49% of teachers report teaching in the suburban and rural
areas surrounding the city. Beyond the geographic boundaries of Philadelphia,
teachers' responses indicate that workplaces are split almost evenly between public
and private schools. For suburban teachers, 41% report teaching at public schools
and 47% report teaching at private schools. The remaining respondents are affiliated with post-secondary institutions, community organizations, or other educa-
tion-related institutions. No suburban or rural teachers report teaching in public
charter schools.

A final indication of teacher characteristics, place of residence, reveals that
40% of participants reside in the city of Philadelphia. Sixty percent reside in the surrounding suburban or rural areas. A slight majority of participants teaches in schools
located within the geographic boundaries of Philadelphia, revealing that teachers
who are suburban residents commute to teach in schools located with the city limits.

Teacher Knowledge and Interest

Pre-survey responses were analyzed to understand workshop participants'
use of and knowledge of HHBE prior to the workshop. Post-survey responses
allow us to understand if Schooling Ourselves increased basic knowledge of
hip-hop and encouraged the likelihood that participants would attempt HHBE
in their classes. Table 5.2 summarizes findings from pre- and post-survey responses. Presented for each item is an abbreviated version of the survey question

Table 5.2. Pre- and Post-Survey Responses

Pre- (N = 29) & Post- (N = 45) Survey Questions and Responses	Number (n)	Percent (%)	Response Rate (n/N)	Source (Pre-survey or Post-survey)
Pre- Knowledge Level of Hip-hop's History and Development			.367	Pre-survey
A great deal	0	0		
Some	7	24		
Very little	15	52		
Nothing	7	24		
Pre- Knowledge Level of Today's Hip-hop Culture			.367	Pre-survey
A great deal	2	7		
Some	13	44		
Very little	7	24		
Nothing	7	24		
Workshop Improved Understanding(s) of Hip-hop			.570	Post-survey
A great deal	27	60		
Some	17	37		
Very little	1	2		
Have Used Hip-hop in Class			.367	Pre-survey
Often	0	0		
Occasionally	9	31		
Never	20	69		
Pre- Prepared to Use Hip-hop to Improve Literacy & Critical Thinking			.367	Pre-survey
Very prepared	0	0		
Somewhat prepared	8	27		
Not prepared	21	72		
Post- Prepared to Use Hip-hop to Improve Literacy & Critical Thinking			.570	Post-survey
Very prepared	14	31		
Somewhat prepared	30	67		
Not prepared	1	7		
Plan to Use Information Learned in Your Classroom			.570	Post-Survey
Often	14	31		
Occasionally	28	66		
Never	3	7		

to which participants responded, the total number of answers, percentages, response rates, and the data source.

Seventy-five percent of pre-survey respondents report knowing very little or nothing about the history and development of hip-hop culture. Roughly half reports knowing some or a great deal about hip-hop culture today. The findings are consistent with the percentage of teachers who indicate not using hip-hop in their classroom. No respondents answered "often" when asked "Have you ever used hip-hop in your classroom?" Thirty percent acknowledge that they have done so occasionally.

Many participants' understandings of the history of hip-hop's development and culture improved either a great deal (60%) or some (37%) after attending the Schooling Ourselves workshops. Although respondents feel their knowledge of the history and development of hip-hop improved, the surveys display less optimism concerning their preparedness to use hip-hop to improve literacy and critical thinking: Respondents report feeling very and somewhat prepared at rates of 31% and 66%, respectively.

Despite participants' lack of familiarity with hip-hop's historical and social roots, music and culture, the survey respondents report intentions of using the information presented in the Schooling Ourselves workshops at the rates of 30% ("often") and 63% ("occasionally"). Despite a relatively low understanding of hip-hop's history, development, or contemporary cultural relevance, the workshop's ability to improve the knowledge of the attendees corresponds with their intent of using the information in their classrooms. Pre-existing knowledge of hip-hop history is not an indicator of whether or not teachers plan to introduce HHBE into their teaching and learning repertoire. Instead, enhancing teachers' understandings of the historical and social significance of hip-hop and HHBE pedagogical practices, through workshops such as Schooling Ourselves, encourages teachers to attempt HHBE. Most Schooling Ourselves workshop participants indicated a willingness to implement what they learned in the workshops into their teaching practices. Given this finding, we thought it important to understand the characteristics of schools and educational institutions to which teachers would take these practices.

WHERE DO THE TEACHERS WORK?

School Characteristics

As many attendees work at the same schools and attended the workshops in groups, the 69 participants who reported working in K–12 settings represented a total of 31 different schools. Using school names and addresses to identify schools, we examine locale and basic demographic characteristics of the 31 schools by referencing NCES Common Core Data set for 2006–2007 school year. Based on the limited availability of income-level indicators (free/reduced lunch), we only report the racial composition of schools. An overview of school characteristics—school locale, grade level, school type, and racial makeup—are presented in Table 5.3. A breakdown of school characteristics by locale appear in subsequent figures.

The school grade levels reflect teacher workplaces reported in the previous section. The similarities underscore the likelihood that most workshop participants will take their newfound knowledge of HHBE to primary school settings. Additionally, most participants will return to private school settings, institutions that have not been explored within the literature. Of the 31 schools, data on the racial demographics are only available for a total of 24 schools; of these 24 schools, 55% contain majority White student populations. HHBE research has yet to consider this population and the implications of hip-hop based interventions and outcomes in majority White K–12 educational settings. Our analysis is limited to the school level. Therefore, classroom-level demographics are unknown. The fact that teachers from majority White schools show interest in HHBE, by virtue of their attendance at Schooling Ourselves, is an emergent finding that the current literature does not address.

Table 5.3. Summary of School Characteristics (All)

School Characteristics (All) (N=31)	Number (n)	Percent Within Category (%)	Percent of All Schools (n/N)	Source (Reg., NCES, PDE)
All Schools	31	100	.1	Reg.
Grade Level				
Primary	25	81		
Secondary	5	16		
Other	1	0		
School Type			.90	Reg.
Public (traditional)	9	32		
Public (charter)	2	1		
Private	16	57		
Other	1	0		
Racial Makeup			.77	Reg., NCES
Maj. Students of Color	11	45		
Maj. White Students	13	55		

Schools in the Urban Setting

Urban school characteristics (Table 5.4) complicate assumptions about what urban schooling contexts entail. Our population of schools reveals that a diversity of educational settings and student populations may be exposed to HHBE.

In the city of Philadelphia, traditional (noncharter or magnet) public schools are not well represented in our sample: Of 31 schools, only three are traditional urban public schools. One school is identified as a public charter school. Within the geographical boundaries of Philadelphia, 73% of the schools in which Schooling Ourselves participants work are private. Relying solely on geography as a measuring rod for "urban" implies that teachers work primarily in traditional urban public schools. If other factors, such as school type and racial composition, are used as proxies for "urban," a picture with different implications emerges. Students' and teachers' experiences in private and charter schools settings may be very different from those of their counterparts in traditional urban public schools. What it means

Table 5.4. Urban (Philadelphia) School Characteristics

Urban School Characteristics (N=17)	Total Number (n)	Percent Within Category (%)	Percent of All Schools (n/31)	Source (Reg., NCES)
Urban (Philadelphia) Schools	17	100	.55	Reg.
Grade Level				
Primary	15	88	.48	
Secondary	2	12	.06	
School Type				
Public (traditional)	3	20	.09	
Public (charter)	1	7	.03	
Private	11	73	.37	
Racial Makeup				Reg., NCES
Maj. Students of Color	10	67	.32	
Maj. White Students	5	33	.16	
School Type x Race				Reg., NCES
Public w/ Maj. Stud. of Color	0	0	.0	
Private w/ Maj. Stud. of Color	8	62	.25	
Public w/ Maj. White Stud.	2	15	.06	
Private w/ Maj. White Stud.	3	23	.09	

to attend an urban school and whether school location and school type shape the likelihood of HHBE curricula and pedagogy and what the curricula and pedagogy are able to accomplish is a line of inquiry that warrants further exploration. This is particularly salient if HHBE scholarship is to become more relevant to theory and practice for nonresearching teachers working in diverse school settings.

The racial compositions of Philadelphia city schools in our sample are indicative of shortcomings of current HHBE research. Of the three public schools with urban locale, racial composition data is available for two: Both have majority White student populations. Contrarily, eight of 11 private schools located in the urban district serve populations that are primarily students of color. Because the student of color category considers all non-White students, the fact that in eight of the 11 private schools, students of color comprise a pure majority masks the possibility that White students make up a proportional majority. This is important to note because the wide range of racial diversity in the urban school context may complicate how HHBE looks and what it accomplishes in comparison to urban educational settings that are more racially homogeneous.

Schools in Suburban Settings

A diverse set of teachers from a diverse set of school settings in both urban and suburban districts is interested in HHBE (a topic that will be explored with more depth in the following section). The suburban districts surrounding the city of Philadelphia reveal a different set of patterns from the analysis of urban schools, as presented in Table 5.5—Suburban School Characteristics. Within the surrounding suburban areas, 100% of schools reported are majority White. Traditional suburban public schools account for 50% of the school settings.

Diversity of School Settings

In summary, our data suggest that HHBE may be occurring in a variety of K–12 educational settings, including majority White urban public schools, majority students of color private schools located in urban school districts, and majority White suburban district schools. If private schooling, suburban, and majority White are used as proxies for privilege, our findings suggest that HHBE may find its way into "privileged" rather than marginal K–12 settings. These findings run counter to the descriptions of urban educational settings that are reflected in the HHBE literature.

SUMMARY OF RESULTS

The findings presented underscore the fact that Schooling Ourselves participants differ greatly from the teacher-researchers who produce HHBE scholarship.

Table 5.5. Suburban School Characteristics

Suburban School Characteristics (N = 14)	Total Number (n)	Percent Within Category (%)	Percent of All Schools (n/31)	Source (Reg., NCES)
Suburban Schools	**14**	**100**	**.45**	Reg.
Grade Level				
Primary	10	77	.32	
Secondary	3	23	.10	
School Type				
Public (traditional)	6	50	.19	
Public (charter)	1	8	.03	
Private	4	33	.13	
Other	1	8	.03	
Racial Makeup				Reg., NCES
Maj. Students of Color		0	.0	
Maj. White Students	8	100	.26	
School Type x Race				Reg., NCES
Public w/ Maj. Stud. of Color	0	0	.0	
Private w/ Maj. Stud. of Color	0	0	.0	
Public w/ Maj. White Stud.	6*	86	.19	
Private w/ Maj. White Stud.	1	14	.03	

*This figure collapses the one public charter school with the five traditional public schools.

Participants in the sample teach at similar rates in urban and suburban school settings, albeit at different rates within each locale. Most teachers work in primary schools, are certified in their respective subject areas, and reside in suburban residential areas. The general profile of participants that emerges is a new face for HHBE: suburban certified primary school teachers with more than 10 years of teaching experience who are likely to work in either a suburban school with a majority White student population or in a nontraditional urban school (private or charter) that serves a majority of students of color.

DISCUSSION: FRESH FACES, NEW PLACES

Nonresearching teachers who use HHBE remain a subaltern population; however, this research confirms that teacher populations who are not represented within the current HHBE literature are indeed interested in learning about using hip-hop to engage students in learning. Additionally, teachers indicate a willingness to incorporate HHBE into their teaching and learning repertoire, given the right guidance through teacher education and professional development. It remains uncertain if and how Schooling Ourselves participants actually use what they learn from the workshops in their classrooms. Despite this uncertainty, our findings, along with the absence of accounts of how HHBE might be taken up by non-researching teachers, point to the need for new approaches to HHBE research, practice, and theory.

Three central concerns about HHBE that relate to our findings illuminate critical issues relevant to nonresearching teachers: teacher diversity and identity, the motivations behind the increased interest in HHBE, and the constraints and affordances of places of practice. First, we revisit the narrowness of teacher-researcher perspectives in HHBE scholarship and contextualize our critique by considering the demographic imperative (Banks, 1995; Dilworth, 1992; Gay & Howard, 2000) and the ongoing discussion of multicultural teacher preparation (Lowenstein, 2009). We address the selection bias of the workshop population and wrestle with why this particular group of teachers attended the workshops and what their attendance might signal for the field of HHBE. Next, we make problematic the ambiguity of place through discussing the constraints that nonresearching teachers might face in their attempt to implement a program of HHBE.

Fresh Faces: Exploring the Diversity of Teachers Interested in HHBE

HHBE literature, produced largely by teacher-researchers, many of whom hold the status of hip-hop cultural insiders, fails to consider the diversity of teachers interested in the practices espoused within the literature. Nonresearching teachers who lack foundational knowledge of hip-hop are interested in incorporating hip-hop culture into their teaching and learning practices. The workshop participants' lack of foundational hip-hop knowledge underscores their status as hip-hop cultural outsiders. In the same way multicultural educators identify a "demographic imperative" among an increasingly White and middle-class teaching force and increasingly diverse student population (Banks, 1995; Dilworth, 1992; Gay & Howard, 2000), our findings suggest the existence of an analogous demographic imperative between teacher-researchers who use HHBE for critical and culturally relevant pedagogical aims and nonresearching teachers (i.e., cultural outsiders) who may hold different motivations for using HHBE (as will be discussed shortly in this section).

Schooling Ourselves participants more accurately reflect the actual teaching population than do teacher-researchers who produce HHBE literature. Thus, it is critical that HHBE researchers consider what contributions can be made to the broader discussion of how to prepare a largely White middle-class teaching force to become multicultural learners capable of understanding and appreciating diversity (Lowenstein, 2009) across multiple educational contexts. If offered the opportunity, teachers such as those at Schooling Ourselves will likely continue to self-select to learn and subsequently employ HHBE, ultimately becoming the new faces of these teaching practices.

As the field shifts inquiry from teacher-researchers like Hill (2009), Emdin (2008), Stovall (2006), and Morrell and Duncan-Andrade (2002) toward subaltern nonresearching teacher populations, critical questions surrounding issues of teacher identity, practice, and student outcomes beg for further exploration. More expansive, penetrative, methodologically diverse studies are required that: (1) capture how personal (e.g., race/ethnicity, class, gender, sexuality, cultural disposition) and professional (teaching experience, educational background, grade level, subject area, and so on) identities shape the ways hip-hop pedagogies are implemented and to what ends, and (2) better understand the relations between teachers' respective identities, pedagogies, and student outcomes. An example of such a study might use interviews and observations to compare and contrast the identities, pedagogies, and outcomes evidenced across a cohort of nonresearching hip-hop based educators. Additionally, survey research could be conducted to explore teachers' perceptions about, content knowledge of, and willingness to learn and use various aspects of HHBE.

Schooling Ourselves participants self-selected to attend the workshops. The process of self-selection leads us to ponder why the teachers who attended the workshops did so. Discovering who might be interested and why certain teachers are interested are two central questions that the HHBE literature does not address. Our findings illustrate that teachers who are less informed of the history, content, and aesthetics of hip-hop are interested in learning about HHBE; as a consequence, the motivating factors of teachers may not be situated in the theoretical and practical objectives of critical and culturally relevant pedagogies. There is a strong likelihood that what nonresearching teachers want and need from HHBE—history, aesthetics, and content—is different from what teacher-researchers cite as their wants and needs regarding HHBE.

A range of intrinsic and extrinsic factors may compel teachers to consult HHBE resources. Among these unexplored factors are professional development credits and other incentives, a genuine curiosity about the history and development of hip-hop culture, and the opportunity to explore the pedagogical possibilities of HHBE. Many educators in our study may have been interested in learning more about hip-hop content as a means of increasing their own cultural competence and/or understanding students' cultural frames of reference. Contrarily, some teachers may have attended Schooling Ourselves as a matter of spectacle of the "other" absent of the intent of using the content and practices covered in the workshop.

Our findings highlight the need to understand why teachers are interested in learning about HHBE and what motivates them to seek opportunities to develop the competencies required to effectively implement the practices. Enhancing our understanding of motivations by investigating self-selection processes would address one shortcoming of teacher-researcher perspectives. Current teacher-researcher perspectives mistakenly presume that nonresearching educators interested in HHBE possess funds of hip-hop knowledge that are essential prerequisites to engaging in hip-hop pedagogies. This implicit assumption has resulted in a body of work that is not well suited for the diverse pool of educators who do not possess similar cultural competencies (i.e., hip-hop) as HHBE teacher-researchers.

Scholarship produced by teacher-researchers succeeds in substantiating HHBE as relevant, effective, and acceptable in the minds of many teachers. The fact that nonresearcher teachers who are hip-hop outsiders (as reflected by teacher knowledge) rather than cultural insiders comprise a majority of workshop participants highlights the need to educate teachers about the history, content, and aesthetics of hip-hop culture. The findings also signal the need to move beyond concerns about legitimating HHBE. As teachers become more interested and committed to using hip-hop as a means of educating students in formal learning contexts, then the work of legitimating HHBE in and of itself as a useful pedagogical aim should become less tantamount within the field.

New Places: The Importance of Place as a Site of Inquiry

Teacher educators and researchers engaging in HHBE must be mindful of the constraints teachers may face as they attempt to take the practices back to their home institutions. Place-based variables such as school location, school type, institutional characteristics, and grade level require additional attention. Depending on these variables, professional, cultural, administrative, and personally held convictions may run counter to HHBE. The variable of place should consider whether the imperatives and interventions of HHBE collide and conflate with the varying definitions of teacher effectiveness and student achievement operating within urban and suburban, public and private, and secondary and elementary schools. Additionally, a focus on place and how urban is obfuscated with student demographics would unpack the loaded and often ambiguous use of the term *urban* within this body of work.

The literature depicts practices primarily in marginalized educational settings that serve urban youth (i.e. poor, racial and ethnic minorities) and higher education settings. Ironically, many of the marginalized settings benefit from having talented academic-oriented teacher researchers leading the HHBE curricula and programs. But HHBE may also be occurring in majority White schools in urban and suburban districts, as well as in public and private K–12 educational spaces. If private schooling and/or majority White are used as proxies for privilege, many of the schools identified in our study may be considered "privileged" K–12 spaces, even within locales that are defined as urban. Consequently, understanding where

HHBE practices might be attempted and the possibilities and limitations inherent to particular places and populations is warranted.

Places beyond the locations where teacher-researchers' studies occur have been theorized but not empirically examined. For example, Pardue's (2004) argument that hip-hop "is about restructuring institutional spaces, especially those places of discipline and surveillance (e.g., prisons, schools) that have historically and systematically been indifferent if not hostile to popular culture in any organized fashion" (p. 423) fails to take into account the real institutional constraints on curricula and pedagogy, together with daunting pressures to improve students' performance on high-stakes tests. Both of these factors are critical areas of concern that have contributed to the frustrations of teachers, especially in urban districts where the curriculum has become increasingly narrowed (Crocco & Costican, 2007). The expectation that HHBE transforms institutional spaces presumes that teachers intend to use HHBE for such ends. It may be the case that teachers wish to use HHBE, not for transformative purposes, but to improve reading or make annual state testing goals. The literature would benefit from additional portraits of hip-hop based educators employing HHBE in response (or resistance) to the politics of accountability in public schools and in various contexts that account for the diversity of urban school (and suburban) settings.

Whereas the practices and outcomes of HHBE may be compatible with the cultures of institutions chosen or established by teacher-researchers, non-researching teachers will likely face unique challenges in workplaces (public or parochial, urban or secondary, secondary or elementary) where critical interrogation of Eurocentric epistemologies and culture are discouraged, if not disallowed altogether. What might HHBE look like in urban Catholic schools with predominantly students of color and working-class students? What about in suburban public or elite private schools with predominantly White and upper-class student populations—does HHBE have a future in these places? If the answer is yes, how, then, might HHBE be modified given new sets of place-based and population-related constraints?

Elementary schools may pose another set of challenges to HHBE. The majority of Schooling Ourselves respondents teach in K–8 schools; however, the teacher-researchers who depict hip-hop based interventions and outcomes function almost exclusively in high schools and post-secondary learning environments. Such glaring incongruence within the literature raises concerns pertaining to the prevalence, effectiveness, and appropriateness of HHBE theory and practice in primary grades. Until the canon considers the primary school context and pursues questions such as "Is it ever too early for teachers to draw on students' hip-hop literacies to begin cultivating in-school literacies?" the field will remain unaware of the possibilities and pitfalls of HHBE in these settings. HHBE scholars should take issue with whether the sociocultural objectives presented in the literature are achievable for students and teachers of various age groups. If the field wishes to move beyond romanticized portraits of how effective HHBE is for at-risk urban youth, researchers must explore the nuances of various institutions where HHBE is attempted.

CONCLUSION

The data presented in this chapter illustrate that nonresearching teachers who work in a variety of educational settings are interested in learning about hip-hop based education. These findings underscore shortcomings of teacher-researcher perspectives that dominate the field of HHBE. Taking into account the new faces and places of HHBE, it is imperative that the investigative lens of academic research move in new directions. As a matter of teacher education, research, and professional development, we recommend that the field consider the differences between teacher-researchers and nonresearching teachers, explore teachers' motivation to learn about and use HHBE, and take seriously the place-based constraints that nonresearching teachers face. Inherent in such discussions are issues of place, diversity, identity, and the ability of teachers to effectively implement a program of HHBE, given the wants and needs of their teaching and learning contexts.

REFERENCES

Abowitz, K. (1997). Horatio Alger and hip-hop. *The Review of Education/ Pedagogy/Cultural Studies, 19*(4), 409–425.

Alexander-Smith, A. C. (2004). Feeling the rhythm of the critically conscious mind. *English Journal, 93*(3), 58–63.

Anderson, E. (1993). Positive use of rap music in the classroom. *Teaching English in the Two-Year College, 20*(3), 214–221.

Baker, H. (1991). Hybridity, the rap race, and pedagogy for the 1990s. *Black Music Research Journal, 11*(2), 217–228.

Banks, J. A. (1995). Multicultural education: Historical development, dimensions, and practice. In J. A. Banks & C. A. McGee Banks (Eds.), *Handbook of research on multicultural education* (pp. 1–24). New York: MacMillan.

Baumann, J., & Duffy, A. (2001). Teacher-researcher methodology: Themes, variations, and possibilities. *The Reading Teacher, 54*(6), 608–615.

Bracey, G. (1991). Teachers as researchers. *The Phi Delta Kappan, 72*(5), 404–405.

Bitz, M. (1998). Rap music and choral education. *Teaching Music, 5*(5), 36–37.

Cochran-Smith, M., & Lytle, S.L. (Eds.) (1993). *Inside/outside: Teacher research and knowledge.* New York: Teachers College Press.

Cochran-Smith, M., & Lytle, L. (1998). Teacher research: The question that persists. *International Journal of Leadership in Education, 1*(1), 19–36.

Cooks, J. (2004). Writing for something: Essay, raps, and writing preferences. *English Journal, 94*(1), 72–76.

Crocco, M., & Costigan, A. (2007). The narrowing of curriculum and pedagogy in the age of accountability: Urban educators speak out. *Urban Education, 42*, 512.

Dilworth, M. E. (Ed.) (1992). *Diversity in teacher education.* San Francisco: Jossey-Bass.

Dimitriadis, G. (2001). *Performing identity/performing culture: Hip-hop as text, pedagogy, and lived practice.* New York: Peter Lang.

Duncan-Andrade, J. M. R., & Morrell, E. (2005). Turn up that radio, teacher: Popular cultural pedagogy in new century. *Journal of School Leadership, 15,* 284–302.

Emdin, C. (2008). The three C's for urban science education, *Phi Delta Kappan, 89*(10), 772–775.

Emdin, C. (2009). Urban science classrooms and new possibilities: Intersubjectivity and grammar in the third space. *Cultural Studies of Science Education, 4,* 239–254.

Gay, G., & Howard, T. (2000). Multicultural teacher education in the 21st century. *The Teacher Educator, 36*(1), 1–16.

Hill, M. L. (2009). *Beats, rhymes, and classroom life: Hip-hop pedagogy and the politics of identity.* New York: Teachers College Press.

Hill, M. L., Perez, B., & Irby, D. (2008). Street fiction: What is it and what does it mean for English teachers? *English Journal, 97*(3), 76–81.

Irby, D. J. (2006). *Do the knowledge: A standards-based hip hop learning guide.* Philadelphia: Art Sanctuary. Retrieved from http://artsanctuary.org/wp-content/uploads/2011/12/Do-The-Knowledge-A-Standards-Based-Hip-Hop-Learning-Guide-Updated-11-06.pdf

Jeremiah, M. (1992). Rap lyrics: Instruments for language arts instruction. *Western Journal of Black Studies, 16*(2), 98–102.

Ladson-Billings, G. (1994). *The dreamkeepers: Successful teaching for African American students.* San Francisco: Jossey-Bass.

Ladson-Billings, G. (1995). Toward a theory of culturally relevant pedagogy. *American Educational Research Journal, 32*(3), 465–491.

Lowenstein, K. (2009). The work of multicultural teacher education: Reconceptualizing white teacher candidates as learners. *Review of Educational Research, 79*(1), 163–196.

Macklis, K. (1989). Fifth graders "rap" English elements. *Reading Teacher, 42*(4), 340.

McLaren, P. (2007). *Life in schools: An introduction to critical pedagogy in the foundations of education* (5th ed.). Boston: Pearson Allyn & Bacon.

Morrell, E., & Duncan-Andrade, J. M. R. (2002). Promoting academic literacy with urban youth through engaging hip-hop culture. *English Journal, 91*(6), 88–92.

Pardue, D. (2004). "Writing in the margins": Brazilian hip-hop as an educational project. *Anthropology and Education Quarterly, 35*(4), 411–432.

Petchauer, E. (2009). Framing and reviewing hip-hop educational research. *Review of Educational Research, 79,* 946.

Petchauer, E. (2012). *Hip-hop culture in college students' lives: Elements, embodiment, and higher edutainment.* New York: Routledge.

Pike, S. (2000, September). Hip-hop sport education. *Teaching Elementary Physical Education,* 19–21.

Powell, C. (1991). Rap music: An education with a beat from the street. *Journal of Negro Education, 60*(3), 245–259.

Rice, J. (2003). The 1963 hip-hop machine: Hip-hop pedagogy as composition. *College Composition and Communication, 54*(3), 453–471.

Rose, T. (1994). *Black noise: Rap music and Black culture in contemporary America.* Hanover, CT: Wesleyan University Press.

Saunders, R. (1999). Teaching rap: The politics of race in the classroom. *Journal of Geography, 98*(4), 185–188.

Stephens, T., Braithwaite, R., & Taylor, S. (1998). Model for using hip-hop music for small group HIV/AIDS prevention counseling with African American adolescents and young adults. *Patient Education and Counseling, 35*(2), 127–137.

Stino, Z. (1995). Writing as therapy in a county jail. *Journal of Poetry Therapy, 9*(1), 13–23.

Stovall, D. (2006). We can relate: Hip-hop culture, critical pedagogy, and the secondary classroom. *Urban Education, 41*(6), 585–602.

Sullivan, R. (2003). Rap and race: It's got a nice beat, but what about the message? *Journal of Black Studies, 33*(5), 605–622.

Sundeen, J. (2003). Teaching literacy as rap at southeast community college. *Teaching English in the Two-Year College, 31*(1), 8–15.

CHAPTER 6

The Limits of "Keepin' It Real"

The Challenges for Critical Hip-Hop Pedagogies of Discourses of Authenticity

Bronwen Low, Eloise Tan,
and Jacqueline Celemencki

I'm not gonna say I'm from anywhere else. I don't expect you to say you're from anywhere else except where you come from. I don't expect to hear from your rap that you did this, or you're doing that, and you know, if shit comes down to defend, don't say you're drivin' hard when you ain't got no car!

—Alex, 15 years old

ip-hop journalist "Angela N." complained in a newsgroup posting that "You haven't lived until you've edited a 2-hour interview and heard 'keepin it real' after every other sentence, tried to cut most of them out of the finished product, then have your boss ask could you do 'something' about all of these 'keeping it real's?'"(McLeod, 1999, p. 139). This suggests that the phrase is so ubiquitous that it is now a speech mannerism or habit, in the mode of "you know what I'm sayin." But as we will see below, the charge to "keep it real" has so many different, sometimes conflicting, meanings that one might wonder if it continues to mean anything it all. We want to argue instead that this polysemy and malleability is at the heart of its power and usefulness. The concept contains an entire hip-hop belief system, even an ideology, which gets used in ways that are both generative and restricting, creative and policing. Speakers use the concept to do different kinds of identity, aesthetic, cultural, and political work, drawing upon their context of utterance and audience expectations and knowledge in order to make "realness" signify. This does not, however, mean that the signification is always clear.

This chapter works to better understand authenticity and realness in hip-hop as well as their implications for critical hip-hop pedagogies, for in our educational work with hip-hop identified youth we have found that "keepin' it real" can create a very rigid template for what it might mean to be a young, urban, person of color.

Hip-hop culture is a framework that informs how youth interpret, represent, and negotiate aspects of their sociocultural identities, including race, ethnicity, class, sexuality, and gender. Given that hip-hop is a means by which "youth and young adults conceive of themselves, others, and the world around them" (Petchauer, 2009, p. 947), youth such as the participants in our research perform a variety of hip-hop narratives in their everyday lives. This happens even in activities that are not directly related to their consumption or production of hip-hop culture, making intelligible, for instance, one project participant's claim that "I brush my teeth hip-hop." The importance of those narratives to identity and thus to education, given that who one thinks one is will shape how and what and why one learns, makes them worth analyzing, critiquing, and sometimes reworking.

Close attention to the stories that young people tell about their identities in relation to hip-hop is also valuable for educators working with youth affiliated with other popular scenes such as "emo" or "rave" because a popular culture lens offers an additional heuristic that can complicate, complement, and intersect with traditional sociocultural frameworks such as race, gender, and class. While we here advocate the importance of popular culture to identity, we are also wary of reifying notions of "hip-hop identities"; identity is not something one can possess or lose (Côté, 2006), nor should it be "fetishized" as static and essential (Sfard & Prusak, 2005). Although in this chapter we focus specifically on how the youth participants in our projects and studies are constructing their identities in relation to hip-hop culture, we remain aware that these identities are built, and rebuilt, in relation to other cultures, communities, and affiliations.

In this chapter, we explore the workings of authenticity in identity in relation to two community-based educational projects. In 2007, Jacqueline created an afterschool writing group called Writing Our Minds Through Rap with six young men from ages 15 to 18, each a member of a racialized minority, each a writer of rap lyrics. Their monthly meetings provided the young men with opportunities to share their experiences of racial profiling, poverty, and neighborhood violence in their original rap lyrics. In 2008, Eloise collaborated with a community media production company called Chronicle Creations (a pseudonym) to create a participatory documentary with a team of hip-hop youth artists in four elements— b-boying, graffiti, emceeing, and DJing (see Tan, 2009). The documentary was designed to explore the role of hip-hop culture in the lives of 13 youth and in the lives of Montreal youth more broadly. Eloise worked with the two producers, two youth coordinators, and 13 youth as a participant-observer over 4 months in their preproduction working sessions.

Given the centrality of discourses of authenticity to hip-hop culture writ large, it is not surprising that the concept of "the real" played an important part in the two pedagogic projects we describe in this paper. We present a typology of hip-hop realness that works to make sense of the many things being referenced, sometimes simultaneously, when members of hip-hop culture invoke authenticity. Its elements are the following:

1. The "streets"
2. "Hard" heterosexual masculinity
3. "Blackness"
4. The importance of representing the place and culture you are from
5. The importance of being true to yourself
6. Politically conscious, "underground" hip-hop[1]

Our data analyses will concentrate on the workings of discourses of "the streets" and "hardness."

CRITICAL HIP-HOP PEDAGOGIES

As this edited collection makes clear, there has been an explosion of academic interest in existing and potential relationships between education and hip-hop (Petchauer, 2009). Much of the literature documents current curricula and programs, many in the "informal" educational sector, including community centers and afterschool programs, given the relative curricular freedom these spaces often have in relation to schools as well as the frequent presence of hip-hop generation youth as facilitators and organizers in community programs in urban centers. (See the appendix in Rose, 2008, for a listing of some of the hip-hop programs found across the United States, as well as Hall, 2009.) Our experiences as and with hip-hop educators outside of schools have made clear how powerful this work can be, with youth and facilitators often building important relationships and developing innovative pedagogies. However, these are not utopian spaces, for difficulties of inclusion and exclusion can shape the dynamics of teaching and learning in informal educational settings as well as in schools (Kim, 2007). This chapter takes up some of these difficulties.

While much of the work on hip-hop pedagogies disrupts the business as usual of mainstream schooling by bringing urban popular culture into curriculum, some educators have worked to do more explicitly political work by using hip-hop as a lens for sociopolitical critique (e.g., Alim, 2001, 2004; Baszile, 2009; Rodriguez, 2009; Stovall, 2006). Williams (2009) provides a helpful definition of critical hip-hop consciousness that works to create counternarratives and develop a language of critique and transcendence in relation to hip-hop culture.

However, very few educators detailing their critical rap pedagogies grapple with the tensions that hip-hop culture's contradictory politics of representation around issues such as violence, gender, race, and materialism pose to education; this is in large part because scholars and educators are working in an advocacy mode to legitimize knowledge and literacy practices that are either ignored or disparaged by mainstream schooling. In advocating for this work, scholars often gloss over the tensions between hip-hop and school. An important exception to this is Hill's (2009) recent study of a language arts course that taught students the elements of literary analysis through close examinations of rap lyrics. Despite the powerful exchanges made possible by Hill's culturally responsive teaching and curriculum, including the sharing of stories by students and teacher in a process of "wounded healing," Hill (2009) also described how this curriculum based in hip-hop "inevitably creates spaces of both voice and silence, centering and marginalization, empowerment and domination" (p. 10). Resonating with this chapter's analysis, Hill found that a politics of hip-hop authenticity was complicit in the silencing and that some hurtful comments "were in direct conversation with, and sometimes buttressed, prominent themes within mainstream hip-hop culture" (p. 10). We argue that *critical* rap pedagogies not only need to use rap texts to do critical thinking about the world, but they also need to be aware that the students themselves might be invested in some of the more oppressive representations provided by hip-hop, and that these investments can prove powerfully resistant to the pedagogic impulses of progressive teachers. According to Tan (2009), this means that critical hip-hop pedagogies need to be:

1. Rooted in hip-hop culture while recognizing that its histories and ideologies are socially produced and at times must be challenged and reworked.
2. Socially conscious of how hegemony operates within society, while paying particular attention to how hegemony and power operate within hip-hop culture to marginalize populations it seeks to liberate.
3. Responsive to marginalization whether it be through structures of gender, class, race, religion, sexuality, or ability.
4. Culturally productive by encouraging learners to be producers of their own hip-hop culture.
5. Inclusive of multiliteracies across forms of media, technology, and culture. (p. 59)

Tan (2009) includes a sixth element for researchers of critical hip-hop pedagogies, indicating that they need be "cognizant of the complex ways that positioning (including hip-hop insider or outsider) affects research within the [critical hip-hop pedagogy] community" (p. 59). This framework informs our analysis of both projects.

"KEEPIN' IT REAL" IN HIP-HOP CULTURE

A preoccupation with authenticity shapes many other music subcultures, including rave, country, and rock (McLeod, 1999), but the emphasis on authenticity in hip-hop culture verges on obsession and conveys so many values and commitments (some of which are contradictory) that it deserves its own examination. Although we concentrate mostly on the "streets" and "hardness" elements of the typology of hip-hop authenticity in our analysis, we first offer a brief overview of all of them in order to map out the complexity and contradictions of "keepin' it real."

The Streets

With its geographic and symbolic origins in the streets of the South Bronx (Toop, 1991), hip-hop has from its inception been envisioned as a conduit for the voices of the dispossessed. Implied in popular phrases like "keepin' it real" and "representin'" is that the space of the real, of the represented and in need of representing, is the "street" (Keyes, 2002; Spady, Lee, & Alim, 1999). As part of hip-hop's "ghetto-centricity" (Kelley, 1994), this stands as a metaphor for the Black underclass. The romance of the streets also takes part in the "rags to riches" narratives so central to the American dream, particularly when voiced by rappers who have "made it." Perry (2004) posits that hip-hop is the first popular cultural space in which one's origins in the "projects" get celebrated rather than rejected "as an embarrassment," a move that signals street-smart toughness and resilience as well as a class-based identification with poor Black people (p. 89). Busta Rhymes's 1998 track "In the Ghetto," which samples Rick James's "Ghetto Life," paints a portrait of this space, both real and symbolic, in which one needs to become a hustler in order to survive and support a family. While the rapper points to the irony of the fact that "we romance the street," given the dangers there of attacks by police and other gangs and the limited opportunities it offers, the ghetto is intrinsic to the narrator's identity as he explains that you can take a person out of the ghetto, but you can't take the ghetto out of the person.

"Hard" Heterosexual Masculinity

This dimension of hip-hop authenticity is closely linked to the "streets," and its investigation requires an understanding of how the gangster rap genre reworked the idea of rap as street social realism. Gangsta rap describes "gang life, or more generally, life in the ghetto from the perspective of a criminal (or liminal, transgressive) figure" (Krims, 2000, p. 70). It became popular in the late 1980s and early 1990s particularly on the West coast of the United States, first in South Central, Los Angeles, with artists such as N.W.A, whose explicit stories of gang life and warfare burned a virtual template of what realness should look like into hip-hop consciousness. This template included an elaborated set of criteria for "hardness" by which an MC's credibility continues to be measured by many.[2] Hip-hop hardness is also steeped in particularly narrow narratives of heterosexual masculinity that make heterosexuality compulsory, exclude and silence the voices of queer men and women in hip-hop who contribute and participate in the culture (Hill, 2009), and equate masculinity with dominating women (Hurt, 2006). This has posed particular difficulties for women rappers (see Pough, Richardson, Durham, & Raimist, 2007; Rose 1994) and hip-hop identified women more generally, who must reconcile feelings of love and hate for a culture in which they are frequently debased (Morgan, 1999).

Hard hip-hop heterosexual masculinity defines a woman's value in whether she can support, pleasure, and serve men, making available only two identity options: either the low-status bitch/slut/ho who sexually satisfies her man or the higher-status sister who supports her man in a multitude of ways (Rose, 2008). This dichotomy between bad ho and good sister is "a key to belonging" (Rose, 2008, p. 173) to hip-hop culture. This can obviously have a harmful impact on the identity formation of young Black women; for instance, the teenage girls in Richardson's (2006) work were keen to question hegemonic structures of race and class but did not extend this to issues of gender, which meant, ironically, that "in their quest to keep it real, they also display instances of succumbing to racist stereotypes and controlling myths of Black womanhood" (p. 49).

Blackness

Blackness comes together with the streets and hard heterosexual masculinity to form the image of the MC that dominates popular representations in outlets like BET (Black Entertainment Television) and perceptions of hip-hop both within and outside the community, while eliding the participation in hip-hop of groups other than African Americans (see, for instance, Rivera 2003; Wang 2004), as well as hip-hop's global reach and its evolving forms (Chang, 2006).

Representing Place, Culture, and Where You Are From

An extension of the emphasis on representing the street is that hip-hop identities are firmly grounded in the particulars of place. Soon after hip-hop's birth in the Bronx, it spread to the West coast and across the country, and every major (and arguably minor) urban center in the United States now has some kind of hip-hop scene. Regions have distinct styles, and rappers regularly make claims to authenticity by calling out their area codes or the names of their neighborhoods.

Being True to Yourself

The equation of authenticity in hip-hop with being "true to oneself" bears most kinship to a wider North American preoccupation with authenticity. This element is heavily promoted by central figures in what gets considered "old school" as well as "conscious" hip-hop, for instance by "Teacha" KRS-One who explained that "Hip-Hop begins with the courage to be yourself. Being you has consequences" (quoted in Zafar, 2007).

Politically Conscious and Underground

This final dimension of keepin' it real reacts against and critiques mainstream hip-hop, and in particular excessive bling-bling materialism, violence, formulaic and uncreative lyrics, and videos with their emphasis on expensive cars, big "cribs," and "video hos." These critiques work in the tradition of conscious hip-hop, which includes all those rappers who use their music as a platform for education, often striving to return the culture to its more community-based "old school" grassroots and realizing its political potential.

THE LIMITS OF AUTHENTICITY

Our work with youth in these and other educational projects has made clear that the elements of the typology regularly play themselves out in students' hip-hop identities, coming together, clashing, and producing sometimes disabling contradictions, as social criticism collides with sensationalism, documentary realism with fantasy, and masculine strength with sexism. Although hip-hop authenticity was important to the students' ability to connect with curricula in which they felt their lives and experiences were prominently featured, the rap "real" also worked to set up some fairly strict dictates about what it could mean to be young, Black, immigrant, male, female, or poor in urban Montreal.

Jacqueline created and led the Writing Our Minds Through Rap project in 2007 as a series of writing workshops in a high school designed for youth at risk of dropping out. In Jacqueline's project, we see how participants' lyrics continually perform authenticity by invoking "the streets," with their implications of violence, urban neighborhoods and poverty, and "hard" heterosexual masculinity, which intersect to reproduce the familiar tropes of gangster rap.

Eloise worked in 2008 as a participant observer over 4 months in the weekly preproduction sessions of a documentary project that explored the role of the elements of hip-hop in the lives of youth hip-hop artists in Montreal. Through Eloise's work with Chronicle Creations, we focus on how hip-hop discourses of "hard" heterosexual masculinity and their attendant economy of stereotypes of women, organized around a dichotomy between female/ho or bitches/sisters, limit how both male and female participants categorize women. We then map out some of the possibilities for critical engagement with the stranglehold of authenticity in hip-hop.

WRITING THEIR MINDS THROUGH RAP

In Jacqueline's project, Writing Our Minds Through Rap, she met with a group of six young male rap lyricists once a month for a period of 5 months. These 90-minute meetings were hosted at a local community center located near the young men's high school, a public alternative school for students who have dropped out of the mainstream system. During each of the meetings, Jacqueline used a set of discussion questions that prompted the young men to discuss the challenges they faced in their daily lives, such as poverty and violence in their neighborhoods, as well as academic challenges. These discussions provided a context for the young men to articulate their frustrations and thoughts through writing rap lyrics. The young men talked about how rap music provides a space for them to discuss things that are not mentioned in their classroom, such as being visible minorities and the realities of their violent neighborhoods. They also described how their teachers discredit rap music's potential as a pedagogical tool in the classroom, mostly because of the discourses of moral panic circulating about hip-hop culture (Koza, 1999) and the overrepresentation of commercial gangster rap music in the media and on the airwaves. Each of the young men in Jacqueline's study faced socioeconomic challenges and came from some of the lower-income neighborhoods in the city of Montreal, such as western Notre Dame de Grace, St. Michel, and the Barclay area of Cote des Neiges. They were all second-generation Canadians, with parents from Jamaica, Trinidad, Sri Lanka, and El Salvador.

For all of these young men, the usual tropes for claiming an authentic hip-hop identity resonated powerfully, and they drew upon many elements of our typology in conversation and through their lyrics in order to make a case for their value and legitimacy as hip-hop insiders. Particularly powerful were the discourses of "the streets" and "hardness," both of which got mobilized in terms of respect and street credibility. For instance, Alex described how among his circle of friends it is believed that the more dangerous your neighborhood, the more respect you deserve for having survived it. He spoke about his childhood experiences of growing up in a southeastern United States urban tenement housing project—where drive-by shootings were a regular occurrence—to explain why he uses violent iconography in his rap lyrics: "The place where I was living in Florida, like 2–3 years back, I mean, I used to hear a lot of murders." Given that U.S. cities are plagued by higher rates of crime than their Canadian counterparts,[3] it makes sense that this aspect of Alex's family history was invoked in defense of his lyrics.

Another youth, Michael, advocated strongly for the importance of rap lyrics as a street social realism, or what Chuck D (1997) described as the "Black CNN" (p. 256). He claimed:

Right now around you someone's getting shot or raped or what not, you wanna portray that, you wanna tell people about it and make people open their eyes, 'cause a lot of people are ignorant about it, and they don't want to hear about it. I personally want to open up my eyes to all of these things.

Michael is driven to witness the crimes he sees around him, casting rap lyrics as the vehicle for educating himself and others. He later links the importance of witnessing to "keepin' it real," in contrast with being "fake":

I see a lot of shit. I see people getting robbed with guns to their faces, I see a lot of things. The reason why I'm all, like don't be fake, cuz if people go around saying like yo . . . I see what I see, I don't see everything. On my block alone, there was like four shootings.

Here, authenticity is linked to actively experiencing, through seeing, violent crime. When asked why some adults, including teachers, criticized rap music, Alex responded: "People don't want to hear the truth. They live in this society, but they're boxed in. They're like, okay, this doesn't happen in my neighborhood."

This social witness as critic theory is challenged, however, by lyrics in which the youth seem to fantasize themselves as more active participants in a violent culture, intertwining "the streets" with images of their own hard masculinity as they adopt gangster personae in which they become perpetuators of violent crime. For instance, Michael raps:

You see me pressin' these bitches, don't think you're not included
This is for the motherfuckers these bitches and greedy suckers
Money, money's on my mind,
Gotta grip my balls and I grind
Any niggas try to interfere me, your bodies will be goin' flyin'.

In analysis of such lyrics, it is important to keep in mind that these images of violence in hip-hop are often metaphoric (Hill, 2009), used to describe a rapper's ability to "kill" or "wreck" any contenders in the long tradition of rap and break-dance battles. An instance of this is found in some of Stuart's lyrics, in which he raps: "Your rhymes are repetitious, I'm kickin' it fresh/Spit the wrong words and I'm rippin' your flesh."

Although the notion of street realism persistently shaped participants' discussions of their art, the young men's rap lyrics offered no specifics or nuances that would make more precise and unique the experience of their lives in Montreal. Instead, they invoke the general tropes of "ghetto life" so central to hip-hop authenticity and forged in U.S. contexts. And these tropes are consistent across the boys' lyrics despite their different relationships to "the streets." One of the first sets of lyrics shared with the group came from Mark, who repeatedly discussed the violence in his neighborhood:

> This is DG, these ain't no regular streets, brothers leave you dead for the way that you speak
> This ain't a joke, so don't provoke, the brothers who will choke you by the throat
> You brokeback snitch, you should walk with a clip
> Cuz at any given moment nigga you could get hit
> While you drivin' your four door, you should be strapped with a 4-4
> Kickin' in the front door
> Niggas you want more? Nah you don't, just hope I won't miss

The gangster personae Mark adopts here, linked to Blackness and hardness, seems to bear little relation to his own experiences in his neighborhood; in a discussion about his work, Mark admitted that his mother does not allow him to go out at night and that he has never witnessed violence (though he hears about it from his peers). And although Mark comes from one of the lower-income neighborhoods in the city (or more specifically, from a lower-income pocket in what is largely a middle-class neighborhood), Mark's lyrics suggest that violent crimes such as drive-by shootings are much more prevalent in Montreal than they really are.[3]

In their conversations with Jacqueline, the youth often spoke about the power of rap as a "literacy of lived experience," describing the importance of conveying your true self in your rap lyrics and the lived conditions on the margins. They described how in their high schools they feel they have limited opportunities to express themselves, and turn to rap as a way to come to terms with what are often challenging life circumstances. In hip-hop, these young men feel embraced as they are, both validated and affirmed in their identities as economically insecure, racially marginalized youth. However, these sets of lyrics also reflect the extent to which their hip-hop identities also function as forms of personal armor, as they adopted gangster personas impervious to dissonance between their actual experiences and those found in the rap lyrics they consume. These narratives and personas act to glorify and sensationalize violence, and seem to limit the imaginative possibilities the youth might have for themselves. The draw to tough and street personas is understandable, beyond the way it dominates the rap representations they all consumed, for many of the youth feel actively discriminated against. Many of the participants discussed police racial profiling and the heightened presence of law enforcement where they lived, citing the many times when they felt they were unfairly targeted simply for being young, non-White, and wearing hip-hop attire. Such experiences of racism help make sense of why violence holds court as a major theme in the young men's lyrics; it is through these graphic and violent iconographies that real and imagined narratives are intertwined. The narratives seem to offer a hard, violent, and hyper-masculine identity as a form of self-protection (as in, for instance, Alex's case), and as means of living up to an authentic and "hard" hip-hop identity when it might be in doubt (perhaps for Mark).

THE BOUNDARIES OF BEING FEMALE IN HIP-HOP: BETWEEN "FEMALES" AND "BITCHES"

In the next section of this chapter, we turn to Eloise's work with Chronicle Creations. Of the 13 participants, there were 2 females and 11 males, all between 18 to 23 years old. As each participant was an active artist in at least one hip-hop element, hip-hop culture unified the 13 participants who came from a variety of ethnic, linguistic and, transnational backgrounds. The two situations presented took place during weekly preproduction sessions of Chronicle Creations where 13 participants met to discuss various themes in hip-hop culture with the purpose of brainstorming ideas for their participatory film on hip-hop culture in Montreal. During this project, authenticity regularly emerged in a number of ways. For instance, project participants (all hip-hop "insiders," including artists) used "realness" as a way to control what counted as "true hip-hop," who could "be hip-hop," and who could speak about it. They also regularly invoked the streets in order to validate the informal paths through which they had learned the hip-hop arts, often demeaning in the process formal education (a pattern that poses a real challenge for those interested in building bridges between hip-hop culture and schools). We here explore a moment during Eloise's participant-observant work that illustrates the workings of "hard heterosexual masculinity" in terms of how participants, male and female alike, mobilized binary constructions of the sister/female and the ho/bitch.

The producers and coordinators focused the second weekly meeting on "women and hip-hop." At the end of the 3-hour session, the producers and coordinators opened up the discussion to a debate on the issue of sexual discrimination in hip-hop. Given that the staff (two producers and two youth coordinators) had framed the debate around sexual discrimination, the conversation began with participants discussing the sexist representation of women in hip-hop videos and lyrics. The conversation shifted when emcee Theo interjected:

> Hip-hop is not disgracing women; we're disgracing women ourselves and women are disgracing women. So guys who gotta mention that there's a ho and that there's a slut in every song that they make, or in most of them, need

to find something else to do with their lives. But girls who are going to be
hos and sluts need to find something else to do with their time.

The room was filled with "mmm-hmmms" and "uhh-huhs" and applause from a
few people.

The first female comment came when one of the producers, Marissa, asked
the group to let Leesha, a participant who was starting to learn how to DJ, speak.
Leesha responded, "I was just gonna say, there's a difference between a female, and
there's a difference between a [pause] bitch." At the word *bitch*, there was laughter
from the participants. Ivan, a graffiti writer, piped in and said, "It's true!" Drawing upon the good woman/bad woman dichotomy, Leesha continued, "A female I
would say has the choice to do whatever she wants with herself. She's proud of herself. But um, I dunno." Another participant, Vanessa, went on to explain how the
identity of good sister or bad ho is a conscious choice made by women in hip-hop:
"They basically put it on themselves, you make a choice, you deal with it." After
another participant affirmed, "Yeah," Marissa asked, "I know I'm interrupting, but
how do you two as women feel about that?" Leesha responded, "It's not me!" and
Vanessa said, "I know who I am, I know what I'm doing, I don't care what they do.
They can go shake their little booties and whatever." The conversation continued,
but it revolved around the group consensus that there was an inherent difference
between females and bitches, affirming Leesha's original comment.

Leesha and Vanessa's comments about females and bitches were revealing in
that the debate eventually became a conversation between Leesha, Vanessa, and
Marissa. The focus shifted from the men in the group to the women, given that
Leesha and Vanessa were the ones who were exhibiting the anti-female comments.
Marissa most often took the stance of moderator in the weekly sessions so as to
not impede the voices of the participants, although her facial expressions sometimes betrayed a frustration with the lack of critical thinking displayed. While it
seemed important to Marissa for her to address the two women in the group, she
never turned to the men and explicitly asked them for their opinion on the comments, which suggests a feeling that sexism was more relevant to the women than
to the men in the group.

Though the staff attempted to continue discussions of women and hip-hop
throughout the sessions, they inevitably evolved into the type of discussion in the
previous scene. Moments like this were often met with laughter, though Marissa
often would try to get the participants to speak directly about what was going on.
For the young women in the group, the reproduction of the existing stereotypes
within hip-hop culture is especially harmful, given that the documentary production group was supposed to be a supportive space for participation and exploration of what it means to be hip-hop. Instead, the discussions around women in
hip-hop only reinforced the dichotomous tropes of femininity in hip-hop defined
by the women's relationship to men. Evidence that this dichotomy stems from

hip-hop emerged in a different session where Carlos, a graf writer in the group, insisted that Eloise listen to Jay-Z's (2002) song "Bitches & Sisters" so that she could gain insight into his perception of women in hip-hop. This perpetuation of the "authentic" hip-hop woman is especially frustrating, given that the participants, like those in Richardson (2006), were keen to question hegemonic structures of race and class but not of gender.

Despite the fact that gender is one of the most obvious axes that affect how we inhabit a space (Massey, 1994), it also continues to be an axis that represents great challenges to community educators struggling to develop a critical consciousness among their participants. Although the participants in Eloise's work were more than apt at creating the types of counternarratives Williams (2009) advocates for based on class, immigration experience, education experience, and their hip-hop experiences, they were less able to do so surrounding authentic constructions of gender.

CHALLENGES TO CRITICAL HIP-HOP PEDAGOGIES
FROM THE AUTHENTICITY DEBATES

Many of the conversations and lyrics described above seem like a far cry from critical hip-hop pedagogies, despite our aims and those of the facilitators in Chronicle Creations. This does not mean that there were no critical aspects to both projects. In both projects, the youth did display the development of critical consciousness while they attempted to identify and deconstruct how structures of class and gender affect others. For instance, the young men and women in Chronicle Creations were quick to point out how the hip-hop industry objectifies young women and how those young women objectify themselves. And yet they did not see themselves as implicated in, and potentially limited by, the dichotomy, even for the "good" female participants. And the young men in Chronicle did not see that their perpetuation of hip-hop's dichotomous construction of women as the ho/sister was sexist. In response, we wonder why the youth participants in Eloise's project were not able to see themselves as actors within hip-hop culture who contribute to and perpetuate its conventions of authenticity in relation to gender. Similarly, the participants in Jacqueline's writing project built powerful critiques of racism and socioeconomic marginalization in conversation, but in their lyrics were not able to imagine different roles, in response, other than the gangster.

Why such inconsistencies? Why didn't Jacqueline, Eloise, and the producers feel able to really challenge the youth they were working with? Similar dynamics shaped both projects. In both instances, they relied on the voluntary, uncompensated participation of the youth. The programs ran separately from formal education institutions and, particularly with Chronicle Creations whose meetings lasted over several months, every week was never the same as the last week, and a range of participants would come back. This type of setup can be common in hip-hop education programs. Consequently, informal educators are sometimes overcome by a feeling of "thank goodness they showed up" when entering the community center or recreation room. In Jacqueline's case, the data from her workshops were the basis of her master's thesis. If participants dropped out, she'd have no data. The documentary project also relied heavily on participation because, if no one came, there would be no one to film, and they were working to create a product that could be professionally broadcast. The producers and coordinators were extremely cognizant of the participants' sacrifice of their own time and made every attempt to let participants know that their voices were valued and a priority. However, if the focus is so strongly on "getting them to come back," educators in this environment may shy away from creating instances that might be uncomfortable for youth in favor of perpetuating a "this is really fun" atmosphere. For instance, although the Chronicle Creations participants were all for deconstructing the corporatization and commercialization of hip-hop culture and enjoyed these types of critical debates, it remains to be seen if they would have enjoyed a similarly critical debate about their own role in perpetuating a limiting model authenticity in hip-hop.

Tied to the "thank goodness they came" mentality mentioned above is the push to create cohesion within groups in voluntary informal education settings. This was especially the case with the documentary project, which needed to build a team atmosphere among the participants. If participants saw themselves as a cohesive group, they would want to come back each week, feel a sense of accountability to each other, and be more likely to follow the project through until the end. There were two primary aspects uniting the group as a team: 1) they were all hip-hop artists, and 2) they all shared a common vision of hip-hop culture as revolutionary. In an effort to create cohesion with the group, Eloise and the producers and coordinators may have been shying away from getting participants to ask critical questions of themselves and their role in hip-hop. Specifically related to the moments of sexism examined in this chapter, it would have been difficult to get participants—male and female—to talk about their role in sexism within hip-hop without seeming to be passing judgment.

In both projects, educators attempted to acknowledge, validate, and draw upon the experiences of young people, opening up spaces for students to share their stories. Of primary concern to Jacqueline's work with the young men in her group was supporting their aspirations to be "culturally productive" (Tan, 2009, p. 59), using their own contexts and familiarity with rap music as artistic inspiration. Most of the young men in the group claimed disinterest in classroom writing assignments but drew regularly from hip-hop as a source of inspiration and as a catalyst to write, reflect, and perform what they saw as their lived experiences of poverty and neighborhood violence. She worried that challenging the young men's depictions of their neighborhoods that at times seemed to glorify violence and danger might have limited their sense of the importance of their creative freedom of expression, making the workshops seem more like school.

Chronicle Creations, like many youth media projects, regularly invokes the discourse of "letting the youth tell their stories." As a starting point, that discourse might make it difficult for the project coordinators to ascertain whether or not it is their role to help shape the youth's consciousness and telling of their story or if it is their role to step aside and let the youth speak for themselves. When we throw into the mix that it was a "documentary," it becomes even more complicated, as most people would have the initial reaction that a documentary must be committed to the real, pure telling of the youth's stories.

All of these factors stood in the way of realizing the type of critical hip-hop pedagogy provided by Tan (2009) at the beginning of this chapter. It is easy to say that a critical hip-hop pedagogy will be "responsive to marginalization whether it be through structures of gender, class, race, religion, sexuality, or ability;" however, as we saw from both Jacqueline's and Eloise's projects, it is difficult to see what that "response" will look like or what obstacles will stand in its way. How can educators approach critical hip-hop pedagogy where students move beyond identifying constructions of authenticity and can begin to question how their own identity is bound by these hip-hop authenticity constructions?

STRATEGIES FOR ADDRESSING CHALLENGES

We have been thinking about and developing a few strategies since these experiences. A first strategy that speaks directly to the obstacles in the documentary project Eloise worked with is to let youth participants know from the beginning what critical thinking means, what you will be expecting from them, and what they can expect of you in relation to enacting a critical hip-hop pedagogy. Although the participants in the documentary project knew that they would be asked to think critically about *hip-hop,* they were not told that they would be asked to think critically about *themselves.* If you are working within a critical hip-hop pedagogy framework, write out what that means to you and put it up somewhere participants can see it every time they walk into the program; perhaps they can write their own versions of what it means to them. Let them know that learning in hip-hop does take work and do not be afraid that they will leave because you will be asking them to think. They want to think.

A second strategy is to draw upon critiques from hip-hop insiders, such as some of the "old school" rappers (as discussed in relation to the politically conscious, "underground" hip-hop element of the typology) as well as contemporary ones (such as Nas, who has claimed "hip-hop is dead") who are critics of the banality of violence and the rise of the "studio" gangster that accompanied rap music's commercialization. Given how complex rap's representational politics are, however, the work of these artists also needs to be interrogated for its own contradictions (for instance, artists who will critique bling-bling culture but perpetuate sexist stereotypes). Thoughtful critics also include hip-hop journalists and scholars such as Joan Morgan, Bakari Kitwana, and Greg Tate. This kind of study will reveal that hip-hop can be a contested space and that there is no consensus on what counts as "real."

A third strategy for educators in reworking what it means to be authentic for young people in hip-hop is to engage rap lyrics as artistic rather than mimetic representation. When we approach hip-hop as an art, we call for a more complex debate surrounding hip-hop texts (such as rap lyrics), and urge students to move beyond questioning *if* rappers "really" live the type of life they depict in their songs, and instead ask *why* rappers choose to depict that type of life. This can prompt discussion about why artists make the choices they do, and the value and limits of these choices—thus, denaturalizing the hip-hop "real." One might ask, for instance, following Perry (2004), "Why is the violence of the illegal underground economy, for example, more compelling than other features of community life" (p. 93) as a subject in rap lyrics? This project of denaturalizing is central to a critical hip-hop pedagogy.

As part of this project, rap music and hip-hop culture should be explored with students in light of aesthetic traditions such African American oral storytelling and competition, including the dozens, boasting, and toasting, as well as Black Atlantic cultural forms such as dub poetry, or Jamaican sound system and dance hall history. They can be read in relation to Henry Louis Gates's (1988) treatment of the trope of signifyin(g), a cornerstone of African American cultural and literary theory, which groups together a system of Black vernacular rhetorical strategies that draw upon the arts of indirection in order to trick or play, as in playful punning. Signifying celebrates the multiplicity and even chaos of meaning making, and therefore complicates the notion of a static, knowable "real." Emphasis can also be placed upon the performative, playful, even postmodern aspects of rap music, such as sampling and the ways in which it, like many Black vernacular modes, works in the way of irony and satire—both inside and outside the object of critique, playing on the audience's ability to recognize the difference (Potter 1995).

A fourth strategy for educators working with the stereotypes of authenticity in hip-hop is to open up discussion on the complexity of performing identities. In the projects discussed here, how the students performed their identities in hip-hop culture was the sole focus, and when other aspects of their identity (e.g., race, gender, class, neighborhood affiliation) were discussed, it was primarily in relation to hip-hop culture. In Eloise's work with Chronicle Creations, Leesha and Vanessa spoke of girls "shaking their booties" in the club and in videos and immediately drew the conclusion that they were "hos" and "sluts." In the context of identity performance, Leesha and Vanessa could have been asked if women who seem to represent one type of construction of femininity in one situation can represent a completely different identity in another situation. For instance, educators may ask whether a scantily clad woman dancing in a video could also be a university-educated woman? When we open up a discussion on the performance of identity, educators can help students see its complexities instead of understanding identity through dichotomous notions of authentic/fake. As part of this project, youth could be encouraged to write "persona" raps in which they take on the identity of another and experiment with different voices, exploring the ways that believability and richness in character need not be confined to the factual real.

These strategies ask us to study rap lyrics and songs as texts shaped by particular, historically situated, conventions of representation. Although central to many of the students' sense of themselves as young, urban, perhaps Black, or as men or women, these texts are also open to contestation and reinvention. Rap can also be studied as art, fiction, performance, and product of the imagination. These frameworks should help students gain the critical detachment necessary to explore both the possibilities and limitations of hip-hop's representations of urban youth and life. Here, they can work to gain some of the perspectives on pop culture developed by Stuart Hall (1996):

> Popular culture, commodified and stereotyped as it often is, is not at all, as we sometimes think of it, the area where we find who we really are, the truth of our experience. It is an arena that is profoundly mythic. It is a theatre of popular desires, a theatre of popular fantasies. It is where we discover and play with the identifications of ourselves, where we are imagined, where we are represented, not only to the audiences out there who do not get the message, but to ourselves for the first time. (p. 32)

NOTES

1. For an extended discussion of the hip-hop realness typology, see Low (2011). These categories overlap at points with McLeod's (1999), a six-item typology of the "semantic dimensions" of authenticity in hip-hop developed through discourse analysis of a significant data corpus, which includes interviews with rappers, fans, and music executives; articles in hip-hop magazines; album lyrics; hip-hop newsgroup postings; and press releases for rap albums. He outlined the various dimensions as: social-psychological (staying true to yourself rather than following mass trends); racial (Black versus White); political-economic (underground as opposed to commercial rap); gender-sexual (hard versus soft); social locational (the street); and cultural (the old school versus the mainstream of rap music).

2. Many blame the corporatization of hip-hop in the production and promotion of an apolitical version of gangster rap, including Immortal Technique (2006), who argues that "if you look at Gangsta Rap now and then back then, the Revolutionary element is for the most part completely sanitized by the corporate structure." As music industry executives

recognized the tremendous marketability of the ghetto fantasy, the "Gangsta Entertainment Complex" (Aaron, 1999) was born and the gangster became the predominant persona among mainstream rappers.

3. While there is violent crime in Montreal, the city is fortunate to have a lower homicide rate per capita than any other Canadian city and, less surprisingly, any U.S. city of comparable size. For instance, in 2008, Montreal reportedly had 29 homicides (down from 42 in 2007) while similarly sized Phoenix had more than 200 and Philadelphia had almost 400 (http://www.cbc.ca/canada/montreal/story/2008/12/30/mtl-homicide-rate-1230.html).

REFERENCES

Aaron, C. (1999, May/June). Black like them: Hip-Hop may be the last best hope for healing America's racial divide. Or not. *Utne Reader*. Retrieved from http://www.utne.com/1999-05-01/black-like-them.aspx

Alim, H. S. (2001, December). Diversifying our approaches to language and literacy development. *Language Magazine*, 29–31.

Alim, H. S. (2004). Hip-hop nation language. In E. Finegan & J. R. Rickford (Eds.), *Language in the USA: Themes for the twenty-first century* (pp. 387–409). Cambridge, UK: Cambridge University Press.

Baszile, D. (2009). Deal with it we must: Education, social justice, and the curriculum of hip hop culture. *Equity and Excellence in Education, 42*(1), 6–19.

Chang, J. (2005). Can't stop won't stop: A history of the hip-hop generation. New York: St. Martin's Press.

Chang, J. (2006) (Ed.). *Total chaos: The art and aesthetics of hip-hop*. New York: Basic Civitas.

Chuck D (with Yusuf Jah). (1997). *Fight the power*. New York: Delacorte Press.

Côté, J. (2006). Identity studies: How close are we to developing a social science of identity? An appraisal of the field. *Identity, 6*(1), 3–25.

Gates, H. L., Jr. (1988). *The signifying monkey: A theory of African American literary criticism*. New York: Oxford University Press.

Hall, M. R. (2009). Hip-hop education resources. *Equity and Excellence in Education, 42*(1), 86–94.

Hall, S. (1996). What is this "black" in black popular culture? In D. Morley & C. Kuan-Hsing (Eds.), *Stuart Hall: Critical dialogues in cultural studies* (pp. 468–478). New York: Routledge.

Hill, M. L. (2009). *Beats, rhymes, and classroom life: Hip-hop pedagogy and the politics of identity*. New York: Teachers College Press.

Hurt, B. (Director). (2006). *Beyond beats and rhymes: A hip-hop head weighs in on manhood in hip-hop culture*. [Documentary]. United States: God Bless the Children.

Immortal Technique. (2006). Is gangsta rap hip-hop? Retrieved from http://www.hiphopdx.com/index/columns-editorials/id.692/title.is-gangsta-rap-hip-hop-by-immortal-technique/p.1

Jay-Z. (2002). Bitches & sisters. On *The blueprint 2: The gift and the curse* [CD]. New York: Roc-A-Fella/Def Jam.

Kelley, R. D. G. (1994). *Race rebels: Culture, politics, and the Black working class*. New York: Free Press.

Keyes, C. (2002). *Rap music and street consciousness*. Chicago: University of Chicago Press.

Kim, I. (2007). Youth videomaking projects: A spoken word study (Doctoral dissertation, University of Toronto, 2007). *Dissertation Abstracts International, 69,* 06.

Koza, J. (1999). Rap music: The cultural politics of official representation. In C. McCarthy, G. Hudak, S. Miklaucic, & P. Saukko (Eds.), *Sound identities: Popular music and the cultural politics of education* (pp. 65–96). New York: Peter Lang.

Krims, A. (2000). *Rap music and the poetics of identity*. Cambridge, UK: Cambridge University Press.

Low, B. (2011). *Slam school: Learning through conflict in the hip-hop and spoken word classroom*. Palo Alto, CA: Stanford University Press.

Massey, D. B. (1994) *Space, place, and gender*. Minneapolis: University of Minnesota Press.

McLeod, K. (1999). Authenticity within hip-hop and other cultures threatened with assimilation. *Journal of Communication* 49(4): 134–150.

Morgan, J. (1999). *When chickenheads come home to roost: My life as a hip-hop feminist*. New York: Touchstone First Editions.

Perry, I. (2004). *Prophets of the hood: Politics and poetics in hip-hop*. Durham, NC: Duke University Press.

Petchauer, E. (2009). Framing and reviewing hip-hop educational research. *Review of Educational Research, 79(2),* 946–978.

Potter, R. A. (1995). *Spectacular vernaculars: Hip-Hop and the politics of postmodernism*. Albany, NY: SUNY Press.

Pough, G. D., Richardson, E., Durham, A., & Raimist, R. (Eds.). (2007). *Home girls make some noise: Hip-Hop feminism anthology*. Mira Loma, CA: Parker Publishing.

Richardson, E. (2006). *Hip-hop literacies*. New York: Routledge.

Rivera, R. (2003). *New York Ricans from the hip-hop zone*. New York: Palgrave Macmillan.

Rodriguez, L. (2009). Dialoguing cultural capital and student engagement: Toward a hip hop pedagogy in the high school. *Equity and Excellence in Education, 42(1),* 20–35.

Rose, T. (1994). *Black noise: Rap music and Black culture in contemporary America*. Middletown, CT: Wesleyan University Press.

Rose, T. (2008). *The hip-hop wars*. New York: Basic Books.

Sfard, A., & Prusak, A. (2005). Telling identities: In search of an analytic tool for investigating learning as a culturally shaped activity. *Educational Researcher, 34(4),* 14–22.

Spady, J., Lee, C., & Alim, H. S. (1999). *Street conscious rap*. Philadelphia: Black History Museum/Umum Loh Publishers.

Stovall, D. (2006). We can relate: Hip-hop culture, critical pedagogy, and the secondary classroom. *Urban Education, 41(6):* 585–602.

Tan, E. (2009). *Participatory and critical out-of-school learning for urban youth: Building community through popular culture*. Unpublished dissertation. McGill University, Montreal.

Toop, D. (1991). *Rap attack 2: African rap to global hip-hop*. London: Serpent's Tail.

Wang, O. (2004). *Spinning identities: A social history of Filipino American DJs in the San Francisco Bay area*. Unpublished dissertation. University of California, Berkeley.

Williams, A. D. (2009). The critical cultural cipher: Remaking Paulo Freire's cultural circles using hip-hop culture. *International Journal of Critical Pedagogy, 2(1),* 1–29.

Zafar, A. (2007). Hip-hop 101 with KRS-One. Retrieved from http://www.hiphopcongress.com/press/hip-hop-101-with-krs-one/

CHAPTER 7

Who Are We?
Hip-Hoppers' Influence in the Brazilian Understanding of Citizenship and Education

Derek Pardue

People often refer to a great basketball center as a "man-child"
The physical force of an undeniable masculinity
Coupled with the playfulness and charm of a boy . . .
Today I saw a version of the contrary
Trivial yet absolutely revealing
A moment of release from my iPod
Remembering my youth with the Bad Brains
The bus stopped and I observed an "infant-teen"
A grown boy with a pacifier
Carrying boxes, crates, bags creating his place under the urban avenue overpass . . .

In early 2009 I scribbled these notes down on one of the many long bus rides part of everyday life in São Paulo, Brazil. The anonymous boy protagonist here is not donning the pacifier in a gesture to an Ice Cube sidekick from the 1990s (see, for example, the film *Boyz in the Hood* [1991]). Over the past decade, I have seen dozens of toddlers in Brazil with pacifiers but never a full-sized boy, perhaps, given his probable diet, a preteen of 10 or 11 years of age. As I watched the "infant-teen" perform his menial tasks over a span of several days, I came to see the pacifier as a metaphoric symbol of the serious systemic problems in Brazilian citizenship.

For more than a decade I have spent hundreds of hours shuttling from one periphery neighborhood to another meeting with hip-hoppers, educators, and community activists. I have witnessed not only the steady popularization across various mainstream media in urban Brazil of Hip Hop in all of its elements (MC, DJ, graffiti, street dance) but also the development and cultivation of homegrown messages regarding community among local Hip Hop organizations. Rap lyrics of groups such as Racionais MCs have become part of college entrance exams and public discourse around urban living conditions. As the visual design of the Brazilian city represents standardized templates of the global modern (i.e., multinational, corporate buildings) underscored by the unique dramas of national and city pride such as soccer along with neighborhood happenings such as police violence or local youth groups, graffiti artists, once condemned as deviant vandals, have gained increasingly positive attention among business owners and neighborhood families as gatekeepers of local distinction. These are just two examples of the proliferation and impact of Hip Hop on everyday life in urban Brazil. Since 2000, the growth of Hip Hop, once relegated to São Paulo in the late 1980s and throughout much of the 1990s, has become a significant part of youth and popular culture in cities throughout the enormous country of Brazil. But, on this day, I wondered again about the impact of Hip Hop as a force in the social dimensions of education and citizenship. If the "infant-teen" represents maladjustment of age and habit or life cycle and knowledge, what sort of contribution has Hip Hop made in this area? Do hip-hoppers offer a path and a system of epistemology so that curious youth gain access to information and cultivate skills into knowledge of self and other?

It is important to remember that Brazilian society does not demonstrate the tragic postcolonial stories of nations such as Mozambique, Angola, Guinea-Bissau, Cape Verde, or other former Portuguese colonies, which have struggled with civil war, Cold War proxy wars, and large-scale emigration. Brazil is a "successful" nation-state, a bedrock of democracy and liberal capitalism in Latin America. At the time of this writing, many Americans have begun to take notice of the "sleeping giant" in South America as we become more concerned about a potential loss of global economic hegemony. Statistically speaking, according to the United Nations, if one were to consider the wealthiest 20% of the Brazilian population, the Human Development Index (HDI) would exceed that of Iceland, the leading country in this category. By contrast, if one were to consider solely the poorest 20%, the HDI would compare with that of India. The report goes on to conclude that indices of education such as literacy rates correlate positively to HDI ranking.[1]

Before proceeding any further, I must underscore a fundamental affirmation, one I believe is a common thread among all the contributions to this volume. Namely, Hip Hop is best understood as a set of practices and network formations rather than simply as a line of products. This underlying theory has engendered a dialogue between those invested in culture and education. Described as a nation, attitude, style, creative force, generation, or a state of mind, Hip Hop has undeniably influenced much of what scholars refer to as *identity formation* and *self-cultivation*. It is the latter term, *cultivation*, that one can locate the etymological and theoretical nexus of culture and education as personal and social development.[2]

The relationship between Hip Hop culture and education has attracted a number of ethnographically rich and theoretically sound studies over the past decade. For the most part, they focus on U.S. contexts and divide into two approaches. On the one hand, there are those that focus on the value of Hip Hop as part of conventional school curricula and pedagogy (e.g., Cooks, 2004; Hanley, 2007; Hill, 2009; Izarry, 2009; Morrell 2008; Morrell & Duncan-Andrade, 2002; Price, 2005; Stovall, 2006). The overarching research question, to borrow from Greg Dimitriadis's assessment, has been how teachers use Hip Hop to provoke students to engage in the learning process (2009, p. 48) or, more pragmatically, to appreciate math, English, poetry, sound engineering, fashion, and other core or elective fields of conventional school course work. Following the work of Freire, Giroux, and other leading theorists of pedagogy, scholars have moved beyond the pragmatic and have argued that the overtly performative, poetic, and philosophical nature of Hip Hop has led many to "reconsider the relationship between curriculum and instruction, reader and text, and teacher and student" (Hill, 2008, p. 143).

In a complementary manner, scholars and journalists have also concluded that forums of Hip Hop outside of the school proper can function as alternative spaces of education (e.g., Bruce & Davis, 2000; Hill, 2008; Isaac, 2003; Pardue, 2007). If one is to expand the notion of education to include a range of rule- and skill-based activities devoted to contextualized knowledge of self and other, then Hip Hop emerges as a potentially vibrant field of popular pedagogy. Furthermore, scholars have argued that rappers often articulate themselves as pedagogues, following the precedent of KRS-ONE (Dimitriadis, 2009) and Afrika Bambaataa (Alim & Pennycook, 2007; Oehler & Hanley, 2009; Pardue, 2007).

I hope to contribute to this discussion not only by simply expanding the data field to include observations from the Brazilian urban milieu, but, perhaps more significantly, by addressing the relationships between local hip-hoppers and governmental agencies in a new recognition of popular culture as a legitimate forum for education and citizenship. Furthermore, such recognition is systematic and institutional in nature. At the time of this writing, many people in the United States are experiencing, first- or secondhand, a financial and existential shock based on rising unemployment, significantly reduced state budgets in the fields of secondary education, and home mortgage defaults. Returning to the United Nations Human Development Index, the United States sits outside of the top 10 at number 15. Thus, as the U. S. administration strives to reorganize essential parts of civic life, with health care most debated presently, perhaps we can learn something from Brazilian and other Latin American as well as European systems of "cultural management" in the development of contemporary projects of education and citizenship empowerment. In short, the case of Hip Hop pedagogy in Brazil could have implications for a more general (re)consideration of education in the public sphere and by extension the role of agency in the practice of citizenship.

Ultimately, Hip Hop, when approached at the level of everyday practice among everyday people, has proven throughout its history to be most successful as a gateway to knowledge among those who are disenfranchised, whether along lines of race, ethnicity, language, class, and to a growing extent, gender and sexuality.[3] To be an expression of the marginalized is/was Hip Hop's *raison d'etre* and thus it is logical that those who have utilized and creatively expanded the purview of Hip Hop have emerged from such social groups. Likewise, it is logical that the state—in the case of Brazil, the Department of Culture—would specifically identify Hip Hop in any formal plan of popular education as a productive segue from culture to citizenship. In the next sections, I contextualize, describe, and interpret the Brazilian Cultural Points (CP) project and then ethnographically ground the CP initiative through an analysis of the Hip Hop House (*Casa de Cultura Hip Hop*).

THE URBAN BRAZILIAN CONTEXT

Brazilians and Brazilianists enjoy citing an adage made popular by the legendary *bossa nova* music composer Tom Jobim: "Brazil is not for beginners." Normally, this phrase is uttered to take account of the stark contradictions evident in Brazilian society in almost every social category. Certainly, Brazil is a challenging puzzle. However, another way to approach Brazil is to assert, in fact, that Brazil is a Weberian ideal type. It is perfect for the beginner to understand many of the dynamics of post–World War II urbanization and its relationship to socioeconomic development in much of Latin America, Africa, and beyond. The emergence of São Paulo, Rio de Janeiro, along with Lagos, Mexico City, and Abidjan as mega-cities is a result of contemporary migration patterns, the majority of which involve a rural to urban flow. Consequently, one of the strongest dynamics of social interaction in contemporary cities is the reckoning of knowledge and value based on assumptions of the urban–rural divide. Historically, this fissure has been particularly pronounced in Brazil due to its colonization and the ensuing demarcation of the coastline and its cities as a harbor of modernity and future promises and the countryside as a place of raw material, tradition, and nostalgia.[4]

These brief comments on Brazilian history help introduce the phenomenon of São Paulo because the shock and mixture of the urban and the rural constitute, in part, the ideological and material world of the *periferia,* the heterogeneous, (sub)urban zones where most people reside. Current discourses around race, class, and religion in urban Brazil are often articulated and interpreted in shifting terms of "being modern." When pushed further, Brazilians usually give examples demonstrating different levels of "education" and "culture." Just as we in the United States have become increasingly aware of quantifiable measures of education through policies such as No Child Left Behind and the host of standardized tests necessary for formal advancement, Brazilians tell stories and attempt to position themselves as "educated" and "having culture."

The dimensions of "being modern" and "Brazilian" are more complicated than a simple White–Black, rural–urban, zero-sum game. Simply put, the "periphery" is too large and visible to be ignored, and one of the persistent puzzles of the Brazilian public sector is the management of the *periferia*. In this sense, the Cultural Points program, the Hip Hop House institution, and the meaning of Hip Hop are expressions of a longstanding relationship between the state and the popular in the name of citizenship. I argue that the potential brilliance of Hip Hop is that for the first time, performers directly address the parameters of citizenship and are forcefully expanding its purview. Likewise, the Cultural Points program represents an official recognition of this new vision of the relationship between the state, popular education, culture, and citizenship.

State attention to the popular is not new. Cultural historians such as Bryan McCann (2004) and Daryle Williams (2001) have rightly concentrated on the first administration of the populist dictator Getúlio Vargas (1930–1945) and his efforts to literally incorporate culture as a state project of citizenship and a viable industry for export. For example, McCann argues that the music/dance genre of *samba* was always a challenge for state "cultural managers." While samba performers often highlighted the racial mixture embodied in the "mulatto/a" and the sonic mixture of perceived African percussion and rhythm with European melodies and harmonic progressions, the frequent protagonist of the *malandro* ("hustler") or the culturally rich life skills of *malandragem* ("hustling" or "street smarts") was, indeed, a sticking point with national radio programming managers. Censors did exercise their power (McCann, 2004, pp. 65–67), but, more interestingly, state culture brokers lobbied for "education" to control more effectively the meaning of samba.[5] In short, this is what Álvaro Salgado, music critic employed by the Department of Press and Propaganda, referred to in his 1941 column as the "social factor" in the "circulation of radio" (Salgado, 1941, p. 79).

Similar to other Latin American states, the Brazilian track record in cultural management, as it relates to folk and popular music, is conflicted. The legacy of "incorporation" and "education" of culture as a top-down model of implementation has been patronizing at best and violent at worst. Although part of this tension has arisen from the equation of culture with a Eurocentric notion of civilization, another factor in the continual gap between the state and marginalized social groups is a systematic lack of recognition as to how ordinary people make meaning through creative, cultural expressions. That education and citizenship could be structured from below was one of pedagogue Paulo Freire's central themes and flagship programs as Minister of Education at the municipal level in São Paulo during the late 1980s and the boom of nongovernmental organizations (NGOs) in the 1990s.

When I arrived in São Paulo in 1995, many of my consultants in the periphery neighborhoods were just beginning to use the term *NGO* as a new presence in their lives. By the late 1990s, some hip-hoppers saw an opportunity to transition from a "posse" to a more visible "NGO" while still maintaining the community ethic of the posse (Pardue, 2008). For some in the periphery, the state signifies abandonment and total frustration. The symbol of the school is empty. Longtime neighborhood activist Paulo Magrão and president of Capão Cidadão[6] explains that "the youth don't have any connection with the school, but they do with the NGO, and so, the entire neighborhood gives it [the NGO] respect" (Vieira, 2008, p. 8). For others, such as the members of the Força Ativa cultural group from the extreme East Side, there is a hesitancy to move too quickly into the neoliberal world of Ford Foundations and UNICEF grants. In November 2001, prior to an event celebrating the opening of a neighborhood library, based primarily on the efforts of Força Ativa, Moisés explained it to me in conversation this way: "This event [library inauguration] is from public support, not private donors. This is a problem with NGOs. We cannot let the state off the hook like that. It is their obligation to provide for the people."

After more than a decade of Hip Hop practice and debate about the relationship between the state, the periphery, and Hip Hop on the meaning of education and citizenship, there is no consensus in opinion. However, one can state that hip-hoppers as well as the state have become more flexible as the former pushes for recognition and representation and the latter strives to show a visible mark of inclusion and a systematic plan for the role of education and culture in a sustained democracy.

THE CULTURAL POINTS PROJECT

Now, here's a deal. The Brazilian state has, as of the writing of this text, recognized approximately a thousand *points* of culture. In this context, the term *point* (i.e., *ponto*) refers to a locale or a meeting place where Brazilians regularly congregate as an organization related to some kind of expressive cultural practice. In addition, there are roughly 35 *pontões* or "big points" that act as regional places for connecting local points. In traditional Hip Hop terms, the analogy would be *ponto* is to *pontão* as rap group is to posse. Such recognition involves an investment by the state of approximately 200 million *reais*, or 85 million U.S. dollars a year. Furthermore, the Cultural Points program is specifically oriented toward already existing cultural practices in marginalized social spaces (*áreas sociais mais degredadas*). This is but one federal program in the promotion of civil society through cultural performance and social networking. As former cultural minister Gilberto Gil reminded reporters, state investment in culture is not charity.[7] Most assuredly, there is a return. In brute terms, according to statistics from the United Nations, 8% of the wealth produced globally is from "cultural creativity." In more concrete terms, cultural products and services generate $1.3 trillion annually, with an average increase of 10% per year (Ramsdale, 2000).

In this section, I explain the precarious position of Hip Hop as a state-sponsored cultural practice. In order to demonstrate such a position, I discuss the essential paradox of the relationship between the state and culture, especially popular culture in contemporary Brazil. Although one can argue that the present administration represents a continuity from past state projects of cultural sponsorship, I believe that the Cultural Points project, as part of the Live Culture initiative spearheaded by Gilberto Gil from 2003 to 2008 and given continuity by the acting minister of culture during that period, Juca Ferreira, does, in fact, mark a significant break from the past. Furthermore, judging from the rhetoric of Gil and the project criteria he presented, hip-hoppers stand to gain a great deal of financial and ideological support from the Cultural Points project. Yet, the long history of paternalism endemic to Brazilian governance along with the strong entrepreneurial spirit of Hip Hop economics and philosophy of skills and information cause many local hip-hoppers to pause and consider carefully the Cultural Points project. The success of Cultural Points does not *depend* on Hip Hop approval; however, with the increasing popularity of Hip Hop in the periphery of (sub)urban neighborhoods throughout Brazilian cities, the relationship between Hip Hop and the program may well provide insight into the current status of cultural citizenship and educational management in urban Brazil.

As mentioned above, the legacy of Vargas in the management of culture in Brazil is one of selective inclusion based on institutional judgment of what counts as culture and, more dynamically, how to transform the popular into an effective discourse of the national. Such transformations involved an "education" or an elite-based directive to "improve" the popular as part of inclusion. In short, then, selective inclusion involves a quantitative process of numeration and documentation, or an account of Brazilian cultural areas and their respective forms. In addition, selection involves a process of positivist cultivation around issues, as in the case of *samba,* of taste, class, race, and space. From the point of view of state culture, the *malandro* was problematic due to his obviation of formal labor, location in the impoverished hills of Rio de Janeiro, his representation of phenotypic "Blackness," and his demonstration of confrontational attitude. Again, cultural selection was not about eliminating the *malandro* but "recasting" him through the efforts of censorship pressures on samba composers and artists. In the case of samba, the main pressure point was with regard to labor, as the emerging ideology of *racial democracy* under Vargas took account of Afro-Brazilian traits as part of a vibrant urban popular within the new, modern Brazil.

The Cultural Points project is theoretically less concerned with listing cultures and more preoccupied with providing the technological infrastructure for local communities whose cultural projects speak to the global in a recognized Brazilian idiom. The keyword for the Ministry of Culture (MinC), according to their official website, is *transversalidade*, or transversatility, a curious neologism referring to the two major themes of network and adaptive performativity. For ex-minister Gil, the role of the state is to "provide information, libraries, video archives, circuits, forums for debate, tools, workshops, opportunities to produce, show and circulate . . . to provide a point for the hundreds of diverse, capable expressions of our plural, mestizo collage."[8] As Claudio Prado (2008) has explained in an interview, popular culture

> works this way, as it is, we [in the Ministry of Culture] are simply trying to facilitate the process by which Brazilians in the underserved periphery neighborhoods are able more readily to connect their realities and experiences with the millions of potentially interested parties both inside and outside of Brazil about a range of topics that are global in nature. We as part of the Brazilian government must facilitate this exchange through the Free Software Multimedia Project because it is undeniable that the challenges that face Brazil face everyone.

As Prado, the coordinator of Digital Technologies in the MinC, and Gil have emphasized, the idea of culture from the perspective of the Brazilian state is not *dirigismo*, a term with a long history throughout Latin America which connotes a top-down model of direction, but rather autonomy and protagonism.[9] Such a perspective represents an expression of social agency. For Gil, this invigorated sense of the state and society can provoke a real practice of civil society or literally "public politics" (*política pública*).

In 2007, Gil gave a lecture in the city of Belo Horizonte to launch the second "web," or *teia*, of the Cultural Points program in which he underlined several concepts of civil society and the role of culture therein. Gil's poetic description and explanation of the program demonstrates a remarkable suitability to Hip Hop and helps contextualize the admittance and relative success of the Hip Hop Culture House in Diadema, an industrial satellite city in the São Paulo metro area.

Gilberto Gil rose to prominence as one of the most important and entertaining musicians in Brazilian history. Whether he is provoking audiences to reflect on the constructed nature of spirituality and pop culture in the late '60s song "Bat Macumba"[10] or in his public lectures about the Brazilian state and culture, Gil productively mixes a memorable sound bite with thoughtful theory. In 2007, Gil peppered his speech in Belo Horizonte with allusions to not only webs and ramps of social and cultural networking, but also invigorating phrases such as "It's good to live life live (i.e., live performance)" (*É bom viver a vida ao vivo*), "I think, I want, I am, I do, I change" (*Eu penso, eu quero, eu sou, eu faço, eu mudo*), and perhaps even more provocative, "the creation of power comes from the power to create" (*a criação do poder vem do poder da criação*).

Gil's rhetorical performance is not simply show. Also in his 2007 speech, he repeatedly explained the Ministry's program as "points" in the sense of "connecting one to another" that require "action" to "announce an idea." Furthermore, he has insisted that the program is not about "inviting society for something *ready,* produced in an agency laboratory. [Rather], we open a relationship of co-existence." Such an action-based model of culture correlates with local hip hoppers' discourse of knowledge and power mediated through the categories of information and experience or *vivência,* as described below.

THE CASA

When I arrived at the Cultural Center in Canhema, a neighborhood in the industrial satellite city of Diadema, in July 1999 at the request of Nino Brown, I shared the general feeling that something was different and exciting. By the end of 1999, local rappers, DJs, b-boys, b-girls, graffiti artists, and historians joined forces with neighborhood politicians and journalists to persuade the Diadema Department of Culture to cede the government-run cultural center to an elected committee's management. Since then, the Canhema Cultural Center has been known as the Hip Hop House.

The widely respected and proclaimed "godfather" of the Hip Hop House as well as many rap groups and various Hip Hop posses around São Paulo, Nino Brown was glowing when we met back in July 1999. A normally soft-spoken Nino was excited at the prospect of having a fixed place for Hip Hop:

> More importantly, this house can be a place where kids can learn about the continuities (*continuidade*) between funk, soul, R&B, disco, and rap. This is fundamental in my opinion. I can move all those files and stuff you saw back in my house [in 1997] to a room here and make it into a real archive. A patrimony of soul, funk, and Hip Hop. (Personal Communication)

The *Casa,* as it is referred to locally, quickly became not only a meeting place in Diadema for youth to practice the four elements of Hip Hop and develop social networks, but also, more important in the long run, an institution of Hip Hop pedagogy. In this case, *Hip Hop pedagogy* refers to not only the teaching of Hip Hop's elements to local youth but also collective conversations, debates, presentations about the links between Hip Hop skills and knowledge, and a general way of living one's life—a pedagogy of citizenship. The *Casa* consists of a series of one-story, concrete slab buildings surrounded by a 9-foot brick wall and in some places a spiked metal fence. In other words, it looks like a typical public service building—"a state thing" (*coisa do governo*). In addition to the ranch-style layout, there is a concrete stage with a covering and a covered place for an audience with a capacity of 500 people.

According to Nino, the establishment of the *Casa* as a Hip Hop institution emerged from the collaborative work and roundtable discussions in the Diadema neighborhood of Inamar between Hip Hop pioneers such as Nelsão Triunfo and local community activists such as Sueli Chan and Oswaldinho Fausto. The result was a plan to link expressive art and community project with the goal of bridging the social concerns of working-class educators and the political concerns of Afro-Brazilian youth. Nino's reflections are fresh, since the *Casa* celebrated its 10-year anniversary in July 2009. Nino explained the idea of the *Casa* in a recent email this way:

> in those early meetings around 1993, we discussed not only the fifth element of Afrika Bambaataa of universal understanding as it relates to Hip Hop but also how it related to teenage pregnancy, AIDS, agrarian reform, and the historical importance of Afro-Brazilians. . . . The *Casa* is different from the conventional school, because we use Hip Hop as our medium to learn. We really value experience and idea exchange as a way toward knowledge.

Every month the *Casa* holds an event called *Hip Hop Em Ação* (Hip Hop in Action), which features groups from the ongoing workshops, local professional artists representing all the elements, and a headlining rapper and DJ. According to well-known Brazilian rappers Thaíde, Jamal, and Rappin' Hood, everyone performs "*na moral*," which literally translates as "along moral lines" but is better understood as "in solidarity" and, practically speaking, "for free." By 2003, virtually all well-known rappers from the São Paulo area as well as many famous rappers and DJs from Rio, Brasília, Campinas, and Porto Alegre, had performed *na moral* at the *Casa*. According to longtime DJ professor Erry-G and graffiti workshop instructor Tota, the Hip Hop in Action events serve to not only make the *Casa* more publicly visible through advertisement but also "are learning experiences for everyone involved." Erry-G goes on to explain:

> We learn how to organize and publicize Hip Hop events. Perhaps most importantly, though, are the experiences of the local kids who wander in to the Casa and the kids who are just beginning in the workshops. Why? The Hip Hop in Action days are positive; the kids here in the neighborhood hear the music, see the dancing, the spray art, and then they see kids who look like them, some of whom they may recognize from around the way, and they see them *doing* something. They are up there next to Mano Brown, Rappin' Hood, Thaíde, DJ Hum, SNJ, Gog, Ieda Hills, all the Hip Hop idols. They get interested. They come back. They sign up (for free) for the workshops and they get turned on to the history, the fun, the art, the idea of saying

something, the power of expression, and they become more positive about themselves and where they come from.

Sometimes they make new friends and that's also important. The beginners from the workshops learn what it means to perform. They develop their self-esteem and that gives them confidence and an attitude that they take with them into whatever they do with their lives. We hope they stay for another round of workshops. We hope they get involved with all the elements. For many, just to get up on that stage is an achievement. (Personal communication)

DJ Erry-G's description of the *Casa* is strikingly exemplary of Gil's notion of *costura*, or weaving in the collective action of exchanging ideas. In a 2009 interview, DJ Preto EL contextualized the *Casa* in more pedagogic terms of teacher/ student relationship:

One of the most important points [of the *Casa*] to me is that I [as a teacher] do not consider myself as the master with all the answers. In our discussions, I try to create a scene where they [the students] feel comfortable in contributing. And, in fact, they do help me build up my own knowledge. This is significantly different than what happens at the formal school, where the direction is only one way. Students just "receive" information. . . . Here kids come and the idea is that they come to add up (*somar*) with a group. The teacher or educator serves as bait or a "start" for the students to speak out, to express themselves, and to see what they could not or did not see before due to social or other forces. They begin to speak their minds. This collective effort is what we call *vivência*. (Personal communication)

For Gil, Preto EL, Nino Brown, and Erry-G, it is the circulation that is the culture; the *Casa* Hip Hop workshop is an instantiation of the federal government's "point." For Preto EL, education is essentially collaborative; the goal is to come to *somar*, to "add up" to something. However, as DJ Erry-G implies, the belief of the wandering local teen is precarious; she is naturally dubious of a "state thing" like the *Casa*. Yet, as she sees others actually break the threshold of audience-stage, her imagination potentially begins. The apocryphal texts of rap lyrics, DJ soundscapes, graffiti images, and street dance moves are tangentially authentic in the conventional definitions of Brazilian culture or *Brasilidade*. Be that as it may, it is difficult to deny that Hip Hop in the *Casa* represents a practice of *costura*, a reassemblage of very real Brazilian experiences and categorical skills, or what Preto EL referred to as *vivência*. The Cultural Points project has attempted to shift semiotic focus regarding *cultura* so that it approximates *costura*, and as this holds steady, hip-hoppers have organized themselves and submitted dozens of proposals to participate.

PROBLEMS IN CULTURAL MANAGEMENT

Until recently, the scale of interaction between the state and culture in the case of the *Casa* remained at the municipal level. The political administrations in Diadema have kept a fairly tight leash on employment contracts and general funding of the *Casa*. Meanwhile, in other venues, public officials have pronounced Diadema as the "Hip Hop City" and declared November 12 to be an officially recognized "Hip Hop Day" under the auspices of the municipality government in association with Universal Zulu Nation Brasil.[11] In my conversations with veteran hip-hoppers employed at the *Casa* and with young resident teenagers, either hanging out at one of the monthly Hip Hop in Action shows or beginning students in one of the free Hip Hop workshops held regularly on the weekends, the message is consistent. They feel a certain respect about being associated with the *Casa* and being from Diadema.

The relationship was more or less comfortable for the Labor Party officials and relatively positive for the hip-hoppers, albeit the hip-hoppers often complained about late salary payments and other ineffective bureaucratic mechanisms. Nevertheless, veteran hip-hoppers recognized that, given the general milieu of state involvement in popular culture, Diadema and the *Casa* had something good going. This helps explain the high percentage of workshop teachers from outside of Diadema and the high number of free performances or colloquially termed "moral" shows (*na moral*) at the *Casa* as mentioned above.

Such value began to change in 2007 when the Department of Culture at the federal level recognized the *Casa* as a Cultural Point. What was once a relatively organic development of Hip Hop culture, institutional "occupation" (keyword in local Hip Hop discourse), and social reputation has begun to be tested by competing interests. Such interests reveal contested notions of culture and the parameters of effective citizenship.

It is not the case that the *Casa* was the first point in Diadema. By 2007, there were already nine recognized points, including organizations of popular poetry, audiovisual production, dance, theater, a pop art museum, and *folia de reis* (Reily, 2002).[12] The federal government provides 185,000 *reais*, or approximately $80,000 U.S. dollars, per year to each of these nine points in five installments. The municipal government must supply the infrastructure and professional and maintenance labor force.[13] Yet, the inclusion of the *Casa* as one point within the larger Cultural Points project incited a sharp debate on the longstanding polemic over whether Hip Hop is, in fact, culture. DJ Preto El, member of Universal Zulu Nation Brasil and workshop teacher at the *Casa*, described the scene this way:

> You see, there's an official sign from "Ponto de Cultura," which was supposed to be installed a while back. It's going [to be posted] here at the Casa. It will reinforce the importance of this space, the struggle we've endured to

conquer this space. It's not just about the ABC [an acronym referring to the industrial cities of the Southeast region of the São Paulo metro area], but about all of São Paulo and Brazil as a whole. This was the first Hip Hop center in Brazil. The problem is that some people at the current municipal department of culture see this as a farce. They don't like our culture and don't want to see us grow and be strong. It's a simple space. In short, there is a misunderstanding about what the Casa is and what the Cultural Points program is. What's worse is that these two factions are in the same building, one of the buildings in the place that you have visited several times. Right there! Truthfully, I don't understand and am confused, as I feel many are right about now. (Personal communication)

In a 2009 email exchange, Tota, a longtime consultant, legendary graffiti artist, and veteran workshop teacher, underscored the difference between municipal and São Paulo state bureaucracy, on the one hand, and the federal department as a significant matter in assessing the state–culture relationship:

Thank God, we've got another project. It's all about the "graffiti poético" [the name of Tota's project]. The state government initiative under the rubric of "cultural action" is great. They make the red tape easy—less worry about receipts, strict budgets. We don't have to produce all of this paperwork up front. This gives us a certain distance from the bureaucracy and allows us to do what we know. They give us time after the fact to do the bookkeeping. The problem with the "cultural points" program is that they delay their payment. I'm still waiting for the money they owe me from the spray cans I bought over two years ago.

CONCLUSION: LESSONS FROM BRAZIL

The case of Hip Hop education and the Brazilian state in the form of the Cultural Points program is instructive for those in the United States and beyond for several reasons. In theoretical terms, the CP initiative has forced state representatives and local hip-hoppers to consider the notion of education and pedagogy and articulate their respective senses of purpose. For some, both in Brazil and the United States, Hip Hop's educational value is mostly vocational. The information is in the technique and can lead to a viable life path of rhetoric, engineering, visual art, body movement, business, advertising, politics, and so on. For others, Hip Hop is a distinct form of creative expression that links the diverse real-world experience of social relationships to the quantifiable, rule-based systems of rhyme, beat-matching, graffiti tagging or lettering, and rhythm-based dance genres. For DJ Preto EL, this is encapsulated in the *Casa* members' use of the term *vivência*, a concept akin to what Greg Dimitriadis has articulated as *lived practice* (Dimitriadis, 2009). Recalling the observations made by Preto EL, teachers try to motivate students to move beyond mere experience and into the realm of interpretation made manifest in a range of technique-based activities or practices. These are the Hip Hop elements—the philosophical and aesthetic pillars of Hip Hop identity.

The Cultural Points project also demonstrates the political aspect of popular education. Hip hop pedagogy is a negotiated phenomenon dependent on engaged actors from various hierarchical levels of society, including, at the very least, generally disenfranchised youth from the periphery neighborhoods; "organic intellectuals" such as Preto EL, Erry-G, and Nino Brown, who act often as both Hip Hop teachers/ performers and bureaucratic intermediaries; and interested, bourgeois members of municipal, state, or federal governing administrations. In short, the Cultural Points project obliges people from various backgrounds to negotiate with each other in a productive manner and come to a mutual understanding about civic responsibility, event organization, and theoretically, the parameters of culture itself. If one can glean anything from the life experiences of individuals such as Preto EL, Erry-G, and Nino Brown, it is that the production of Hip Hop is a political classroom because it requires bargaining, persuasion, and consensus across lines of difference. The political lesson of the CP project is one of *vivência*—negotiation through robust social networking.

At the time of this writing, daily rallies around the United States have emerged to express the need for health care as a public option. The case of Brazil reminds us that, at its historical basis and its soul, Hip Hop is likewise a public sector practice. "Public" and "private" education or health policies are not as Manichean as they may appear. In both areas of life, the neoliberalism of the 1990s in both the United States and in Brazil has augmented exclusionary practices and worsened social inequalities based on predominantly class, race, gender, and sexuality. However, a real solution is not simply about going public or "turning it over to the state." It is about the dynamic of state involvement in the public sector. That dynamic hinges on the extent to which local actors are able to articulate *vivência* into policy measures, whether they are Cultural Points, medical remuneration based on health rather than number of operations, ending coal-based energy, installing public gardens, or public bicycle lanes.

Early in Obama's first term as president, U.S. media outlets ranging from Fox news to the *Daily Show* to *The Nation* have compared the Obama administration to a number of popular and not-so-popular former presidencies. I was struck by one such comparison with Franklin D. Roosevelt and find it most apropos for the purposes of this text. The story goes that after a meeting about the "plight of the Negro" with A. Philip Randolph, the African American union and civil rights leader, President Roosevelt stated that he agreed with everything Randolph had said, but ended his meeting by stating that for Randolph's and other civil rights leaders' demands to be realized, they must force the president's hand. Similarly, early in his presidency, Obama recalled Roosevelt's position and stated that the public must organize and articulate its position forcefully for the president effectively to bring change.

Aspects such as public performativity, expression of experience, and collective culture are the strengths of Hip Hop. Although the terrain of state culture requires delicate negotiations around issues of popular pedagogy and "the popular" overall, the history of Brazil demonstrates that now is the time to push *vivência*, the rich texture of intersubjective experience and artistic, material production, to the front of discussions around democratic citizenship and education policies. Whether in Brazil or in the United States, the determination of measurable benchmarks of educational success or progress (if one were to consider the logic of No Child Left Behind, for example) must involve a dialogue, a *vivência*, which involves state-civil management rooted in an organic sense of local realities and local skills. In this manner, notions of "education," "politics," "the classroom," and "culture" become less socioeconomically elitist and more inclusive and action-based. For those who historically and structurally have been marginalized from the centers of power and influence, this perspective on pedagogy is promising. The case of the Hip Hop House in Diadema represents a dynamic example of a new form of popular education, one that is politicized not in terms of party affiliation but in the more essential sense of civic engagement and social identity formation. The title of De La Soul's 1993 song "I Am I Be" can then symbolize a state programmatic project: "I live live" (as a live performance). We can see a Hip Hop opportunity of global dimensions.

NOTES

1. See "Desigualdade faz Brasil ter índice de 'Islíndia'" in the daily newspaper *Folha de São Paulo,* December 19, 2008: A15–16. Author not given. Brazil ranked in 70th position overall. All translations in this text unless otherwise stated are by the author.

2. A discussion of the relationship between "culture" and "cultivation" is beyond the scope of this essay. I would, however, direct interested readers to the 19th-century essays of British statesmen such as Matthew Arnold and German intellectuals such as Johann Gottfried Herder. For a review of pertinent debates, see Eagleton (2000) and Lloyd and Thomas (1998).

3. See Mitchell (2001), Pardue (2008), Fernandes (2006), Condry (2006), Durand (2002), and Maxwell (2003) for a survey of global Hip Hop and the theme of marginality in various cultural contexts. With regard to the latter claim, see Perry (2004), Rivera (2003), Keyes (2003), and Pough (2004) for discussions of gender and sexuality empowerment in Hip Hop performance.

4. Of course, this is a generalization. The construction of Brasília as the nation's federal district was a gesture toward distributing not only population in the center of the country but also social capital throughout the territory. See Holston (1989) for a detailed

discussion of the "idea of Brasília" and the general struggle Brazilians have faced regarding the tension between the shoreline and the countryside. In terms of music and imagination, see Dent (2009) and his discussion of *música sertaneja* in the interior of the state of São Paulo.

5. See also Guilbault (2007, pp. 44–46) for a discussion of British colonial and local Creole middle-class management of carnival music in Trinidad.

6. "Capão" refers to the (in)famous neighborhood on the south side, Capão Redondo, where the leader of the popular rap group Racionais MCs hails from and where the indices of violence are among the highest in the metro area. *Cidadão* means "citizen" and thus the alliterative rhyme is completed.

7. The Cultural Points program is one of several initiatives. In July 2009 Brazilian president "Lula" da Silva signed a law for the creation of "Culture Voucher" (*Vale Cultura*), which stipulates that working-class families would receive a voucher for 50 reais (US $27.50) per month dedicated for "cultural" consumption. The details are under debate in the Congress and not clear at the time of this writing.

8. The excerpts from Gil's speech come from the MinC website. The speech was part of the award ceremony Prêmio Cultura Viva, retrieved from http://www.cultura.gov.br

9. The debate around government participation in civic life, negatively referred to as *dirigismo*, continues around the issue of cultural management in Brazil. See the exchanges between the current cultural minister Juca Ferreira and his critics in the online journal Interesse Nacional (www.interessenacional.com) from July 2009.

10. Gil recorded the song "Bat Macumba" in 1968 as part of the legendary "Tropicália" collective recording with Caetano Veloso, Gal Costa, Tom Zé, Os Mutantes, and others. The song is an exercise in concrete poetry with the lyrics taking the phrase "*bat macumba iê iê, bat macumba ai ya*" as if it were a structure. Over time, the singing builds it up and breaks the phrase down syllable by syllable. *Macumba*, in its conventional spelling, is a popular term referring to the Afro-Brazilian religion of *candomblé*. In usual Brazilian colloquial speech, *macumba* carries negative connotations with racist overtones. Here, Gil playfully subverts such meanings.

11. See regional newspaper articles, such as http://www.diadema.sp.gov.br/municipio/224-hip-hop-e-opcao-para-final-de-semana.html and http://www.metodista.br/rronline/noticias/entretenimento/copy_of_pasta-2/dia-mundial-do-hip-hopi-tem-comemoracao-em-diadema, regarding Diadema as "Hip Hop City." On September 4, 2008, Mayor José de Filippi Junior authorized November 12 as "Hip Hop Day," decreed as law #2791/08 (*Lei Ordinária No. 2791/08*). According to King Zulu Nino Brown of the Hip Hop House and Zulu Nation Brasil, November 12 refers to when Afrika Bambaataa coordinated all of the Hip Hop "elements" including emcee, DJ, graffiti, street dance, and the fifth element of "knowledge."

12. *Folia de Reis* is a popular Catholic practice originally from the rural countryside areas of the states of São Paulo and Minas Gerais. The *folias* feature music, dance, and parade and are based on the narrative of the journey of the Wise Men to Bethlehem and back to the Orient.

13. See the official MinC website: http://www.cultura.gov.br/cultura_viva/?page_id = 3

REFERENCES

Alim, H. S., & Pennycook, A. (2007) Glocal linguistic flows: Hip hop culture(s), identities, and the politics of language education. *Journal of Language, Identity, and Education, 6*(2), 89–100.

Bruce, H. E., & Davis, B. D. (2000) Slam: Hip-hop meets poetry—A Strategy for violence intervention." *English Journal, 89*(5), 119–127.

Condry, I. (2006). *Hip-hop Japan: Rap and the paths of cultural globalization.* Durham, NC: Duke University Press.

Cooks, J. A. (2004). Writing for something: Essays, raps, and writing preferences. *English Journal, 94*(1), 72–76.

De La Soul. (1993). "I am I be." *Buhloone Mindstate.* Rhino Records.

Dent, A. (2009). *Country critics: Rural public culture and remembrance in Brazil.* Durham, NC: Duke University Press.

Dimitriadis, G. (2009). *Performing identity/performing culture: Hip hop as text, pedagogy, and lived practice* (Rev. ed.). New York: Peter Lang.

Durand, A. P. (Ed.) (2002). *Black, blanc, beur: Rap music and hip-hop culture in the Francophone world.* Oxford, UK: The Scarecrow Press.

Eagleton, T. (2000). *The idea of culture.* Oxford, UK: Blackwell.

Fernandes, S. (2006). *Cuba represent!: Cuban arts, state power and the making of new revolutionary cultures.* Durham, NC: Duke University Press.

Guilbault, J. (2007). *Governing sound: The cultural politics of Trinidad's carnival musics.* Chicago: University of Chicago Press.

Hanley, M. S. (2007). Old school crossings: Hip hop in teacher education and beyond. *New Directions for Adult and Continuing Education, 115,* 35–44.

Hill, M. L. (2008). Toward a pedagogy of the popular: Bourdieu, hip-hop, and out-of-school literacies. In J. Albright & A. Luke (Eds.), *Pierre Bourdieu and literacy education* (pp. 136–161). New York: Routledge.

Hill, M. L. (2009). Wounded healing: Forming a storytelling community in hip-hop lit. *Teachers College Record, 111*(1), 248–293.

Holston, J. (1989). *The modernist city: An anthropological critique of Brasília.* Chicago: University of Chicago Press.

Isaac, A. (2003). Um espaço que pulsa. *Jornal Sou da Paz, 8*(3), 3.

Izarry, J. G. (2009). Representin': Drawing from hip-hop and urban youth culture to inform teacher education. *Education and Urban Society, 41,* 489–515.

Keyes, C. (2003). *Rap music and street consciousness.* Urbana, IL: University of Illinois Press.

Lloyd, D., & Thomas, P. (1998). *Culture and the state.* New York: Routledge.

Maxwell, I. (2003). *Phat beats, dope rhymes: Hip hop down under comin' upper.* Middletown, CT: Wesleyan University Press.

McCann, B. (2004). *Hello hello Brazil: Popular music in the making of modern Brazil.* Durham, NC: Duke University Press.

Mitchell, T. (Ed.) (2001). *Global noise: Rap and hip hop outside of the U.S.* Middletown, CT.: Wesleyan University Press.

Morrell, E. (2008). *Critical literacy and urban youth: Pedagogies of access, dissent, and liberation.* New York: Routledge.

Morrell, E., & Duncan-Andrade, J. M. R. (2002). Promoting academic literacy with urban youth through engaging hip hop culture." *English Journal, 91*(6), 88–92.

Oehler, S., & Hanley, J. (2009). Perspective of popular music pedagogy in practice: An introduction. *Journal of Popular Music Studies, 21*(1), 2–19.

Pardue, D. (2007). Hip hop as pedagogy: A look into "Heaven" and "Soul" in São Paulo, Brazil. *Anthropological Quarterly, 80*(3), 673–708.

Pardue, D. (2008). *Ideologies of marginality in Brazilian Hip Hop*. New York: Palgrave.

Perry, I. (2004). *Prophets of the hood: Politics and poetics in hip hop*. Durham, NC: Duke University Press.

Pough, G. (2004). *Check it while I wreck it: Black womanhood, hip-hop culture, and the public sphere*. Boston: Northeastern University Press.

Prado, C. (2008). Interview. Retrieved from http://www.youtube.com/watch?v = WJbbqHbAjuI

Price, R. J., Jr. (2005). Hegemony, hope, and the Harlem Renaissance: Taking hip hop culture seriously. *Convergence, 38*(2), 55–64.

Ramsdale, P. (2000). *International flows of selected cultural goods, 1980–1998*. Paris: UNESCO Institute for Statistics publication.

Reily, A. S. (2002). *Voices of the magi: Enchanted journey in Southeast Brazil*. Chicago: University of Chicago Press.

Rivera, R. Z. (2003). *New York Ricans from the hip hop zone*. New York: Palgrave Macmillan.

Salgado, Á. (1941). Radiodifusão, fator social. *Cultural Política, 1*(6), 79–93.

Singleton, J. (Director). (1991). *Boyz in the Hood*. Columbia Pictures.

Stovall, D. (2006). We can relate: Hip-hop culture, critical pedagogy, and the secondary classroom." *Urban Education, 41*(6), 585–602.

Vieira, W. (2008, September 7). Professor ensina rap para combater violência no Capão Redondo. *Folha de São Paulo*, p. 8.

Williams, D. (2001). *Culture wars in Brazil: The first Vargas Regime, 1930–1945*. Durham, NC: Duke University Press.

CHAPTER 8

Hip-Hop and the New Response to Urban Renewal

Youth, Social Studies, and the Bridge to College

David Stovall

Where there have been numerous accounts that identify the uses of hip-hop in the classroom (Alim & Baugh, 2007; Fisher, 2007; Hill 2009; Duncan-Andrade & Morrell, 2008), this chapter seeks to unpack, synergize, and problematize the ways in which hip-hop is understood and utilized by both youth and adults who consider themselves part of the hip-hop generation. Taking place in a high school/college bridge class in Chicago called "Education, Youth, and Social Justice," the pages that follow are an attempt to contribute to the larger conversation aimed at the examination and process of meaning making through hip-hop in urban classrooms.

Hip-hop is a rapidly moving phenomenon in its relationship to style, culture, technology, and economics. Consequently, as soon as this chapter is printed, the information may appear outdated to some people. As popular media conflate the way in which hip-hop is consumed, contextualized, and understood by way of music videos, radio playlists, and social networking Internet sites, there are numerous contradictions to dispel. Central to these contradictions are the continued presence of misogyny and portrayals of violence in hip-hop. As these components do not represent the totality of hip-hop, many of the aforementioned contradictions are fueled by corporate entities that push product to a particular demographic. In light of said realities, it is important to locate my work as an educator in making the attempt to address the contradictions while grappling with differing perspectives surrounding the utility of hip-hop in classroom space. As my attempt occurred in a hybrid between a high school social studies class and an introductory college urban sociology class (discussed in later sections), the social context of hip-hop became central to the discussions and assignments in the unit. As a social studies/urban sociology course, we sought to interrogate the various contradictions and challenges brought forth in social contexts (e.g., political, social, economic, racial, and so on). Hip-hop, as art form, cultural practice, and material commodity, embodies said contradictions, from its genesis to the present.

Because hip-hop locates its beginnings in a response to injustices by way of urban renewal and disinvestment, the concept of social justice is central to this chapter. For the purposes of this chapter, social justice in education is understood as the process by which teachers and students make informed decisions while participating in efforts to dismantle all systems of oppression (e.g., racism, sexism, classism, ableism, patriarchy, homophobia, and so forth; Stovall & Morales-Doyle, 2011). The described classroom space, as a site of praxis (i.e., action and reflection in the world in order to change it), also serves as a site to unpack the contradictions and disconnects that are underreported in discussions of hip-hop and the realities of urban life. By entering this conversation earlier rather than later, the idea is to establish a baseline from which this essay operates.

To create a sense of continuity, the chapter is organized with the hope of allowing the reader to understand the simultaneous nature of the work that was internal and external to the class. Because the course was centered on the idea of young people making sense of their realities and consciously deciding to address them, it served as a space to put theory to practice. In talking the reader through the ideas that were integral for the creation of the unit, the chapter also highlights classroom reflections that demonstrate how we (myself and the students who took the course) grappled with our opinions and insights as we discussed and processed the unit.

OVER THE BRIDGE: COLLEGE BRIDGE AND THE COMMITMENT TO COMMUNITY ENGAGEMENT

In order to understand the premise for the course, the context of the high school deserves some unpacking. The curricular unit took place at the Lawndale/Little Village School for Social Justice (SOJO) during a college bridge course. The college bridge component came about by way of my and another university faculty member (Eric "Rico" Gutstein) contributing to the design team for the high school. The events leading to the creation of SOJO, including a community-driven 19-day hunger strike, are critical to understanding the origins of the class. Because Rico and I were invited to be members of the design team, our accountability to the community process informed our work tremendously.

Opening its doors in the fall of 2005, the building where SOJO is housed contains four schools, each with its own theme (the other three are multicultural arts, math and science, and world languages). The population of SOJO is approximately 30% African American and 70% Latino/a. Students from our school come from the communities of North Lawndale, a predominantly African American community just north of Little Village, and Little Village itself.

During the first 3 years of the high school (2005–2008), Rico and I worked with faculty and students in math and social studies, respectively, largely in the capacity of developing curriculum and modeling lessons for the faculty. As the students who began at SOJO in the fall of 2005 approached their senior year, we along with SOJO faculty and administration began discussing the possibilities of students obtaining early college credit. Utilizing our networks as university professors, we were able to contact the university while the SOJO administration addressed our concerns with Chicago Public Schools (CPS).

During this time, officials at our local university alerted us that they currently offered a college bridge program on campus. University officials wanted to revitalize the program, which was virtually dormant, with fewer than 10 students enrolled in it. However, because the university had established a partnership with CPS, we figured that we could place our students into their existing structure. Similar to college bridge programs across the country, students at SOJO would be enrolled in an actual university course and take that course on the campus with other college students. Where this sounded optimal, we presented it to SOJO's administration. The idea sounded good in theory, but SOJO administration forewarned us of potential scheduling conflicts, specifically concerning transportation between SOJO and the university. My course would be called "Education, Youth, and Justice," and Rico's course would be called "Using Mathematics to Write the World."

Confronted with the practical realities of coordinating high school and college schedules, we thought the best way to provide the course would be for Rico and me to teach the classes on-site at SOJO. This would include us being on campus 4 days per week, one period per day, in addition to any time we used to update the administration on the progress of the course. The course would be the equivalent of two semesters long and would run for the entire school year at SOJO. Our work would be in concert with the likes of Duncan-Andrade and Morrell (2008) and Yang (2009), all of whom are university professors who have taught high school courses while holding positions as university faculty. Personally, my interactions with the aforementioned authors have been influential in positioning my work. Remaining accountable to the community-driven initiative, our decision to teach the class on campus allowed for a more tangible connection to the intent of the initial proposal for SOJO.

THE COURSE: EDUCATION, YOUTH, AND JUSTICE

In reference to the work communities of color have engaged in to demand justice in education from a critical historical, political, and contemporary perspective, I decided to call the course Education, Youth, and Justice. Pairing concepts of social justice with current and historical interpretations of youth culture, one of the objectives of the course was to apply interpretations of social justice to analyze urban public education. In Chicago (and in other cities across the United States), because many students, families, and community members are in an epic battle to save their schools and homes, investigating the different perspectives of justice allowed for rich inquiry and exchange. Even with SOJO existing as a new school, students understood the threat of how the intended purpose of the community-driven initiative that led to the high school could be hijacked under the false guise of "development."

Materials for the course included four books and a course packet. Supplemental materials such as handouts, poster boards, markers, MP3s, video cameras, and so on were generated as needed, depending on the research projects of the students. Because education for the purposes of this course operated from a broader perspective, one of the books (Howard Zinn's 2008 *On Democratic Education*) and the course packet had an educational focus. In addition to articles that addressed education, the packet contained a section on youth and community organizing. Both the text and the packet framed education broadly as the process by which people are able to ask critical questions while making informed decisions concerning themselves and others. Using Zinn (2008) as the template, the second text used critical historiography to highlight justice movements of people of color throughout the world (Vijay Prashad's 2007 *The Darker Nations*). The last two texts investigated the philosophy of race (Charles Mills's 1999 *The Racial Contract*) and legal scholarship (Richard Delgado and Jean Stefancic's 2001 *Critical Race Theory: An Introduction*). Although the uses of these texts are not discussed in detail in this account, they were critical in developing the course. Discussed in detail in the next section, the packet was instrumental in the unit of the course designed to unpack the relationship among hip-hop, gentrification, and education.

THE UNIT: HIP-HOP, URBAN RENEWAL, AND GENTRIFICATION

The primary goal of the unit on hip-hop, urban renewal, and gentrification was for students to make a connection between the history of hip-hop and their current experiences as young people in Chicago. As social justice education, another goal was to provide an opportunity to interrogate the contexts that mediate their world, such as mass media and popular culture, while identifying personal and community connections to the contexts in question. In maintaining the connection to critical praxis (i.e., action and reflection in the world in order to change it), a final goal of the unit was to identify other sites of resistance that they could possibly engage, as part of the process of changing their condition. Where many high school lesson plans have a section that state, "Students will be able to" (often referenced as SWBAT), this unit contained a section that listed some specific objectives. One was for students to be able to identify the key elements that shaped the formation of hip-hop. Additionally, the unit plan stated that after the unit, students would be able to identify the foundational elements of hip-hop culture (i.e., MCing, DJing, writing graffiti, and b-boying/b-girling). Directly connected to the concept of social justice education stated in the aforementioned sections, another objective was to have students compare the policies of urban renewal surrounding hip-hop's genesis in New York City in the early 1970s with current urban renewal/gentrification policies in Chicago, also originating in the same decade.

TANGIBLE CONNECTIONS BETWEEN
URBAN RENEWAL/GENTRIFICATION AND HIP-HOP

There were several pedagogical connections between urban renewal/gentrification and hip-hop from the outset of this course. Where Chicago is in the midst of a 38-year wave of gentrification, the parallels to New York City are evident. To contextualize this reality, we used Chapter 1 of Jeff Chang's 2005 book *Can't Stop Won't Stop* to provide a social, political, and economic context for hip-hop. The provocative title of the chapter ("Necropolis") allowed the class to engage in some lively discussion around what we would consider to be a "city of death." When I asked students to describe what a necropolis could be, they talked about a place that was infested with drugs, high crime, poverty, and few social services. I continued to probe if there were any necropolises that they knew about. A few students responded, "We could say that about some parts of Chicago." As others nodded their heads, some chimed in that Chicago is more complex than that. When I asked them to speak to the complexities, they returned that there are a number of experiences in Chicago that would allow us to consider it a necropolis, while it could still be a city of dreams to others. I asked them for whom Chicago would be a city of dreams. Some students said that it would be that way for the folks who were gentrifying the city. Others thought that it would be a city of dreams for families who immigrated to the city to make a better life for their families.

If students could grasp how Chicago could be considered a city of death to some, I felt that we could smoothly transition into Chang's (2005) interpretation of New York City as a necropolis. Beginning with the World Series of 1977, Chang leads readers into the context of White flight and insurance arson.[1] As the people who could not move out of the city were largely African American, Puerto Rican, and Caribbean, hip-hop became an instrument by which young people were able to respond to their conditions. With the construction of the Cross-Bronx Expressway, the residents who remained after the raising of property were largely poor and unable to relocate. Coupled with the removal of music and art programs in

New York City Public Schools, hip-hop, through DJing, MCing, writing graffiti, and b-boying/b-girling, became the musical and physical expression of young people in these conditions in the South Bronx.

This connection resonated with my students in that they saw what young people at that time were creating in the midst of gentrification. There was a historical connection to Chicago in that the 1977 city of New York report called *The South Bronx: A Plan for Revitalization* acknowledged that the damage done to the South Bronx "could not be measured in numbers" (Chang, 2005, p. 17). In Chicago, some 6 years earlier, a plan called the "Chicago 21" plan was created that identified 21 geographic wards as sites that were beyond repair and needed to be "revitalized." Because urban planning policies of the 1970s were steeped in the language of urban renewal, students were able to identify the connection to gentrification in Chicago. As the city of New York made a concerted effort to "remove" residents that were deemed disposable, a similar plan was in place in Chicago. Coupled with the economic downturn, disinvestment in public infrastructure and services (transportation, streets and sanitation services, education, state and federal employment programs), New York City (and urban cities throughout the country) found itself in a major crisis. Instead of reaching its desired outcome of moving African American and Latino/a residents out of the five boroughs, the move resulted in the reconcentration of poverty.

Because my students were high school seniors, their previous 3 years at SOJO were centered in grappling with the real-life issues of race, place, class, and gender. Although SOJO is physically housed in the predominantly Latino/a neighborhood of Little Village while also serving students from North Lawndale, it is often considered a "Latino/a" school. My students, in addressing this perception, were very clear as to how their school was positioned and spoke to these realities in their assignments throughout the class. My class, with 28 students, was comprised of 4 African Americans and 24 Latinos/as. Despite the stark division in terms of racial/ethnic distribution, students were very clear as to where their lives converged and diverged. Because both groups of students were from low-income working-class communities that were immersed in the policies of immigration, gentrification, and development, hip-hop's historical context provided a relevant portal from which to connect to their lives.

The historical realities of urban renewal/gentrification in New York City resonated with my students in Chicago for several reasons. The neighborhoods that they come from (North Lawndale and Little Village) are witnessing the effects of a massive gentrification project. Although Little Village is densely populated, North Lawndale has the highest number of vacant lots in the city. Over the last 10 years, rents have doubled on some blocks, and property taxes have tripled in some areas of North Lawndale. Similar to the Cross-Bronx Expressway in New York City, Ogden Avenue, which cuts through North Lawndale and Little Village, provides direct access to downtown and the central business district in Chicago. Because property along Ogden has been identified as desirable, developers have target-ed vacant lots in North Lawndale for high-end condominium and single-family homes. At SOJO, this has resulted in students having to change addresses up to three or four times while new residents move to the area. Where Little Village and North Lawndale provide one context, it should be considered part of a larger plan to remove residents out of the city who have been deemed "undesirable." Similar to the conditions in New York, these "undesirable" populations continue to consist mainly of African American and Latino/a residents.

ENTERING THE DISCONNECT

It should be noted that not all of my students were avid fans of hip-hop. Where some felt themselves to be deeply engrained in the culture of hip-hop, other stu-dents were fans of Mexican Cumbia, R&B, country and western, and speed metal. Hip-hop, however, provided a point of recognition in that they were at mini-mum familiar with the music and the culture. As a class that sought to transition concepts learned in high school social studies to a college-level urban sociology course, I wanted to excavate the potential disconnects between how I understood hip-hop and the music they felt was most relevant to them.

In order to do this, I wanted students to get a sense of the music young people were listening to during the late 1970s in Chicago and New York City. Hip-hop, as a hybrid of musical genres, was a mix of funk, disco, soul, R&B, and in some cases, rock and roll music. Although there are often debates about who was the first to recite lyrics over an instrumental while using a microphone in front of an audience, there were several pivotal artists that were marked as pioneers in the culture. One of the lesser-known albums was by a group from Brooklyn called The Fatback Band. Their 1979 song "King Tim III (Personality Jock)" is often credited as one of the first songs to feature an MC. With a very simplistic rhyme scheme and disco-music backing, the song sounds very different from the hip-hop music that most young people listen to today.

When I played this song for the class, many of the students started laughing. Some students thought it was "lame" and "didn't even have a good beat." When I asked them if they thought the record would do well in the current music indus-try, many of them laughed and asked me if I was serious. After I laughed out loud with them, I shared an experience I had with my mother in 4th grade. While she was driving me to school, a song was being played on the radio. I had never heard it before and wanted to hear the name of the song. I wasn't able to hear all of it, so I just remembered telling my classmates during recess how "cold" (a Chicago term we used to describe something we really liked) this song was. I could memorize the chorus ("Don't push me 'cus I'm close to the edge/ I'm tryin' not to lose my head/ Huh-huh, huh, huh/ It's like a jungle sometimes, it makes me wonder how

I keep from going under"), but I couldn't remember much else. I continued to explain to my students that the chorus was so captivating that I was compelled to find out more of the song. When I finally learned more of the song, the introductory verse proved to be the most gripping.

> Broken glass everywhere
> People pissin' on the stairs you know they just don't care
> I can't take the smell, can't take the noise
> Got no money to move out, I guess I got no choice
> Rats in the front room, roaches in the back
> Junkies in the alley with a baseball bat
> I tried to get away but I couldn't get far
> 'cus the man with the tow truck repossessed my car.

When I recited the lyrics to the class, I screamed out loud in explaining how excited I was to have memorized the verse. The song was called "The Message" and it was by a group called Grandmaster Flash and the Furious Five (1982). Upon playing the song for the class, they liked it better than "King Tim III (Personality Jock)," but they still thought it wouldn't do well in today's market. Some liked the lyrics, while others scrunched their faces to express their dislike. I continued to explain to the class that in 1982 as a 10-year-old, what made the song so compelling was the beat and the fact that the lyrics spoke to many of the realities of what was happening in my neighborhood. For many communities of color, the late 1970s and early 1980s were a time of devastating government cutbacks in the form of welfare reductions, loss of job training programs, deindustrialization, and disinvestment in safety-net programs. To hear someone talk about that in a song was captivating to me. On a personal note, my father, as an employee of the Illinois Department of Employment Security (IDES) actually supervised a job-readiness program for those who were trying to re-enter the workforce after some form of hardship. I remember when the program was cut and how disappointed he was to have to tell the people he was working with that funds were pulled from the program. Although artists and songs that spoke to the realities of inner-city life and resistance were not new (e.g., the works of Marvin Gaye, Curtis Mayfield, Abbey Lincoln, the Staples Singers, and so on), it was something about "The Message" that resonated with me.

The students appeared to understand where I was coming from, but they felt that I was a little too excited about the song. They joked with me about how I yelled out, I was "on ten" (a Chicago term meaning that a person is physically excited). Their comments, while true to their experiences, were interesting for me to hear in that they provided me some perspective on tangible disconnects between my perspective and their own. Where I am no longer 18 years old, I have to remember that there are some experiences that we share and also places where our experiences diverge. This becomes particularly important in hip-hop because some of my students and I would identify with hip-hop as pivotal in our upbringing. Instead of viewing this as a "generational gap," I understand it as the recognition that there are many things that are different for my students than they were for me when I was the same age. In recognition of those differences, the challenge is to discover ways in which each of our experiences can inform the other in the larger quest for justice in education. Even though many of our experiences are different, many are the same or similar. The major difference, however, often lies in the intensity with which young people of color are persecuted and vilified. For example, where the issue of police brutality has consistently been an issue in working-class/low-income African American and Latino/a communities, urban police forces have militarized themselves in light of a perceived "threat" in these areas. In Chicago, there was recently an ordinance to arm every squad car with M-4 assault rifles, which are designed to penetrate tank armor. Despite these differences, the music served as the necessary entry point by which to engage an example of how hip-hop, in many instances, was a response to the political, economic, and social conditions of the late 1970s and early 1980s. Just like "The Message" provided context for me, I was making the attempt to provide context for them. Now understood as culturally relevant or culturally relevant teaching, the idea is to use the views, values, opinions, and culture of young people as a portal by which to develop analytical and concrete skills (Ladson-Billings, 1994).

Returning to hip-hop, I had the students write a reflection about responses to gentrification. Because many students in this class were activists in their own right (many of the students in the class participated in developing policy initiatives, conference presentations, and curriculum development addressing police brutality, predatory lending, and standardized testing), I was familiar with their abilities to synthesize information and develop an argument. In my own reflections, I wondered whether or not they saw any connection between the responses of African American and Puerto Rican youth of the South Bronx in the 1970s to what was happening currently in Chicago. To my surprise, when I first posed the question, there was a lot of dead silence. Many of the students responded with confused looks. When I began to ask students to recall the conditions in the South Bronx, they began to pepper me with the information they read in Chang's (2005) chapter. I continued by asking them to talk about gentrification in Chicago, and they responded with information they had given me earlier in class. From there, I asked them to connect the two and write down their reflections. Once they made the connection, they were able to engage the writing exercise.

The reflection prompt contained two questions. The first was "Why do you feel hip-hop was the response of young people to urban renewal/gentrification in New York City in the 1970s?" Second was "What is your creative response as a young person to urban renewal/gentrification in Chicago? Where the first question may be read as a reiteration of the earlier discussion, I wanted to focus on the second prompt, as it would signal the students' abilities to analyze and process information to develop a cogent argument. Many of them felt their activism was the creative response, while others thought their connection to visual arts could be considered a creative form of resistance similar to hip-hop. One of my students was a painter and sculptor, while another was an avid guitarist who dedicated much of his time to composing music. Both felt that attending a social justice high school allowed them to hone their creative skills as visual and performing artists and to address issues of injustice in their communities.

In understanding hip-hop as a response to urban renewal/gentrification, I often wonder what will be the next creative response of young people to conditions they determine to be unjust. When I asked my students, some shrugged their shoulders, while others felt it would be their activism around specific issues. Others felt as if the answer was still in the works. Nevertheless, we agreed that hip-hop, in its original conception, should be considered as another creative response to injustice and oppression.

REVISITING THE DISCONNECTS AND CONTRADICTIONS FOR LIBERATION

For many of us who work with communities, families, and young people, we need to recognize the various disconnects we experience with young people in terms of their day-to-day understandings. Where we can experience deep and tangible connections with young people in the fight for justice in education, there are other spaces where generational divisions are apparent. Instead of viewing this reality as a point of contention, these sites should be viewed as spaces of recognition and accountability. At this moment, teachers have the opportunity to create a space where they can learn from their students. In my own classroom, I have numerous technological challenges that my students often correct. Additionally, if I do not understand a term or a position that they are communicating, I ask them to explain or demonstrate how the term is used. This process of "putting me on" has proven integral to strengthening relationships with my students, allowing me to experience a level of comfort in dealing with my own ignorance in reference to their understandings.[2]

Because discussion was an integral component of the course, many of our conversations would focus on their understandings as young people. Because I'm older, our dialogues and reflections allowed me to realize how much the world has changed for young people. Although many concerns remain the same in the quest for justice (e.g., food, clothing, shelter, employment, quality education, self-determination, peace of mind, and so forth), there are nuances that deserve some attention. Technology, through access and distribution, conflates and democratizes many dimensions of the world. In the same light, policies aimed at repressing youth have also intensified. Zero-tolerance school policies, drug sentencing laws, felony disenfranchisement, and corporate mass media can inundate and misdirect young people if there is no critical analysis. Instead of seeing this as a disconnect, I used it as a space for solidarity. If our concern is liberation, we cannot hold on to the sentiment of "things were better in my day." Instead, we must understand the times as different and should embrace the idea that the new understandings of young people have the potential to serve as sites for liberation. The idea is not to privilege, fetishize, or romanticize the contributions of young people. Instead, the sentiment is to build from their contributions in the quest to create quality, relevant, and liberatory education. If used with humility, our experiences can provide some insight to the questions young people may have concerning their lives. More important, by providing guidance through examples, spaces like a college bridge class can contribute to the liberation of our minds for the purposes of engaging the broad project of social justice in education.

NOTES

1. Insurance arson is the process of a landlord/property owner hiring a third party to burn the property while executing insurance fraud for the purposes of securing a settlement for the destruction of the property.
2. "Putting me on" is in reference to a euphemism requesting assistance in developing an understanding of a particular issue or concern.

REFERENCES

Alim, H. S., & Baugh, J. (Eds.) (2007). *Talkin' Black talk: Language, education and social change.* New York: Teachers College.

Chang, J. (2005). *Can't stop won't stop: A history of the hip-hop generation.* New York: St. Martin's.

Delgado, R., & Stefancic, J. (2001). *Critical race theory: An introduction.* New York: New York University Press.

Duncan-Andrade, J. M. R., & Morrell, E. (2008). *The art of critical pedagogy: Possibilities for moving from theory to practice in urban schools.* New York: Peter Lang.

Fatback Band. (1979). King Tim III (Personality jock). On *XII.* New York: Spring Records.

Fisher, M. (2007). *Walking in rhythm: Spoken word poetry in urban classrooms.* New York: Teachers College Press.

Grandmaster Flash & The Furious Five. (1982). "The Message." On *The Message.* United States: Sugar Hill Records.

Hill, M. L. (2009). *Beats, rhymes, and classroom life: Hip-hop pedagogy and the politics of identity.* New York: Teachers College Press.

Ladson-Billings, G. (1994). *The dreamkeepers: Successful teachers of African American children.* Boston: Jossey-Bass.

Mills, C. (1999). *The racial contract.* Ithaca, NY: Cornell University Press.

Prashad, V. (2007). *The darker nations: A people's history of the third world.* New York: The New Press.

Stovall, D., & Morales-Doyle, D. (2010). Critical media inquiry as high school social studies for social justice: Doc your bloc. In T. K. Chapman & N. Hobbel (Eds.), *Social justice pedagogy across the curriculum* (pp. 283–298). New York: Routledge.

Yang, K. W. (2009). Discipline and punish: Some suggestions for teacher practice and policy. *Language Arts, 87*(11), 49–61.

Zinn, H. (2008). *On democratic education.* Boulder, CO: Paradigm.

About the Editors and Contributors

Marc Lamont Hill is an associate professor of English education at Teachers College, Columbia University. He is the author of the award-winning *Beats, Rhymes, and Classroom Life: Hip-Hop Pedagogy and the Politics of Identity* (Teachers College Press). He is also the co-author of *The Classroom and the Cell: Conversations on Black Life in America* (Third World Press).

Emery Petchauer is an assistant professor of urban education in the Teacher Development and Educational Studies department at Oakland University. His research focuses on the cultural dimensions of teaching and learning in urban schools and universities as well as teacher development and licensure. An award-winning teacher, he is the author of *Hip-Hop Culture in College Students' Lives: Elements, Embodiment, and Higher Edutainment* (Routledge), the first scholarly study of hip-hop culture on college campuses. In addition to these academic pursuits, Dr. Petchauer has over 15 years of experience organizing urban arts spaces across the United States.

Jacqueline Celemencki is a doctoral candidate in the Department of Integrated Studies in Education at McGill University in Montreal. Her research looks at how the experience of racial profiling at school affects the educational trajectories of Black youth in Montreal. She is also the education coordinator at the Montreal Holocaust Memorial Centre.

Christopher Emdin is an associate professor of science education at Teachers College, Columbia University and a nationally acclaimed expert on urban public education. He also oversees secondary school initiatives at the Urban Science Education Center, which is a research-based institution associated with Teachers College. He holds a PhD in urban education with a concentration in mathematics, science and technology, an MS in natural sciences, an advanced certificate in education administration, and bachelor's degrees in physical anthropology, biology, and chemistry.

H. Bernard Hall is an assistant professor of English at West Chester University. His research interests include English education, urban teacher education and development, hip-hop based education theory and praxis, and the relationships between teacher cultural identity and pedagogical effectiveness.

Decoteau J. Irby is an assistant professor in the Department of Administrative Leadership at University of Wisconsin–Milwaukee, where he teaches in the Educational Leadership and Urban Education Doctoral programs. His scholarly interests include the cultural politics of urban school reform; zero-tolerance, school safety, and discipline policies; and schooling and labor experiences of Black males.

Bronwen Low is an associate professor in the Faculty of Education, McGill University. In her research she explores the implications and challenges of popular youth culture for curriculum theory, literacy studies, and pedagogy. Current research includes community-media projects and pedagogies, translanguaging and the multilingual Montreal hip-hop scene, and life stories of Montrealers who have survived genocide and other human rights violations. She is the author of *Reading Youth Writing: "New" Literacies, Cultural Studies in Education* (Peter Lang, 2008) with Michael Hoechsmann, and most recently, *Slam School: Learning through Conflict in the Hip-Hop and Spoken Word Classroom* (Stanford University Press, 2011).

Derek Pardue is an assistant professor of Anthropology and International Studies at Washington University in St. Louis. His initial work was on the ways hip-hoppers in São Paulo "designed" culture and in so doing redesigned aspects of Brazilian society, including race, class, and space. His current book project, *Creole Citizenship*, details the links between *kriolu* language, space, and history in Lisbon, Portugal, and addresses the urgent concerns of migration and identity in the "New Europe."

James Braxton Peterson is the director of Africana Studies and an associate professor of English at Lehigh University. He is also the founder of Hip Hop Scholars, LLC, an association of Hip Hop generational scholars dedicated to researching and developing the educational potential of hip-hop, urban, and youth cultures. He is a contributor to TheGrio.com and he has appeared on CNN, HLN, Fox News, MSNBC, and various local television networks as an expert on race, politics, and popular culture.

David Stovall is an associate professor of educational policy studies and African American studies at the University of Illinois at Chicago. Currently, his research is centered in critical race theory, youth culture, community organizing and education and concepts of social justice in education. He also serves as a volunteer social studies teacher at Social Justice High School in Chicago.

Eloise Tan is a teaching and learning developer at Dublin City University. She acts as a consultant and facilitator for local and national organizations in curriculum and community development in Ireland. Her dissertation, *Participation and Critical out of School Learning for Urban Youth: Building Community Through Popular Culture*, is an ethnography of a documentary process with Montreal hip-hop artists.

Joycelyn A. Wilson is an assistant professor of educational foundations in the Department of Learning Sciences and Technologies at Virginia Tech and a former Hiphop Archive Fellow at the W. E. B. Du Bois Institute for African and African American Research at Harvard University. The founding director of HipHop2020, her current research focuses on schooling and leadership practices of the post–civil rights generation.

Index

Aaron, C., 135n2
Abowitz, K., 98, 99
Achievement gap, in science education, 17–18, 24
Aerosol art. *See* Graffiti writing
Aesthetics. *See* Hip-hop aesthetics
Afrika Bambaataa, 48, 74, 139, 146, 152n11
Akbar, N., 31
Akom, A. A., 1
Alexander-Smith, A. C., 1, 28, 95, 98
Alim, H. S., 1, 30, 33, 58, 64n4, 120, 122, 139, 155
Alridge, D. P., 2
"Amazing" (song), 88n2
Anderson, E., 99
Andre 3000, 72, 80, 88n2
Annie (film), 52
Appiah, K. A., 20
"Aquemini" (song), 82–86
   domain analysis in, 84–86
   kinds of justice found in, taxonomy of, 85
Area codes, in rap lyrics, 123
Argumentation
   communication and, in urban science education, 11–25
   hip-hop supporting, 16, 17
   between realist and relativist scientists, 14–15
   in Reality Pedagogy instructional approach, 24–25
Arrested Development, 80
Arson, insurance, 159, 165n1
Art form, hip-hop as, 133
Asante, M. K., 31, 71, 76, 83
Asante, M. K., Jnr., 67
Ault, C. R., 17
Austin, J. L., 55

Authentic leadership
   HipHop2020 Curriculum Project and, 67–68
   schoolin' on, 75–76
   teaching with hip-hop aesthetics, 70–78
Authenticity, discourses of
   challenging critical hip-hop pedagogies, 130–134
   from community-based educational workshops, 125–130. *See also* "Keepin' It Real," in hip-hop culture
   limits of, 124
   reworking, 133
Autonomy/distance aesthetic, 30
   activity critique and improvement, 43–44
   learning activities based upon, 31, 33
   practices identified in, 38–41
Avolio, B. J., 75
Ayers, W., 44

B-boying/b-girling, 2, 29
   in community-based educational project, 119
   origins of, 53
Baber, C., 70
Bad Boy Records, 80, 89n8
Bad ho–good sister dichotomy, 123, 129
Baker, H., 99
Bambaataa, A. *See* Afrika Bambaataa
Banks, J. A., 111
bard/naamu-sayer continuum, 86, 88n2
Barnett, Robert "T-Mo," 73
Baszile, D., 120
"Bat Macumba" (song), 144, 152n10
Battling, competitive, 3, 9, 13–14
   East Coast–West Coast feud, 89n8
   in hip-hop creative practices, 30, 133

169